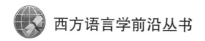

西方语言学前沿丛书

交际中的人际关系仪式
群内仪式互动研究
中文导读注释版

RELATIONAL RITUALS AND COMMUNICATION

RITUAL INTERACTION IN GROUPS

〔匈〕丹尼尔·卡达尔（Dániel Z. Kádár） 著

陈新仁 导读

北京大学出版社
PEKING UNIVERSITY PRESS

著作权合同登记号　图字：01-2016-1053

图书在版编目(CIP)数据

交际中的人际关系仪式：群内仪式互动研究：中文导读注释版：英文/(匈)丹尼尔·卡达尔(Dániel Kádár)著．—北京：北京大学出版社，2016.10

（西方语言学前沿丛书）

ISBN 978-7-301-27615-0

Ⅰ.①交… Ⅱ.①丹… Ⅲ.①人际关系学—研究—英文 Ⅳ.①C912.11

中国版本图书馆CIP数据核字（2016）第236475号

© Dániel Z. Kádár 2013

First published in English by Palgrave Macmillan, a division of Macmillan Publishers Limited under the title Relational Rituals and Communication: Ritual Interaction in Groups, by Daniel Z. Kadar. This edition has been reprinted under licence from Palgrave Macmillan. The author has asserted his right to be identified as the authors of this Work.

For copyright reasons this edition is not for sale outside of China Mainland exc. Hong Kong and Macao.

书　　名	交际中的人际关系仪式——群内仪式互动研究 JIAOJI ZHONG DE RENJI GUANXI YISHI
著作责任者	〔匈〕丹尼尔·卡达尔（Dániel Z.Kádár）著
责任编辑	朱丽娜
标准书号	ISBN 978-7-301-27615-0
出版发行	北京大学出版社
地　　址	北京市海淀区成府路205号　100871
网　　址	http://www.pup.cn　新浪微博：@北京大学出版社
电子信箱	zln0120@163.com
电　　话	邮购部62752015　发行部62750672　编辑部62754382
印　刷　者	三河市北燕印装有限公司
经　销　者	新华书店
	650毫米×980毫米　16开本　15.5印张　200千字 2016年10月第1版　2016年10月第1次印刷
定　　价	46.00元

未经许可，不得以任何方式复制或抄袭本书之部分或全部内容。

版权所有，侵权必究

举报电话：010-62752024　电子信箱：fd@pup.pku.edu.cn

图书如有印装质量问题，请与出版部联系，电话：010-62756370

专家委员会

陈新仁	程晓堂	丁建新	丁言仁
封宗信	高一虹	顾曰国	胡壮麟
黄国文	姜望琪	李　兵	李福印
李战子	廖美珍	刘世生	卢　植
马秋武	毛浩然	苗兴伟	彭宣维
齐振海	钱　军	冉永平	申　丹
史宝辉	田贵森	王初明	王克非
王立非	王　寅	王振华	文　军
文　旭	熊学亮	杨永林	张德禄
张　辉	张绍杰	张应林	赵蓉晖

总　序

马年甫始，喜讯频传。北京大学出版社自2012年起着手准备影印出版"西方语言学前沿丛书"，经过国内专家多方推荐和认真论证，并与国外出版社谈判版权，已取得很大进展，最近将陆续出版。就我所知悉的内容，这套丛书的选题涉及句法学、心理语言学、社会语言学、语用学、认知语言学、隐喻学、话语分析、文体学、多模态语言学等。"丛书"的出版无疑具有巨大的现实意义和深远意义。

就现实意义而言，我国外语教育界近年来不时受到种种骚扰，最典型的、危害最大的论调是有人不把高校的外语教育看作一个专业，以致我国高校的外语专业学生除了学习听、说、读、写四个技能外，被要求到外系学习专业课；也有人不能正确认识我国改革开放后在外语教育方面所取得的成就，不图进取，走新中国成立前老路的片面观点。在此关键时刻，"丛书"的出版，将有助于外语教育界的决策者和高校老师树立正确的全面的认识。

就深远意义而言，北京大学出版社继2011年出版"语言学论丛"系列论著外，再接再厉，如今又出版"西方语言学前沿丛书"，其用意无非是让国内高校和研究机构了解国际上在语言学研究方面的动向和进展。我认为此举还具有深层次的意义，就我国治学情况说，这将有利于扭转我国学术研究中不重视理论研究的陋习，如改革开放前我国外语界主要为编纂词典和教材；其次，这将帮助我们了解国外不同学派的出现和争鸣以推动学术创新；不仅如此，这也帮助我们了解国外学者如何注意把握理论与实践的关系，将理论应用于实践，在实践中发现问题和对理论不断修正。应该说，我们对实践还是一贯重视的，但对于如何以先进理论指导实践的认识有待提高。

这里，我还想就"西方语言学前沿丛书"的"前沿"二字谈一些看法。"前沿"的一层意思指"处于领先地位的"。我们平时常说要将我国外语教学和科研达到国际水平，就是要达到国际上的前沿水平。在这一点上，我们已取得很大进步。读者会发现本次出版的上下两集的 *LANGAUGE AND STYLE* 的论文集中，就收录了我国北京大学学者申丹教授的论文，这表明我国已有学者达到"前沿"水平，与国外学者平起平坐了。我相信这一趋势将日益明显。"前沿"的另一层意思是"前部的边儿"，它隐含的意义是一个学科或一门专业必然与其他学科或专业有这样那样的相邻关系，从其他学科和专业获得营养，拓宽视野。这是反映学术发展的交叉学科得以出现的前提。因此本语言学丛书既有传统意义的句法学、词汇学、语音学等选题，也有心理语言学、认知语言学、文体学、隐喻学等选题，特别是与现代信息技术密切结合的多模态语言学。这便为我国学者指引了努力方向。

本套丛书采取英文原版影印，同时配有中文导读，并对目录主题等主要段落进行中文翻译的方式，以促进高校教师与学生更充分地汲取国内外语言学研究的最新理论和成果。这体现了"丛书"策划者和编者能为读者着想、为读者服务的敬业精神。

最后，我对各书导读作者的学术水平和辛勤劳动非常钦佩，导读作者们不仅帮助我们如何正确理解和掌握各书的内容和要点，而且能够勇于对一些问题或观点发表评论，引导读者批判学习，殊非易事。可见，"前沿"的丛书需要"前沿"的导读执笔者、"前沿"的编者，谨向各位"者"们致敬！

胡壮麟
北京大学外国语学院
2014 年 3 月

导　读

陈新仁

《交际中的人际关系仪式[1]——群内仪式互动研究》(*Relational Rituals and Communication: Ritual Interaction in Groups*)（为行文方便起见，以下简称"本书"）的作者是来自英国哈德斯菲尔德大学跨文化礼貌研究中心主任、教授、匈牙利人 Dániel Kádár。Kádár 教授是一位年轻有为的语用学专家，主要从事语言礼貌研究，近年来取得丰硕研究成果，代表作包括《礼貌新解》(*Understanding Politeness*, 2013)（与 Michael Haugh 合著）、《东亚礼貌研究》(*Politeness in East Asia*, 2011)（与 Sara Mills 合编）、《(不)礼貌术语研究》(*Terms of (Im)Politeness*, 2007)、《历史(不)礼貌研究》(*Historical (Im)Politeness*, 2010)（与 Jonathan Culpeper 合编）、《历史(不)礼貌新解》(*Understanding Historical (Im)Politeness*, 2011)（与 Marcel Bax 合编）、《跨文化礼貌研究》(*Politeness Across Cultures*, 2010)（与 Francesca Bargiela-Chiappini 合编）、《古代汉语信函研究》(*Historical Chinese Letter Writing*, 2010)。本书是 Kádár 教授的最新力作之一，英文版于 2013 年由麦克米伦出版社出版。

作者写作本书的目的是挑战一些历史学家、哲学家、人类学家所持有的西方语言随着现代化、全球化的深入以及宗教信仰的退化发生"去仪式化"(deritualization)以致已经没有多少仪式可言的观点，通过分析交际者在不同文化、不同社会语境中的行为，捕捉带有仪式特点的会话现象，呈现"关于仪式的基于话语的人际关系分析框架"

---

[1] 这里将 relational ritual 中的 ritual 译为"仪式"是为了与 Goffman (1967) 使用该 ritual 的意思保持一致且与 Kádár 教授在本书中挑战"去仪式化"说的主旨呼应。Kádár 教授虽然给该术语赋予了新的内涵，拓宽了其外延，但维持了其基本的意义。钱永红 (2015) 将该术语翻译为"人际关系程式"也是合理的，因为 Kádár 教授笔下的 ritual 要比一般意义上的仪式在外延上更宽泛。

(p.1)。作者发现,交际者往往会通过带有仪式特征的行为或话语实践,建构、维持或解构人际关系,任何面向人际关系的带有仪式特征的会话行为都具有人际关系功能,因此,关注带有仪式特征的互动行为或话语实践对于交际者的影响比关注交际者如何实施仪式行为本身更有价值。

1. 内容简介

全书由图表清单、正文(共七章)、各章注释、术语表、参考文献、索引等部分组成。下面重点介绍正文七章的内容。

第一章为"导论",介绍仪式的由来及本书中对仪式的界定,呈现本书运用的方法论和语料情况。作者首先从人际关系角度,对言语交际中经常出现的仪式现象给出工作定义。作者将仪式看作是人际关系沟通的行为,由会话者在会话互动中通过事先存在的模式加以建构。从传统上看,仪式的概念包括各种仪式行为,从宗教洗礼过程中的祈祷,到使用诸如 Well done("干得好")的话语来对某人的行为或成就予以认可。在大众文化中,该概念一般指某种规定性的、古老的行为形式,其中很多形式非常庄严,有固定的话语及次序,与特定的"仪式性"活动或事件相关联。作者在本书中对仪式持一种更为宽泛的定义,认为日常会话中存在各种带有仪式特征的话语实践现象,在互动中由交际双方或多方共同建构,可以独立成段,与互动的其他部分有明显的分界。

作者基于话语语用学,从人际关系视角,指出群体内部的仪式话语是参与者之间使用的"形式化/图式性的、规约化的语言用法"(formalized/schematic and conventionalized language usage)(p. 13),具有下列重要特征:(1) 性质上,这种仪式是一种群内话语实践,在特定的社会关系网络中具有约定俗成性。该用法不是当下使用者发明的,但却是当下使用者首先把它用来作为仪式表达方式的。(2)频率上,这种仪式话语行为具有反复实施的特征。(3)功能上,这种仪式话语用法具有特定的人际关系功能,可以用来促进群内特定问题的讨论。该功能是情感性的。该仪式表达能够构建一种临时性的仪式"框架"或基调,让交际对方感到当前的基调不同于平时默认的、非仪式的基调,一般具有较好的互动效果。仪式互动可以(重新)塑造、强化人际关系,借助仪式,个体可以传递自身的社会依附性,表达自己希望在特定交际群体中得到位置的想法或愿望。(4)来源上,该仪式的功能源于交际双方的交往关系史(之前彼此曾使用该表达方式开过玩笑),因而具有历史性(historicality),当前使用更准确地说是一种再次激活,与彼此过去的情感相联结,对彼此没有任何伤害。(5)特征上,这种无害特性源于其模仿特性。特定仪式表达的使用原本并非当前说话人的个人声音,而是模仿了所在群体的声音,该仪式表达方式是交际双方的共同"财产"。

第二章"人际关系视角下的仪式界定"由三大部分组成,第一部分从人际关系角度详细界定仪式,区分人际关系仪式与(不)礼貌等其他人际关系现象。在人类学等领域,仪式常被描述为一种独立的分析范畴。然而,从人际关系沟通角度看,仪式隶属"带有图式特征的行为"(schematic acts)以及"带有规约性质的的人际行为"领域中的范畴,如图一所示。

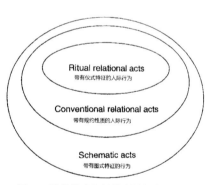

图一:带有仪式特征的人际行为的位置

作者重点区分了人际关系仪式与(不)礼貌,认为二者之间存在一个关键差别,即(不)礼貌源于解读和评价,而人际关系仪式需要从行为视角加以考察。人际关系仪式的发生需要通过实施某种之前业已存在的交际图式。只有当交际者实施特定图式时人际关系仪式才会产生。评价虽然在仪式中也起一定的作用,但不及在(不)礼貌实施中那么关键。研究（不）礼貌重在关注评价，而研究人际关系仪式重在关注行为本身。在第二部分，作者从语用学角度讨论各种带有图式特征的行为，然后聚焦图式性人际关系的规约现象，从具体的、话语的角度界定规约。与一般做法不同，作者从人际关系角度阐释言语交际中的规约现象，认为规约是人际关系网络中的话语实践现象，凡是遵循各种模式的、与人际关系沟通相关的、反复出现的图式行为，如涉及礼貌、幽默、讥讽、反语等的表达与理解，都可以界定为（人际关系）规约或规约类人际行为。在第三部分，作者通过比较方式考察人际关系仪式，将其与其他各种规约区分开来，指出一般规约行为与仪式行为的关键差别，即实施一般规约行为的前提是要强调遵循，需要遵守关系网络的期盼，而实施仪式行为的前提则是强调模仿。

  在第三章"群内仪式的运作：两则个案研究"中，作者分析了群内人际关系仪式，借助两类个案（匈牙利语电子邮件以及中国古代信函），呈现了人际关系仪式在形式和功能方面的主要互动特征。作者指出，人际关系仪式与标准化的社会仪式之间有较为显著的相似性，虽然不总是拥有惯用的语汇、组织方式和功能，但也有可加以明确辨认、相对严格的形式和功能特征，观察者往往也是很容易捕捉到这些特征的。接着，作者在第二部分探讨了群内人际关系仪式的建构性人际关系功能，指出群内人际关系仪式实践通过激活群内道义情感，有助于建构或强化人际关系网络身份。用来建构人际关系网络身份的人际关系仪式，不仅包括特定的语用行为（如选择使用明显带有人际关系仪式的表达形式），也包括多轮展开的话语或互动行为（如具有人际关系仪式特征的、涉及特定图式话题的反复讨论）。此外，如一些案例分析所示，交际者在一些场合下也可以借助仪式实践，刻意将自己与其他社交网络或人群区分开来。

  在第四章"人际关系仪式的分类体系"中，作者将群内概念纳入基于人际关系沟通概念的仪式分类体系，把群内人际关系仪式实践置于人际关系仪式"家族"中。之前关于仪式的分类一般不会考虑人际关系功能，而是基于其出现的社会事件语境加以分析。本书采用互动视角来界定人际关系仪式，就可以不考虑群体的大小，而是关注群内仪式相对于关系网络局外人的"透明性"和"可及性"。人际关系仪式现象包括那些对许多人而言易于辨认、理解、任何语言使用者都可以参与的话语实践(因而是透明、可及的仪式),也包括那些交际者刻意隐蔽、模糊、(作为参与者的)观察者难以辨认、理解的话语实践(因而是不透明、不可及的仪式),二者处于连续统的两端,具体包括下列四类:(1)隐性仪式;(2)个人仪式;(3)群内仪式;(4)社会仪式。在作者看来,由(1)到(4),透明性和可及性依次增强。作者通过个案分析,对上述四种仪式实践进行了阐述和辨析。

在第五章"识别、情感性和情绪性"中,作者从认知角度探讨了群内人际关系仪式的识别与理解问题。作者首先聚焦群内人际关系仪式实践的识别问题,指出此类仪式作为规约化行为具有变异性,对于说话人而言可能是默认的,而对于听话人而言则可能是有标记的。在这种情况下,听话人可能会通过元话语加以提及或评价。接着,作者考察群内人际关系仪式对于交际者的情感和情绪影响,指出群内人际关系仪式没有机构性仪式惯有的目标(如丧礼上相关仪式的作用是引发悲伤),因此,难以预测群内人际关系仪式的情感效应。群内人际关系仪式往往对互动双方而非其他参与者或观察者产生情绪性或情感性效应,也正是这些效应提升了相对于互动者而言的人际关系功能。

在第六章"破坏性人际关系仪式"中,作者从反方面进一步探究人际关系仪式理论,重点剖析了(针对具体对象的)破坏性人际关系仪式行为,尤其是,考察破坏性人际关系仪式,有助于将交际者的感知和评价纳入到人际关系仪式的理论框架中。作者根据相关话语实践对人际关系的影响性质,区分了建设性的群内人际关系仪式实践和破坏性的群内人际关系仪式实践。前者是"强化关系的"(relation forcing),通过实施该行为能激发人际关系向好的方向发展或至少可以维持好的状况,后者是"腐蚀关系的"(relation corrupting),也就是说,实施该行为会导致实施者(以及整个关系网络)与被羞辱者之间的人际关系恶化。作者在介绍了 Goffman 关于 stigma("骂名")的概念后,借助不礼貌研究案例,探讨了最具代表性的破坏性群内人际关系仪式实践,表明破坏性仪式实践的运行往往遵循之前不礼貌研究者发现的一些模式。不过，如同作者强调的那样，破坏性仪式实践与不礼貌之间存在一个根本的区别，那就是，前者的破坏力来自该仪式实践的反复实施，而后者只与表达方式有关。这也进一步说明了区分二者的重要性和必要性。最后，作者从参与者的感知视角，进一步考察了群内人际关系仪式的破坏性和建设性。

在第七章"结论"中，作者总结了本书所构建的群内人际关系仪式框架的优势与不足（如未吸取经济学领域的研究成果、分析的客观性问题），指出未来的研究方向与领域（如跨关系网络之间的人际关系仪式实践研究、古今关系网络中人际关系仪式实施方面的质性差异研究），尤其是跨文化语境中研究人际关系仪式的必要性，并尝试性地为此类研究提出了一个分析模式。

2. 评价

2.1 本书的主要理论贡献

本书的贡献之一在于，作者秉持话语实践观和关系建构观，提出了人际关系仪式理论（theory of relational ritual）（p.21），是对人际关系理论（relational theory）的重要发展。在过去的近二十年里，一些学者开始超越语言（不）礼貌本身，关注语言使用对更为宽广的人际关系的建构、维持、破坏等作用，提出了不同的理论模式，如 Helen Spencer-Oatey（2000, 2002, 2005, 2007, 2008）的 Rapport management theory, Janet Holmes et al（2011）的 neo-politeness theory, Miriam Locher and Richard Watts（2005）和 Watts（1989, 2003）的 theory of relational work, Robert Arundale（1999, 2006, 2010）的 face-constituting theory。学者们尽管使用了不同的术语，如 rapport management, relational practice, relational work, relating, relationality，但都是在探讨语言使用与人际关系的问题，而非传统的礼貌模式(关注的是个人单方面的礼貌实施行为)。在新的理论框架下，礼貌被视为人际关系的一个重要方面，而非全部。作者所建构的人际关系仪式理论具有鲜明的特点，主要包括（1）基于话语而展开；（2）从人际关系视角切入；（3）融入交际者和分析者分析视角；4）融合了多学科的研究成果，具有跨学科性，兼顾关于仪式的规范性、大众性的理解和动态性、互动性的认识；（5）兼顾人际关系仪式的实施与识别、感知及其效应；（6）不仅探讨了建设性人际关系仪式行为，而且探讨了破坏性人际关系仪式行为；（7）将人际关系仪式置于更宽广的图式行为框架中，厘清了人际关系仪式与（不）礼貌、一般规约行为等之间的区别。

　　本书的贡献之二在于，作者发展并拓宽了仪式的概念。首先，在界定上，引入话语语用学理论和人际关系视角，将言语交际中的人际关系仪式现象与其他各种人际关系现象（如礼貌）一同加以考察，并予以明确区分。仪式的概念源于 Goffman（1967）的《互动仪式》。该概念进入语用学研究领域后，相关研究一般都采用源于 Goffman 的传统定义，用它来概括语言使用中各种规约化、形式化的部分，往往与特定的言语行为（如命名、宣誓）有关。这一做法忽略了仪式话语实践具有的复杂的互动和人际关系功能。为此，作者聚焦人际关系仪式，即从人际关系沟通角度界定的各种仪式，这些仪式是由互动话语实践触发的社会行为，包括那些通过话语互动来建构、维持或解构人际关系的仪式话语实践，但不包括暗自发出的诅咒、祝福等，因为后者不是通过话语实践实现的，也看不出其对人际关系会产生什么外在的影响。所研究的仪式必须对实施者有意义、有影响，不包括空洞的、无效果的话语行为。作者从人际关系角度，将仪式看作是社会行为这一点，与 Collins（2004）把仪式看作是带有情感或思想的实体有不同之处。其次，在分类上，作者以透明性、可及性为标准，区分不同性质的仪式。这样的仪式分类方式是作者的创举，一方面有利于洞察所有人际关系仪式的共同特征，即具有人际关系功能（如建构、强化关系网络身份），另一方面有利于阐释为什么特定的仪式话语实践易于辨认、理解，而另外一些仪式话语实践则难以被识别或易被误解。再次，作者探究了（人际关系）仪式的互动感知，填补了之前研究只关注其实施的局限性，丰富了关于仪式的认识。最后，作者探讨了破坏性仪式行为，这同样填补了一个研究空白，因为之前的人类学、社会学、语用学文献始终关注的都是仪式行为的建构作用。通过相关讨论，作者明确指出，人际关系仪式的实施不仅可以建构、强化积极的人际关系，也可能会削弱甚至破坏人际关系，从而让我们对人际关系仪式的社会功能有了更完整的认识。总之，作者从人际关系角度、基于话语建构的理念重新界定仪式，将其纳入人际关系这一宽广的理论体系，打破了传统研究范式（包括人类学、社会学、历史学、博弈学、心理学等）的藩篱，具有明显的创新性。新框架由于强调仪式的人际关系维度，可以融合来自不同学科的研究成果。

2.2 本书的方法论特点

本书在研究方法上采用了多元视角，既有语言使用者的视角（又分为交际参与者与解读者或当事人），又有观察者视角（又分为语料分析者和理论建构者），前者代表了当事人路径（emic approach）或第一阶视角（first-order perspective），后者则代表了局外人路径（etic approach）或第二阶视角（second-order perspective）。尽管前者在诸如礼貌、身份研究中越来越多地被使用，仿佛是一种潮流，但本书作者认为后者同样重要，可以与前者互参、互补，相得益彰。其次，作者以社会关系网络（可大可小，可以是二人组，也可以是多人组成的群）作为分析单位，认为群内仪式指的是在社会关系网络内形成的人际关系实践仪式，这样做一方面有助于区分微观层面上的群内人际关系仪式与宏观层面上的（超越单一关系网络的）社会仪式，另一方面有助于捕捉更多场景下相同仪式的使用情况，比把实践社区作为分析单位更具优势。值得一提的是，作者在语料使用上同样体现了多元性，既有口语语料，又有笔语语料；既有当下语料，又有历史语料；既有对话性语料，又有独白性语料；既有纯文字语料，又有多模态语料；既有交际语料，又有访谈、回溯语料。上述语料分别来自英语、匈牙利语和汉语，体现了多元语言性和多元文化性。

2.3 本书的主要不足

纵观全书，笔者认为本书具有很高的学术价值，论述较充分，结构较严谨，但仍然存在一些可以进一步完善的方面，主要包括：

（一）作者对人际关系仪式对了非常细致的界定（p.12），但略显繁琐、晦涩。诸如"or historicity in general (and related social ethos)" "emotively invested" "as anthropological research has shown"等可删。该定义的优点是包容性，但缺点也是其过于求全，应突出重点。此外，需要说明该定义所采用的人际关系视角与现有的定义方式是互补而非取代关系。

（二）尽管区分了人际关系仪式与（不）礼貌（p.18），对二者的联系虽然也提及但讨论明显不够。其实，仪式使用本身也会被评价为（不）礼貌。换言之，实施仪式有时是实施（不）礼貌的一种手段。在讨论人际关系仪式与身份的关系时也存在类似的问题。

（三）如作者在第七章中指出的那样，本书没有对言语交际中的人际关系仪式进行跨文化比较或对比研究，而是作为未来研究的话题予以提出。笔者认为，本书缺少这样的跨文化比较是一大缺憾，原因是人际关系仪式带有很强的文化个性。诚如作者本人指出的那样，不同社会文化对仪式的预期和评价会存在很大的差异，甚至在同一社会中不同群体之间也会存在很大差异。作者同时使用了三种语言的语料，由于缺乏比较分析而显得有点混杂、随意。此外，作者同时使用了当下语料和历史语料，由于缺乏历史比较，因而也是一大缺憾，毕竟人际关系仪式会随历史发展而有很大的变化。作者原本就是要挑战英语中"去仪式化"的观点，仅采用一种宽式的仪式定义也许并非是最好、最有力的挑战方式，原因是作者与前人对仪式的定义并不等同，因而有偷换概念之嫌。

（四）标题使用及行文方面仍有完善的空间。不同章节之间行文偶尔存在简单重复的问题。一些例子的背景知识交代不够充分。个别标题的使用会引起读者的误解，如 1.1.2 会让读者期盼作者会在此节给出自己关于人际关系仪式的定义，而 1.1.3 易让读者以为作者会给出另一种定义，而实际上，作者是在后一节中才给出自己的定义。个别小节的序号编排欠妥，如第 3 章只有 3.1.1 而无 3.1.2，第 7 章只有 7.1.1 而无 7.1.2 等。

当然，瑕不掩瑜。希望本书能给中国读者带来尽可能多的启迪，对中国语用学的研究起到应有的推导作用，引发更多的中国学者更加深入探究汉语中的人际关系仪式。

参考文献

钱永红. (2015). 《国际通用语视角下关系程式教学模式探究》. 《外语与外语教学》（2）：19—25.

Arundale, Richard. (1999). An alternative model and ideology of communication for an alternative politeness theory. *Pragmatics* 9: 119—153.

Arundale, Richard. (2006). Face as relational and interactional: A communication framework for research on face, facework, and politeness. *Journal of Politeness Research* (2) 2: 193—216.

Arundale, Richard. (2010). Constituting face in conversation: face, facework and interactional achievement. *Journal of Pragmatics* 42 (8): 2078—2105.

Collins, Randall. (2004). *Interaction Ritual Chains*. Princeton: Princeton University Press.

Eelen, Gino. (2001). *Critique of Politeness Theories*. Manchester: St Jerome Press.

Goffman, Erving. (1967). *Interactional Ritual: Essays on Face-to-Face Behavior*. Garden City, NY: Doubleday.

Haugh, Michael. (2003). Anticipated versus Inferred Politeness. *Multilingua* 22, 4: 397—413.

Haugh, Michael. (2007). The discursive challenge to politeness theory: An interactional alternative. *Journal of Politeness Research* 3(2): 295—317.

Haugh, Michael & Francesca Bargiela-Chiappini. (2010). Face in interaction. Special issue of *Journal of Pragmatics* 42(8): 2073—2171.

Holmes, Janet, et al. (2011). *Discourse, Ethnicity and Leadership*. Oxford: Oxford University Press.

Kádár, Daniel. Z. & Haugh Micahel. (2013). *Understanding Politeness*. Cambridge: Cambridge University Press.

Kádár, D. Z. & Yuling, Pan. (2011). Politeness in China. In D. Z. Kádár & S. Mills (eds.). *Politeness in East Asia*. Cambridge: Cambridge University Press. 125—

146.

Kádár, Daniel & Pan, Yuling. (eds.). (2013). *Chinese Discourse and Interaction*. London: Equinox.

Kádár, Daniel Z. & Sara Mills. (2011). *Politeness in East Asia*. Cambridge: Cambridge University Press.

Locher, Miriam & Richard Watts. (2005). Politeness theory and relational work. *Journal of Politeness Research* 1: 9—33.

Locher, Miriam. (2004). *Power and Politeness in Action: Disagreements in Oral Communication*. Berlin: Mouton.

Mills, S. (2003). *Gender and Politeness*. Cambridge: Cambridge University Press.

Spencer-Oatey, Helen. (2000). Rapport management: A framework for analysis. In H. Spencer-Oatey (ed.). *Culturally Speaking: Managing Rapport through Talk across Cultures*. London: Continuum, 11—46.

Spencer-Oatey, Helen. (2002). Managing rapport in talk: using rapport sensitive incidents to explore the motivational concerns underlying the management of relations. *Journal of Pragmatics* 34: 529—545.

Spencer-Oatey, Helen. (2005). (Im)politeness, face and perceptions of rapport: unpacking their bases and interrelationships. *Journal of Politeness Research* 1: 95—119.

Spencer-Oatey, Helen. (2007). Theories of identity and the analysis of face. *Journal of Pragmatics* 39: 639—656.

Spencer-Oatey, Helen. (2008). Face, (im)politeness and rapport. In H. Spencer-Oatey (ed.), Culturally Speaking: *Culture, Communication and Politeness Theory*. London: Continuum, 11—47.

Watts, Richard. (1989). Relevance and relational work: Linguistic politeness as politic behaviour. *Multilingua* 8(2/3): 131—166.

Watts, Richard. (2003). *Politeness*. Cambridge: Cambridge University Press.

Contents

List of Figures and Tables　图表清单　　　　　　　　　　　　　　　1
Acknowledgements　致谢　　　　　　　　　　　　　　　　　　　3

1　Introduction　导论　　　　　　　　　　　　　　　　　　　　1
　1.1　Why this book?　本书目的　　　　　　　　　　　　　　　1
　　　1.1.1　Rituals: the narrow interpretation　仪式：窄式定义　　5
　　　1.1.2　Definitions of ritual　仪式的各种定义　　　　　　　6
　　　1.1.3　An alternative 'relational' definition of ritual　基于"人际关系"的定义　9
　　　1.1.4　In-group ritual: an illustrative example　群内仪式：示例　12
　1.2　Methodology and data　方法论及语料　　　　　　　　　14
　　　1.2.1　Methodology　方法论　　　　　　　　　　　　　14
　　　1.2.2　Data　语料　　　　　　　　　　　　　　　　　　15
　1.3　Structure of the book　本书结构　　　　　　　　　　　18

2　Defining Ritual from a Relational Perspective　人际关系视角下的仪式界定　23
　2.1　Introduction　引言　　　　　　　　　　　　　　　　　23
　　　2.1.1　Ritual and the relational perspective　仪式及人际关系视角　23
　　　2.1.2　Focus on the ritual–(im)politeness interface　聚焦仪式与（不）礼貌界面　24
　　　2.1.3　Structure　结构　　　　　　　　　　　　　　　　28
　2.2　Schematic acts and conventions　图式行为与规约　　　　29
　　　2.2.1　Schematic acts in relating　人际关系沟通中的图式行为　29
　　　2.2.2　Convention　规约　　　　　　　　　　　　　　　33
　2.3　Relational rituals　人际关系仪式　　　　　　　　　　　43
　　　2.3.1　Mimesis　模仿　　　　　　　　　　　　　　　　43
　　　2.3.2　Mimesis in operation　模仿的运作　　　　　　　　46
　　　2.3.3　The visibility of mimesis　模仿的可视性　　　　　48
　2.4　Summary　结语　　　　　　　　　　　　　　　　　　50

3　In-Group Ritual in Operation: Two Case Studies　群内仪式的运作：两则个案研究　51
　3.1　Introduction　引言　　　　　　　　　　　　　　　　　51
　　　3.1.1　Scope　范围　　　　　　　　　　　　　　　　　53
　3.2　Formal and functional features of in-group ritual: a case study of Hungarian e-mails　群内仪式的形式与功能特征：关于匈牙利语电邮的个案研究　53
　　　3.2.1　Data　语料　　　　　　　　　　　　　　　　　　53

2　Contents

  3.2.2　Formal properties: forms, sequences and activations　形式特征：形式、序列与激活　56
  3.2.3　Functional properties　功能特征　60
 3.3　In-group ritual and the construction of network identity: a case study of historical Chinese letters　群内仪式与社交网络身份的构建：关于汉语古代信函的个案研究　64
  3.3.1　Data　语料　66
  3.3.2　The first category: non-contrastive identity formation　第一类：非对比性身份的形成　67
  3.3.3　The second category: contrastive (counter-social conventional) ritual practice　第二类：对比性（反社会规约）仪式实践　73
 3.4　Summary　结语　77

4　Relational Ritual Typology　人际关系仪式的分类体系　78
 4.1　Introduction　引言　78
  4.1.1　Previous typologies of ritual behaviour　关于仪式行为的既往分类体系　78
  4.1.2　The relational typology　基于人际关系的分类体系　81
 4.2　Types of relational ritual　人际关系仪式的类型　85
  4.2.1　Covert ritual　隐性仪式　85
  4.2.2　Personal ritual　个人仪式　93
  4.2.3　In-group and social ritual　群内与社会仪式　98
 4.3　Summary　结语　102

5　Recognition, Affectivity and Emotivity　识别、情感性和情绪性　104
 5.1　Introduction　引言　104
  5.1.1　Recognition　识别　105
  5.1.2　Affectivity and emotivity　情感性和情绪性　111
 5.2　The recognition of rituals in interaction　互动中仪式的识别　114
 5.3　The affective effect and emotivity of relational rituals　人际关系仪式的情感效应及情绪性　125
 5.4　Summary　结语　133

6　Destructive Relational Rituals　破坏性人际关系仪式　135
 6.1　Introduction　引言　135
  6.1.1　Destructive rituals: a definition　破坏性人际关系仪式的定义　135
  6.1.2　Analytic significance　分析该类型仪式的意义　139
  6.1.3　Data and structure　语料及结构　142
 6.2　Stigma　骂名　143
 6.3　Inventory　各种特点　148
  6.3.1　Recurrent non-doing　反复该做不做　149
  6.3.2　Recurrent covert offence　反复隐性冒犯　155
  6.3.3　Recurrent reference to the stigma　反复提及骂名　159
 6.4　Different perceptions of ritual practices　对仪式实践的不同感知　161
  6.4.1　Public evaluation of destructive rituals　对破坏性仪式的公众评价　162

	6.4.2 Participant/onlooker perspectives 参与者/旁观者视角	166
	6.5 Summary 结语	173
7	Conclusion 结论	175
	7.1 The framework 分析框架	175
	7.1.1 The cross-cultural (and intercultural) ritual project 跨文化仪式研究课题	177
	7.2 Looking ahead 研究展望	182

Notes 注释   185
Glossary 术语表   197
References 参考文献   202
Index 索引   217

List of Figures and Tables 图表清单

Figures

2.1	The position of relational rituals	29
4.1	Example 4.1: *Szervusz, üdvözöllek*	83
4.2	The relational function of covert ritual practices	87
4.3	The in-group neutralisation and ritualisation of potentially covert ritual practices	95
5.1	The interactional recognition of relational ritual practices	124
5.2	Ritual and affectivity/emotivity	133
6.1	Example 6.10: Ritual unrecognition	157
6.2	Different perceptions and evaluations of destructive rituals	173
7.1	Difference of normative ritual types across cultures	182

Tables

6.1	Different practices of ritual in the data studied	150

Acknowledgements 致谢

I would like to say a big thank you to Francesca Bargiela-Chiappini for her continuous encouragement and expert comments on the manuscript. I am also greatly indebted to Sara Mills for sharing her expert views with me and inspiring me to develop a discursive pragmatic approach to rituals. Without Francesca and Sara devoting their precious time and energy to help me, this book would have never come into existence.

I would also like to thank Marcel Bax for his advice and inspiration. It was Marcel's fascinating research on ritual, and an impressive lecture of his, which aroused my long-term interest in this area. I owe a great deal of gratitude to Michael Haugh, who commented on my framework in the course of various insightful discussions. Our joint research project, which led to the authoring of the monograph *Understanding Politeness*, gave me some of the key ideas such as the significance of time in understanding the discursive operation of ritual.

My thanks also go to Jim O'Driscoll for commenting on some topics discussed in this book, and for bearing with me while I was nagging him with questions in his office. I would like to say thanks to Lesley Jeffries for tracking funding to cover some practical costs accrued in the present project, and also for sharing example (5.1) in Chapter 5 with me. I am also grateful to Olivia Middleton for inviting me to publish the present book with Palgrave Macmillan.

I would like to say thanks to my doctoral students May Asswae and Chengyu Zhuang for the research work they have undertaken in the Centre for Intercultural Politeness Research of the University of Huddersfield. The research of May and Chengyu provided insightful cross-cultural (and intercultural) data, which not only turned out to be essential for the present volume (Chapter 7) but will also be the basis of future projects in this area. I am also very much indebted to all those friends and acquaintances of mine who agreed to act as (anonymous) informants in the projects that led to the authoring of this book.

My sincere thanks go to the Hungarian blogger Szergej Tamis for allowing me to use the comic strip (4.1) in Chapter 4. I would like to extend my gratitude to the following persons and organisations for permitting me to use their materials: *The Telegraph* for allowing me to use an excerpt on rudeness in Chapter 2; Macon Dee for permitting me to cite from his blog (example 5.2); OnlineColleges.net for giving permission to cite from their website (example 6.13). In the case of some other websites cited I was not able to reach the authors, and I here would like to give credit to these persons/organisations.

Last but not least, I am greatly indebted to members of my family – who sometimes appear on the pages of this book – for their patience and care while I was working on this project. I dedicate this book to them: my wife, daughter, father and mother.

On an institutional level, I would like to express my gratitude to the Chiang Ching-Kuo Foundation for International Scholarly Exchange, for supporting my research through a long-term grant (RG025-P-10).

1
Introduction
导论

1.1 Why this book? 本书目的

This book offers a discursive relational framework of rituals. It examines ritual as a relational action constructed in interaction through pre-existing patterns (cf. Chapter 2), and it captures the features of ritual phenomena by analysing the interactants' behaviour in culturally and socially diverse contexts, hence avoiding a priori predictions (cf. later in the present section; for a detailed introduction to discursive approaches see Haugh et al. 2013). Stereotypically, English and other Western languages are thought of as languages which have dispensed with rituals, and the present volume will be challenging this concept.

Traditionally, the notion of ritual includes a variety of acts, spanning from baptism prayers, through certain acts of etiquette, to utterances such as *Well done* to acknowledge someone's achievements. Whilst interpretations of 'ritual' vary greatly, in popular culture this notion often refers to a prescribed, archaic form of behaviour, as represented by the following extract from the Sherlock Holmes story 'The Musgrave Ritual':[1]

(1.1)

" 'It is rather an absurd business, this ritual of ours,' he answered. 'But it has at least the saving grace of antiquity to excuse it. I have a copy of the questions and answers here if you care to run your eye over them.'

"He handed me the very paper which I have here, Watson, and this is the strange catechism to which each Musgrave had to submit when he came to man's estate. I will read you the questions and answers as they stand.

" 'Whose was it?'

" 'His who is gone.'

" 'Who shall have it?'

" 'He who will come.'

" 'Where was the sun?'

" 'Over the oak.'

" 'Where was the shadow?'

" 'Under the elm.'

" 'How was it stepped?'

" 'North by ten and by ten, east by five and by five, south by two and by two, west by one and by one, and so under.'

" 'What shall we give for it?'

" 'All that is ours.'

" 'Why should we give it?'

" 'For the sake of the trust.'
    (Sir Arthur Conan Doyle: *The Musgrave Ritual* [1893] 2003)

This ritual – meant to be performed when a member of the Musgrave family "came to man's estate" – is a rather archetypal one, due to its solemn nature.

 Although such acts certainly represent an important aspect of rituality, from a discursive perspective – which implies focusing on ritual acts as they occur in interaction – ritual covers a much broader set of phenomena. Indeed, ritual can be an interactionally 'stand-alone' or 'demarcated' (cf. Staal 1979, and Chapter 5) act like the Musgrave ritual, which is clearly codified and institutionalised, and which is meant to be performed at a definite point in time. However, to discourse pragmaticians it is evident that rituals are present in daily conversations, often in interactionally "co-constructed" forms (cf. Schegloff 1995).

 Furthermore, from a relational perspective – i.e. if we examine the effect of language on human identities "being in relation" with each other (see Miller 1984) – ritual plays a significantly more important relational role than marking ceremonies: by means of ritual acts we work out and maintain interpersonal relationships in diverse ways. In pragmatics, the technical terms 'relational' and 'relating' are applied in different contexts (cf. Chapter 2), and here they simply describe the interactional construction (or destruction) of interpersonal relationships vis-à-vis ritual practices.[2] This implies that we focus on the effect of ritual on interactants, rather than examining the individual performing ritual practices (cf. Spencer-Oatey's 2011 work on relationality). In a sense every ritual act has some relational function; the label 'relational ritual' is applied in this book as a collective term for 'rituals approached from the perspective of interpersonal relating'.[3] Nevertheless, the relational perspective implies some limitation of scope: the category of 'relational rituals' only includes those ritual practices which form or maintain relationships through interaction, for example a blessing or a curse is excluded from the analysis if it is a silent one, as it does not have any visible interactional impact on interpersonal relationships (cf. Chapter 6). The relational perspective also implies that the rituals studied here must be meaningful for their performers, i.e. it excludes 'empty', gratuitous performance, as is the case with rituals that have lost their practical significance. As Chapter 4 will argue, ritual practices usually have a distinct lifespan, which means that they 'fade out' after some time, and in the course of their disappearance they tend to become 'empty' rituals.[4]

In accordance with the discursive relational framework, this book focuses on language usage, and it approaches ritual as social action triggered by interactional practices (cf. Kádár and Haugh 2013). Describing language use in this way accords with the view of Clift et al. (2006):

> Talk is [...] a vehicle for social action; and also as a principal means by which social organization in person-to-person interaction is mutually constructed and sustained. (Clift et al. 2006: 5)

Interpreting ritual as social action implies diversity. As with any other social action, ritual practices are understood differently in situated contexts.

The discursive relational approach to rituals fills an important gap in the field because it integrates the phenomenon of ritual into a broader conceptualisation, which goes beyond traditional paradigms. Aspects of rituality have been discussed in various disciplines, including the humanities (e.g. anthropology, linguistics, history, game and play theory), and certain areas of social sciences including, for example, psychology.[5] As this book will argue (see e.g. Chapters 4 and 6), the present framework is suitable for incorporating findings from several of these disciplines due to its focus on the relational aspect of rituality.

Although this book does pursue an interest in ritual per se, it focuses primarily on an important yet generally neglected discursive phenomenon which is described as 'in-group ritual'. In-group ritual refers to the ritualised relational practices formed locally within the social unit of network. Since the term 'network' can take various interpretations, it is worth defining the meaning adopted in the present work. As Milroy and Milroy (1992: 2) claim, a "social network relates to the community and interpersonal level of social organization"; as Chapter 3 will argue, society is constituted through an intersecting nexus of relational networks. The concept of social network (which is used interchangeably with 'group' in this book) provides a useful unit of analysis to study discursively constructed practices of rituality because it allows us to approach rituality in a contextualised way, in accordance with the above-discussed view of ritual as social action. At the same time, the notion of social network helps the analyst to capture ritual in more settings than for example the notion of 'community of practice' (cf. Wenger 1998), which represents social networks primarily (but not exclusively) in the workplace.[6]

In terms of typology (cf. Chapter 4), the in-group rituals of relational networks represent a different type of ritual from practices which are conventionalised on a wider social level beyond single networks (this super-network type of ritual will henceforth be referred to as 'social ritual'). In the present framework, the size of networks/groups can range from the traditional speaker–hearer dyad to much larger groups. In-group ritual practices come into existence if a relational network meets the following criteria: (a) all those engaging in ritual practices have in-group status; and (b) group members have accrued a necessary extent of relational history (see Sections 1.1.2 and 1.1.3).

The notion of locally situated rituals differing from established macro-level social rituals is not new: the phenomenon of locally practised ritual has been widely discussed in psychology and other behavioural disciplines (see Chapter 4 for an overview). It has also been addressed in various studies on language usage (cf. Chapter 3), though it has been approached under different labels (e.g. teasing, mocking, routines). There is an important exception, namely, Collins' (2004) monograph, which theorises ritual on the micro-level. Whilst Collins' sociological framework greatly inspired me, and various references will be made to it (see e.g. Chapter 5), it has a considerably different scope from the present work (which might be due to disciplinary differences). Collins pursues an interest in ritual as an object or idea which is emotionally charged and argues that individuals are, in a sense, interconnected through rituals, i.e. he approaches relationality from the perspective of ritual act as an entity. I, on the other hand, am more interested in relationality per se, i.e. my framework operates the other way around as I approach ritual as a social action from the perspective of relationships (and individual goals) which generate this action. The relational stance brings along some major differences between Collins' and my conceptualisations of ritual; for example, an individual engaged in the performance of a relational ritual, unlike in the case of Collins' 'interaction ritual', has a wide space to transform a ritual act according to her or his preferences; also, the relational approach calls for categorising ritual in radically different ways from sociology (see Section 1.3 and Chapter 2). Thus, a distinctive aspect of the present framework is that it captures various manifestations of the ritual phenomenon within the perspective of relational *and* ritual theories.

The coexistence of social rituals and in-group rituals is not contradictory: for example, Chapter 3 will illustrate that even in historical communities such as imperial China in which much importance was attached to socially conventionalised ritual, both social and in-group rituals used to be practised. Furthermore, as Chapter 2 will argue, these two types of rituality tend to intermix, for example social rituals may develop into in-group rituals (and vice versa).[7]

In what follows, I discuss how the present discursive and micro-level approach to ritual relates to previous theories of rituality, before providing a discursive-relational definition of 'rituality'. An example of in-group ritual will be offered as an illustration.

1.1.1 Rituals: the narrow interpretation 仪式：窄式定义

Since the publication of Erving Goffman's (1967) classic study *Interaction Ritual* (some essays of this work were published earlier, in the 1950s), ritual has been regarded as a pivotal relational phenomenon. Goffman aimed to translate traditional ethnographic concepts of ritual research "to grasp some aspects of urban secular living" (Goffman 1967: 95). Despite this innovative stance, ritual continues to be represented in the field of pragmatic studies in a somewhat traditional way; in fact, ritual is often used as an umbrella term for the conventionalised aspects of language usage (cf. Chapter 2), and it is regularly associated with certain speech acts, such as greetings, performed in specific institutional settings (see e.g. Rash 2004, Zhu 2005). Such a perception of rituality is problematic because it represents ritual as a rather specific and formalised aspect of language usage, and so it fails to capture its complex interactional and relational functions.

It can be argued that this view follows from a narrow interpretation of rituals as phenomena that are, of necessity, recognised by a society, or at least substantial groupings within a society, in order to qualify as rituals (see also Chapter 2 for a detailed discussion of this problem). This criterion of 'public recognition' can be encountered, for example, in the work of historians such as Norbert Elias ([1994] 2000). Defining rituality from a social-constitutive perspective also occurs, quite interestingly (and perhaps somewhat paradoxically), in theories such as Bell's (1997: 43–6), which argues for a rethinking of the elusive notion of society in the context of ritual studies, and sees virtue in Douglas's (1970) concept of 'grid–group' definition of societies.[8] Furthermore, the restricted perspective can also be encountered in perceptive studies on ritual language use; Labov (1972), for one, has analysed ritual formats as widely used macro-level linguistic forms with 'local' (re-)interpretations and modifications. Such narrow interpretations of ritual are debatable since they are essentially at odds with discursive pragmatics in which the emphasis is on the micro-level analysis of pragmatic phenomena (cf. Mills 2011). Furthermore, a narrow sense interpretation of ritual creates an interdisciplinary gap between ritual as it is described in social studies and humanities, and its interpretations in other disciplines such as psychology (cf. Marks 1987, Poyurovsky et al. 2004; for more details see Chapter 4).

1.1.2 Definitions of ritual 仪式的各种定义

With these limitations in mind, an alternative – and more extensive – definition for ritual is due. In order to provide such a discursive definition, it is necessary first to survey the most important properties of ritual behaviour, as represented by scholars from various disciplines such as anthropology, social history and historical pragmatics. It is also necessary to revisit a historical–anthropological notion, 'deritualisation' (the claim that rituals have become insignificant in modern globalised social life), which I have found problematic from a relational perspective. Such an overview is inevitably biased: as experts of ritual research have stated (see e.g. Bell 1997), ritual has many functions which no single theory can capture comprehensively, and the present framework is no exception.

From a Durkheimian vantage point, it can be argued that ever since the dawn of humankind, ritual has been a key social phenomenon because of its 'survival value', specifically its potential to enhance the establishment and reinforcement of interpersonal and/or intragroup relations (cf. Durkheim [1912] 1954; cf. Guttmann 2004 for an elaboration of the Durkheimian view). Given its mimetic (and iconic) make-up – i.e. relational ritual acts are imitative performances which facilitate interpersonal communication (cf. Chapter 2 on mimetic ritual performance and its different interpretations) – ritual favours survival in that it serves as a means of conflict resolution and avoidance. A ritualised utterance is a mimetic performance, which re-enacts certain social or interpersonal values, and as such it facilitates interaction; ritual thus comes into operation as memes, by transmitting cultural/societal/in-group ideologies (see more on this issue in Blackmore 2007). As Potolsky (2006: 160) notes, "mimesis [...] is among the most successful memes in history"; furthermore, Merlin Donald (1991) makes it clear that mimesis, as it occurs in ritual, is a fundamental feature that distinguishes human from animal behaviour:

> Aside from advanced manual skill, there is another aspect of human mimetic behaviour that appears to need a special, modular neural apparatus in addition to a general mimetic capability: facial and vocal mimesis, which combine in the expression of emotion. The combination of vocal and facial emotional expression might have played a paramount role in mimetic culture, as it still does in modern society. (Donald 1991: 180)

Moreover ritual helps individuals to cope with critical situations because of its affection-evoking psychological function (Burke 1987, Muir 2005, Bax 2010a; see also Chapters 3 and 5). Through this prime function, ritual interaction has a strong potential to (re)shape and strengthen interpersonal relationships. By performing rituals, individuals convey their 'social dependence' or express their wish to find a place in the community, and to create new social dependences. "What is important about rituals", said Émile Durkheim, is "that they provide a powerful way in which people's social dependence can be expressed" (cited in Muir 2005: 3). In much the same vein, Kertzer has argued that

> [r]itual is a means by which we express our social dependence; what is important in ritual is our common participation and emotional involvement, not the specific rationalizations by which we account for the rites... Thus, ritual can promote social solidarity without implying that people share the same values, or even the same interpretation of the ritual. (Kertzer 1988: 67, 69)

Indeed, hegemonic and marginalised social groups may well have a different understanding of their joint rituals – and because of this fact such practices are open to be contested (cf. Chapter 4) – but as far as these rituals are normatively performed they tend to reinforce the ideological concept(s) according to which individuals in these groups depend on each other.

In contrast to some anthropologists and historians I claim that the concept of dependence should be taken as a broad notion, as an anthropological synonym for 'relationality', which does not inherently coincide with hierarchy (even though there is of course the potential for such a coincidence). As various historians, anthropologists and philosophers argue (see e.g. Burke 1987, Muir 2005, Naipaul 2005, Kanter 2007; but see Blackmore 2007 as an important exception), many contemporary social-communicative practices seem to be 'deritualised'.[9] This process is claimed to be due to the impact of the overall process (in the globalised world) of rationalisation (Bax 2010b), along with the transformation of many communal social structures into individual ones with the advent of modernisation and globalisation which, as Sifianou (2012) has evinced, brought about substantial changes in the area of sociopragmatic behaviour. In addition, one can argue that the decline of religious belief has also had a massive impact on this diachronic process (Muir 2005).

Deritualisation raises some problems from both a sociological and a relational–interactional aspect. As for the former, several researchers (e.g. Charvat and Kučera 1967) point out that, despite the spread of the ethos of egalitarianism (equality) and the ideology of individualism, social dependences have not ceased to influence human life, including social–interactional behaviour, even in egalitarian and individualistic societies. Deritualisation seems a highly problematic notion from a Foucauldian perspective (Mills 2003a), since it equates rituality with specific formal/functional interpretations, and maps such interpretations onto historical events, instead of dealing with rituality in its broader social function, i.e. as a means to reinforce social dependence (relationality). Furthermore, the notion of deritualisation is problematic because it implies that in modern Western societies egalitarianism is not an ethos but an absolute social reality (i.e. it projects an ideology on reality). Both historical sociology (Henderson et al. 2005) and contemporary sociological research (Western 2006) indicate that even in societies that make egalitarianism their central ideology, social inequality and hierarchy are ever present, although in a potentially more covert form than in societies dominated by hierarchical ideologies. Consequently, it seems logical to argue that rituality exists in every society, even though it is codified differently across societies, that is, hierarchical and conservative societies are more likely to preserve their rituals in codified/written forms, while in modern Western societies rituals are less concerned about codification and centralisation. But these are tendencies only: societies are not homogeneous, i.e. these perceptions are likely to be challenged by certain groups within a society (cf. Chapter 7).

From a relational–interactional perspective, there is a twofold problem with deritualisation, and in fact with any attempt to make a clear comparative distinction between the ritual practices of past and present. Firstly, it seems difficult to support such comparative claims with convincing evidence. Whilst historians such as Muir ([1997] 2005) cite a variety of old texts to illustrate how different historical people's ritual interaction was from today, from a relational perspective there seems to be little difference between the function and practices of ritual in different historical periods. I also agree with Jacobs and Jucker's (1995) claim that historical data is inherently 'faulted': firstly, historical texts transmit the voice and worldviews of the ruling elite (in the past, writing was a privilege reserved to the few); secondly, they also represent data in a less reliable way than, for example, audio recorded interactions. Consequently, one could rightly ask whether historical data is suitable to support claims about differences between past and present rituals (see Kádár and Culpeper 2010 on the problem of representation). This, of course, does not mean that there are no potential qualitative differences between the ritual practices of past and present, but capturing these differences is subject to future research (cf. Chapter 7). Secondly, the concept of deritualisation reflects a specific understanding of time (and diachronic interaction). In this concept, time occurs as a dichotomy, where historical/tribal is contrasted with contemporary/globalised. From a relational–interactional perspective it seems to be more productive to look into the *historicity* of rituals beyond this dichotomy. Historicity is a complex philosophical concept (on this notion and its theoretical implications see Heidegger [1927] 1991, and Foucault 1973); it is sufficient here to limit its interpretation to the following statement: all actions (and entities) in the world have their place and time, and so every action is part of history. In this perspective, every ritual act is 'historical', and what matters for a relational theory of ritual is relational history (or the historically situated feelings and notions which a ritual practice re-enacts), the existence of which is a precondition for relational rituals to operate (cf. Section 1.1.1). As Chapter 2 will illustrate, relational history forms an important link between the past and the present, as historicity influences the formation of the conventions according to which rituals operate.

1.1.3 An alternative 'relational' definition of ritual
基于"人际关系"的定义

Ritual can be approached from various angles, including, most importantly, from the perspective of (post-)interactional perception *by the participants/observers themselves*, or from a *theoretical* perspective, i.e. by rationalising the interactional meaning and function of relational ritual. The former perspective is often referred to as the so-called 'first-order perspective' and the latter one as the 'second-order perspective' (see more in Kádár and Haugh 2013). This distinction has so far been neglected by pragmatics and other theories of rituals. Most scholars describe rituals from their outsider (etic) perspective, and they provide technical (second-order) models for rituals, i.e. first-order expectancies (the etic perspective is a first-order one) are often implicitly present in these models.[10] This is why ritual is often defined in a narrow sense, without making an argument for, or even explicitly describing, this analytic perspective. In fact, objectivity cannot be reached in the examination of a phenomenon as ritual (it is not even self-evident whether objectivity is the prime aim of a qualitative research), and the culture-boundedness of interpretation and modelling probably need to be reflected upon as being 'necessary' components of any analysis of ritual. The interpreter is embedded in his or her own culture(s) which is also an influence on the analytical process. However, it seems necessary to make the first-order/second-order distinction, in order to be able to approach rituals in a self-reflexive way, and also to broaden our definition of ritual.

An important issue that the analyst needs to bear in mind is that the expectancies and evaluation of rituals differ greatly across societies (cf. Chapter 7). Due to this fact, models that implicitly include culture-specific expectancies of 'ritual', especially those which do not make this stance clear, present this phenomenon from specific perspectives, which often contradict each other. In fact, every sociopragmatic phenomenon is subject to different evaluations across cultures and societies, and even across the groups of a given society (cf. Mills 2003b). This seems to be particularly the case for rituals, as the very word 'ritual' tends to have strongly negative connotations in Western cultures and positive ones in East Asian cultures (see also Chapter 4 on such intercultural differences). This difference is due to historical reasons. As the historian Edward Muir (2005: 7–8) notes,

> during the Middle Ages [...] conceptions of what a ceremony or ritual did were very different from modern notions. For medieval Christians the most important distinction was between "good" and "bad" rituals. The Incarnation and Passion of Christ made Jewish ceremonies irrelevant, and the fact that Jews continued to practice them was an example of an empty, useless, or bad ritual. The same logic was applied to pagan ritual observances. But rituals could be bad in another sense. To perform a ritual was risky because it gave

one's enemies an opportunity to disrupt or manipulate it to serve their ends. And thus ritual was always potentially dangerous to the social order, not just an opportunity to create or represent community, providing a lubricant for the social system as much of modern ritual theory would assert.

As this description makes clear, the medieval perception of rituality covered a practice that often became necessary, but which was nevertheless potentially harmful. This somewhat negative meaning continued to pertain after the concept of 'ritual', a relatively late coinage, spread in the sixteenth century. In East Asian cultures the concept of 'ritual' has been interpreted differently, as the Chinese notion of *li* 礼 (ritual) has a considerably different history from 'ritual'. *Li* is a complex notion, which means, among other things, '(religious) rites', 'social rules' and 'respect' (cf. Gou 2002). In a similar way to 'rituality', *li* has a sacred origin: the most ancient meaning of this word is the performance of rites before the spirits of the ancestors. This ancient definition of *li* is positive, and *li* continued to preserve its predominantly positive connotations in the course of its history, to the extent that this notion was integrated into Confucianism (see e.g. Chan 2000), and, through (Neo-)Confucianism, into the state ideology of imperial China (see e.g. Buckley Ebrey 1991) and that of neighbouring countries such as Japan and Korea which were influenced by (Neo-)Confucian ideals.

Due to such differences, it is reasonable to create a theoretical and technical (second-order) interpretation of 'ritual' that is broad enough, and which can consequently accommodate several second-order models based on different (first-order) expectancies. Although such a broad theoretical definition cannot be entirely 'objective', it seeks to bring different views on the ritual phenomenon closer to each other. While the model of ritual proposed in this book is a theoretical one, it is based on the analysis of real-life discourse. This methodological approach can be enriched by including the observer's as well as the participants' perspective as emerging in post-event interviews (cf. Spencer-Oatey 2000 and Section 1.2.2). This is needed in order to understand what a certain ritual implies for those who perform it (see e.g. Chapter 3).[11]

With these methodological considerations and the above-discussed relational properties of rituals in mind, we can define the phenomenon of ritual as follows:

Relational ritual is a formalised/schematic, conventionalised and recurrent act, which is relationship forcing, i.e. by operating it reinforces/

transforms in-group relationships. Ritual is realised as an embedded (mini-)performance (mimesis), and this performance is bound to relational history (and related ethos), or historicity in general (and related social ethos[12]). Ritual is an emotively invested affective action, as anthropological research has shown.

An important advantage of this second-order definition is that it is inclusive, and consequently it avoids restricting rituals to social ones, which are the most visible types of rituals (cf. Chapter 3). Accordingly, the following Section 1.1.4 will illustrate this definition in detail, by citing an example of in-group ritual.

1.1.4 In-group ritual: an illustrative example 群内仪式：示例

My data shows that ritual – in particular its in-group type – often manifests itself in forms that are meaningful primarily to those who perform them (cf. Chapter 4), and so the discursive analysis of rituals makes it possible for us to journey into a relatively hidden realm of language usage. Let us illustrate this point by examining the following Hungarian language extract:

(1.2)

1. A: belegondolva lehetséges=   anyád

   B: =lenne bunkókám (.) ha (.) felfogtad volna időben hogy

2. A: (hhh)

   B: női társaságban az ember nem (.) viselkedik bunkó módon mint aki nem tudja

1. A: thinking about it it might be=   your mother is

   B: =could be yokel (.) should (.) you have realised in time that

2. A: (hhh)

   B: in female company you don't (.) behave in such a yokel-like way as one who doesn't know

This short fragment occurs in a longer recording belonging to a set of recordings of interactions between A and B, two males in their thirties, which was provided by one of the participants (B), who is an acquaintance of mine. In what follows, let us examine the main ritualistic features of this interaction; the key features, which occur in the definition of ritual proposed in Section 1.1.3, are underlined.

As the recordings reveal, A and B used a Hungarian rude form of endearment, *bunkókám* (lit. my little yokel, trans. yokel), in order to tease each other in an amiable way. This is a <u>formalised/schematic</u> and <u>conventionalised</u> language use between these two people (see Chapter 2 for a detailed definition of 'schematic'). Thus, it is clearly an in-group practice as it is conventionalised within the given relational network (cf. Chapter 2 for a detailed definition of conventionalisation and its relationship with rituality). As B disclosed in the course of a post-event interview, this in-group use of the offensive term *bunkókám* originates in secondary school where he and A were classmates. This form occurs in example (1.2) in which B reproaches A for repeatedly failing to secure a date with a girl he liked to go out with. Importantly, *bunkókám* is not an invention of this group as it is a conventional Hungarian swear word (cf. Culpeper 2011a on conventional impoliteness); what *is* the in-group 'invention' of A and B is the adoption of *bunkókám* as ritual teasing.[13]

Bunkókám can be evaluated as a ritual term due to the following interrelated characteristics. Firstly, it is a <u>recurrent</u> form with a specific relational function: in the approximately 4 hour and 30 minute-long recordings that B provided, this word occurs 42 times, in contexts in which A and B negotiate (predominantly dating-related) life strategies, that is, it seems to serve as a tool to facilitate the in-group discussion of certain issues. Secondly, it operates as an <u>emotively invested affective action</u> (cf. González et al. 1998),[14] which becomes obvious from its contextual usage. In an already challenging context (the other's dating skills are questioned) a deprecatory word such as *bunkókám* would normally further increase the imposition, and so the most plausible explanation for its usage resides in its positive affective value (see this expression in Grabenhorst et al. 2008). The 'harmless' affective function of *bunkókám* is illustrated by its interactional effect. Although in line 1, A reacts to this word by using the mild swear word *anyád* (your mother [is a bitch]...)[15] as a ritualistic counter-challenge, *bunkókám* is not visibly evaluated by the interlocutor.[16] And after the very short counter-challenge, A does not attempt to retake the 'floor': *bunkókám* seems to create an affective ritual 'frame', which allows B to freely advise his listener (see Section 1.3 on the pragmatic function of relational rituals). As Chapter 3 (cf. example 3.4) will illustrate, this ritual frame is a temporal one, as it tends to differ from non-ritual (default) feeling. The affective function of this term seems to originate in its specific <u>relational history</u> mentioned above, i.e. it was previously a term used in banter when the interactants were secondary school students. Consequently, the use (or, more precisely, reactivation) of this form is bound to an in-group ethos (A and B's schooldays); its 'harmlessness' resides in its mimetic value: by using *bunkókám* B not so much speaks as an individual, but rather he animates the voice of a historical group of schoolchildren. The difference between the usage of this ritual form and any other non-ritualised form which the members of a relational network used in the past is that *bunkókám* is a common 'property' of A and B.

The definition of ritual provided here will be drawn on and further explained in the following chapters. In what follows, let us overview the methodology and data used in the present book.

1.2 Methodology and data 方法论及语料

1.2.1 Methodology 方法论

In accordance with the discursive approach, the present book will examine ritual in interactional settings. In terms of research methodology this has the following implications:

- We need to include longer stretches of interaction in the scope of our analysis, in order to capture the way in which rituals are co-constructed. This accords with a recent methodology in various topics in linguistics, for example identity research (e.g. Krzyżanowski 2010) and politeness research (e.g. Watts 2003, Mills 2011), as well as in psychology and sociology (e.g. Andrews 2000, Hepburn and Wiggins 2007). Extending our analysis to co-constructed interactions gives a more comprehensive picture of relational ritual than focusing on utterances only. As the following chapters will illustrate, relational ritual – and in-group ritual in particular – manifests itself in many forms, spanning single utterances (and paralinguistic forms) to ritual interaction. In spite of formal differences, such manifestations represent essentially the same relational behaviour. For example, as Chapter 2 will argue (see e.g. example 2.9), relational rituals which are co-constructed in longer stretches of talk are, in a sense, as normative to those who perform them as various demarcated daily used social rituals. Note that the interactionally co-constructed nature of certain ritual acts does not imply that they come into existence simply through what is said in a moment: similarly to any other ritual act like single utterances, ritualised conversation follows certain schematic conventions, i.e. it is characterised by a degree of formal fixity (cf. Chapter 3).
- Observing the way in which rituals are co-constructed and/or utilised within interaction includes taking their context into consideration. As Goodwin and Duranti (1992: 5, cited from Mills 2003b: 49)

note, "the dynamic socially constructive properties of context are inescapable since each additional move within the interaction modifies the existing context while creating a new arena for subsequent interaction". The examination of the context of ritual also requires us to inquire into the relational history of interactants, which "pertains to the prior relationship experiences [...] people have" (West and Turner 2010: 21), as well as the prospects of the relational network.
- Approaching ritual from a discursive angle – which conceptualises ritual as an interactionally situated phenomenon – entails the theoretical stance that no form is inherently ritualistic. Whilst certain utterances are associated with relational ritual behaviour by default – a representative case might be *Welcome on board*, which is associated with the act of a rite of passage (cf. Chapter 2) – arguably rituals do not universally operate as such in any context and in every relational network. Ritual is an action (cf. Section 1.1) which comes into operation vis-à-vis the schematic (and mimetic) usage of forms (network practice), that is, form per se only has an indirect relationship with the actual act of ritual. Consequently, forms and schematically organised co-constructed interaction (cf. Chapter 2) can function as ritual only if and when they occur under interactional conditions that fulfil a relational network's expectations for ritualised behaviour.

1.2.2 Data 语料

The majority of the ritual practices studied in this book were collected between 2008 and 2011, in the course of concurrent projects. In accordance with the discursive scope of this work, the data has been analysed qualitatively rather than quantitatively. As the data will be presented and discussed in detail in individual chapters, in this section I only provide a description of the general features of the database.

The present research is based on multicultural data, including ritual interactions in Hungarian, English and Chinese.[17] Reliance on multicultural data had a rather practical function in my research: examining ritual situated in different cultures helped me to form the second-order framework proposed in Section 1.1, which seems to be broad enough to capture ritual in various cultural contexts. This volume does not include a comparative cross-cultural or intercultural examination of rituals, which is the subject of further research (cf. Chapter 7). Therefore, the database was not deliberately set up to offer a comparable representation of the three languages.

From a diachronic perspective, this book aims to study ritual practices in our time and consequently the majority of examples analysed are contemporary ones. Nevertheless, the database also includes historical data: monologic interactions such as historical correspondence between Chinese men of letters (cf. Chapter 3) and dialogic exchanges taken from novels and educational materials (cf. Chapter 6).[18] Chapter 3 will bring contemporary and historical analysis together. Merging historical and contemporary data is important from the perspective of the theoretical framework: as this book argues against the concept of 'deritualisation' (cf. Section 1.1.2) and claims that we should avoid distinguishing between the notions of 'historical' and 'contemporary' in terms of rituality, it is essential to illustrate that historical data and diachronically situated understandings of rituality are in agreement with the present relational theory.

The contemporary database includes both spoken and written data, including audio-recorded and manually recorded spoken interactions, computer-mediated conversations through e-mail and discussion rooms, extracts from films, literary pieces, cartoons and blogs.[19] Many examples in this book represent recorded spoken conversations and the computer-mediated genres of e-mails and discussion boards. This accords with the aim to capture the way in which ritual is constructed interactionally. Recorded and computer-mediated communication are relatively close to each other; as Thornbury and Slade (2006: 25) note,

> the electronic medium has had the effect of dissolving many of the traditional distinctions between written and spoken interactions: interactants are less writers than co-participants in an exchange that resembles live talk.

Recorded spoken data includes audio-recorded interactions, and short conversations which I wrote down and analysed soon after they had taken place. I obtained much of this data through friends and acquaintances; in one case my acquaintance recorded his in-group conversations for me and in others I was present at them. Audio-recorded data proved to be suitable to capture certain micro-level conversational properties of rituality. As Watts (1991: 13) notes about observing relational phenomena through audio-recorded conversations,

> An omnipresent problem with the data of this kind is that of the observer's paradox. The degree to which the researcher's presence effects [sic] the behaviour of the other participants and the subsequent nature of the data is a factor which must be included in the interpretation of verbal interaction. [...] it is impossible to solve this problem entirely and that it may even be undesirable to go to great

lengths in the attempt to exclude the effects of the observer and/or the equipment.

Accordingly, while I am aware that working with audio-recorded data poses certain problems,[20] it is hoped that the diversity of data used in this book at least partly offsets them.

The data includes fictional literary pieces and film extracts; for example, in Chapter 2 reference will be made to the epic historical film *300* (cf. example 2.8). Fictional sources have a distinct value from the perspective of ritual research: they illustrate the emotive and affective function of relational ritual. Similarly to narrative epics such as *Ilias*, these creative texts not only aim to retell the emotion of (and affection between) those who perform a ritual, but also to provoke emotions in the audience. As Bell (1997) and others argue, there is a gap between the ritual experiences of those who perform rituals and others who observe them, and in fictional sources this gap narrows down.

It is pertinent to note that I also included conversations with my family and friends in the data set for the following reasons:

- I regarded it important to extend the present study to analyses in which I can represent the perspectives of both the observer and the participant (also due to the above-discussed phenomenon of ritual experience);
- I understood the context of these interactions better than in any other interaction studied.

While in such analyses the researcher is inevitably 'biased', no discursive analysis can be entirely objective. Furthermore, including self-analysis in research accords with ethnographic methodologies, which allow "[s]elf-analysis through auto/ethnography and practitioner ethnography" (Kress 2011: 230).

Since not every spoken interaction in this book is audio-recorded, there is some diversity in the representation of spoken face-to-face examples. The extracts which I transcribed from memory appear in a 'plain' dialogic form, whilst audio-recorded data is transcribed following transcription conventions which allowed me to analyse certain micro-level features of rituals such as prosody. Note that the transcription adopted is a fairly simple one, compared for example to the conventions adopted in conversation analysis (see e.g. Jefferson 2002).[21]

Along with interactional data, the present research also involves some retrospective accounts and interviews. This book will argue[22] that in the research of relational ritual it is essential to take different perspectives into account (cf. Section 1.1.3). As Kádár and Haugh (2013) note, relational phenomena can be analysed from the perspective of both participants and emic or 'insider' understandings (which are both first-order *user* perspectives), as well as from the perspective of analysts and theoretical understandings (which are both second-order *observer* perspectives).[23] Although the proposed framework is a second-order one, first-order perspectives are regarded as essential in order to understand the relational function of ritual. Whilst the interactants' understanding of ritual can be captured to some extent by looking at interactional moves and reactions, retrospective accounts complete the picture. The post-event interviews (cf. Spencer-Oatey [2000] 2008 for a detailed discussion) conducted for the present research are quite simple: I usually asked my acquaintances to retell their experiences of a certain ritual event, and I slightly edited most of their accounts.

Interactants in the contemporary data are represented with acronyms. Most of my acquaintances were happy to have their real names used in the transcripts, whilst some preferred to remain anonymous. In order to avoid discrepancies, I decided to represent all interactants by capital letters, except in the case of examples drawn from my family data.

1.3 Structure of the book 本书结构

Chapter 2 will set the ground for the rest of this book by defining the phenomenon of ritual from a relational perspective. In the first part of Chapter 2, I will define the relationship between ritual and other relational phenomena. As will be argued, in some fields such as anthropology, ritual is often described as an analytic category that exists in its own right. However, in terms of relating, ritual is but one, albeit important, category within the domain which can be defined as 'schematic acts', and, in a narrower sense, 'relational conventions'. The relational perspective also entails focusing on an area where ritual and various relational phenomena, such as practices of (im)politeness (most significantly, but not exclusively) coincide. Yet, there is a key difference between ritual and (im)politeness: politeness comes into existence through interpretation and evaluation, whilst relational ritual should be approached from the perspective of action. As ritual is operationalised through certain pre-existing communicational schemata, it comes into existence as the interactants perform these schemata, i.e. via acting (evaluation also plays a part in the interactional operation of rituals, just perhaps not to the same extent as in that of (im)politeness, cf. Chapters 5 and 6). In the second part of Chapter 2, I will examine the collective category of schematic acts from a pragmatic perspective, and then I will narrow the analysis to the schematic relational phenomenon of conventions. The concept of 'convention' will be represented from a specific, discursive angle. Finally, in the third part of the chapter, I will examine relational rituals in a comparative way, i.e. by showing how they differ from the wider category of conventions. It will be proposed that there is a major difference between convention and ritual: utilisation of the former presupposes a particular emphasis on conformance, that is the need to conform to network expectancies, and that of the latter presupposes performance, that is mimesis.

Chapter 3 will focus the present analysis on in-group relational rituals, by discussing their representative features through the analyses of two case studies. I will first overview the major formal and functional (interactional) properties of in-group rituals. Capturing these features is challenging due to the interactionally constructed nature of many in-group ritual practices. Socially 'standardised' ritual acts tend to have a prescribed vocabulary, organisation and function, and these features are often clearly visible to the external observer. However, it will be argued that interactionally constructed in-group ritual practices also have clearly distinguishable and relatively strict formal and functional properties, which show noteworthy resemblances to those of social rituals. In the second part of Chapter 3 I will examine the constructive relational function of in-group rituals in a wider discursive sense, by analysing their role in creating network identity. Whilst every in-group relational ritual practice contributes to the formation of network identity, by animating in-group ethos, there are ritual practices which specifically boost group identity formation. Ritual practices by means of which network identity is constructed, not only include strict-sense pragmatic actions such as the choice of ritualistic forms, but also discursive actions such as the recurrent ritualistic discussion of certain schematic topics which are significant from an in-group perspective. Furthermore, it will be shown that relational networks do in certain cases intentionally form specific ritual practices in order to distinguish themselves from other networks and/or society.

Chapter 4 will integrate the category of in-group into a ritual typology which is based on the concept of relating. Such a categorisation sets in-group ritual practices in their proper place within the 'family' of relational rituals, but it is also needed as the present approach to ritual acts calls for an alternative typology. Relational function as such is hardly relevant to previous typological approaches to rituality, which categorise rituals according to their social event (i.e. context) of occurrence. It will be argued that an interactional approach should depart from categorising ritual types merely according to the size of the group to whom a ritual practice counts as normative. This is because a ritual practice, irrespective of whether it is a schematic script which has been conventionalised on the societal or more local level, is always adopted, (re-)interpreted and contested by and within networks of language users (cf. Section 1.1). Instead of defining ritual on the basis of network size, I will propose an approach to relational rituals vis-à-vis their 'transparency' and 'accessibility' to network outsiders, which of course also reveals information about the type of network that 'codifies' a ritual practice. The phenomenon of relational ritual includes practices that are clearly understandable to many and in which any language user can take part (transparent and accessible rituals), as well as practices that are intentionally hidden and/or obscure and which exclude the involvement of the observer as participant (non-transparent and non-accessible rituals). One can refer to these two practice types as the ends of a scale, and conceptualisation based on this scale results in an alternative, relational typology of ritual practices.

Chapter 5 will examine in-group relational ritual practices from a cognitive angle.[24] I will first focus on the question of how in-group ritual practices are recognised in interaction. The interactional perception of ritual is a relatively ignored issue in the field, and so this is a gap that the present book hopes to fill. From a discursive perspective, conventionalised acts like rituals are subject to variability and the contestation that variability implies, and this entails that rituals can become non-default for the speaker and marked for the hearer. Once a ritual practice becomes non-default and marked, it may also become subject to evaluation and be picked up in metadiscourse, that is, the interactants will tend to reflect on their ritual practices. In the second part of Chapter 5 I will examine the affective and emotive effects of in-group relational rituals on the interactants. I will argue that in-group ritual practices are emotively invested affective acts. Interactionally constructed in-group rituals are 'non-codified' in the sense that they can occur without any institutionally formalised goal (unlike e.g. funeral speeches which are meant to provoke sadness, see Collins 2004). Thus, the emotional effect of these ritual acts is difficult to predict, even though they follow conventionalised schemata and have conventionalised formal elements. Due to their emotively invested nature rituals tend to have affective and emotive effects also on the person who performs them, and this twofold emotional effect boosts the relational function of ritual performances. It is therefore difficult to systematically capture means–ends, intention–effect relationships between the performer's ritual mimesis and the participant's reaction in every interaction. Furthermore, in certain interactions, emotions fluctuate even while the given interaction is being constructed.

Chapter 6 will further elaborate upon the theory of relational rituals by exploring destructive relational ritual acts (i.e. rituals which are targeted against someone). This is a relatively unexplored area: the pragmatic (and, to some extent, anthropological/sociological) anthropological literature to date shows an enduring interest in the constructive aspect of ritual behaviour, and destructive ritual practices have been somewhat marginalised. I will illustrate that whilst destructive in-group ritual practices fit into the present theoretical framework for ritual, there is a substantial difference between constructive and destructive in-group ritual practices, in terms of their relationship-creating character. Constructive ritual is relationship forcing in the sense that its performance stimulates interpersonal relationships to develop or stay in a stasis mode.[25] Destructive ritual practices function differently: their performance causes the corruption of the relationship between the performer (and the relational network) and the stigmatised person(s), and so they should be defined as 'relationship corrupting'. In this chapter I will first discuss the Goffmanian (1963) notion of 'stigma', which is key to examining destructive ritual behaviour. I will then explore the most representative practices of in-group destructive ritual by drawing on some studies of impoliteness. It will be argued that destructive rituals operate according to some patterns identified by impoliteness researchers, even though there is a key difference between impoliteness and ritual offence within relational networks, namely, that destructive in-group rituals obtain their destructive function by being performed again and again. This finding further accentuates the difference between ritual and (im)politeness proposed in Chapter 2. Finally, I will examine de/constructiveness from the perspective of participant perceptions.

Chapter 7 will summarise the advantages and limitations of the framework elaborated in the present book, and some areas for future research will be proposed. Most importantly among these areas, Chapter 7 will explain the necessity of examining relational ritual in the context of cross-cultural and intercultural research, and it will propose a tentative model for such analyses.

To sum up, the present book aims to fill an important knowledge gap by offering a discursive relational framework of rituals. It will be challenging the concept that rituals are relatively insignificant in contemporary interpersonal communication, by analysing the in-group practices of relational networks. The present framework opens up new vistas: it not only helps us to approach ritual as part of a broader phenomenon (Chapter 2), but also it provides an alternative ritual typology (Chapter 4), as well as innovative insights into ritual cognition (Chapter 5) and into the relationship between the relationally constructive and destructive aspects of rituality (Chapter 6). It is hoped that the ideas presented here will provoke discussions and further research in the field.

2
Defining Ritual from a Relational Perspective
人际关系视角下的仪式界定

2.1 Introduction 引言

2.1.1 Ritual and the relational perspective 仪式及人际关系视角

'In-group ritual' is a category which reflects a specific, relational understanding of ritual actions. In order to analyse the properties of in-group rituals (topic of Chapter 3) and integrate them into a typology (see Chapter 4), we need first to position ritual practices per se from the relational perspective proposed in this book.

In anthropology, sociology and other fields, ritual is often described as an analytic category that exists in its own right as, for example, Bell (1992: 14) notes:

> The notion of ritual first emerged as a formal term of analysis in the nineteenth century to identify what was believed to be a universal category of human experience. The term expressed, therefore, the beginnings of a major shift in the way European culture compared itself to other cultures and religions. [...] Many myth-and-ritual theorists, for example, looked at ritual in order to describe 'religion'. Later social functionalists, in contrast, explored ritual actions and values in order to analyze 'society' and the nature of social phenomena. More recently symbolic anthropologists have found ritual to be fundamental to the dynamics of 'culture'.

The situation of ritual as an analytic category is special, in a sense, from a relational perspective. In terms of relating vis-à-vis language, ritual is but one, albeit important, category within the domain which can be defined as *schematic language usage* (see Section 2.2 on the detailed definition of this term). Integrating ritual into this domain and, even more importantly, comparing it with other categories is important because such a comparison can contextualise some of the key properties of ritual practices, in particular mimesis (cf. Chapter 1). These properties have been analysed in-depth in other disciplines (e.g. mimesis has been described in anthropological studies, see e.g. Crane 2002, Wallace 2007; see also Section 2.3 below), but an advantage of the relational approach is that it has the potential to capture the operation of these properties as part of a larger (relational) model.

2.1.2 Focus on the ritual–(im)politeness interface
聚焦仪式与（不）礼貌界面

The relational perspective adopted, and the integration of ritual into the domain of schematic imply that we need to focus on an area where ritual and various relational phenomena – most significantly but not exclusively practices of (im)politeness – coincide. Thus, in the present book the phenomenon of (im)politeness will repeatedly emerge. Although (im)politeness has many conventional and somewhat limited interpretations, here this term is used in a wider sense, in accordance with Kádár and Haugh (2013: 1) who argue as follows:

> Politeness is a key means by which humans work out and maintain interpersonal relationships. Many of us have been educated how to behave politely since childhood; we only have to think about parents prescribing to their children when and how to apologise, to say 'please' and 'thank you' (at least in English), or to call (*jiao*) people by familial titles when greeting them (at least in Chinese). However, politeness is not limited to conventional acts of linguistic etiquette like formal apologies, so-called 'polite' language and address terms, even though it includes all of these acts. Rather it covers something much broader, encompassing all types of interpersonal behaviour through which we take into account the feelings of others as to how they think they should be treated in working out and maintaining our sense of personhood as well as our interpersonal relationships with others.

That is, in a sense (im)politeness covers a wide range of practices and understandings which are described by the technical term 'relating' (see also Chapter 1). It is pertinent to note that almost without exception every approach to politeness that has been proposed in the past 10–15 years has had an explicit focus on relationships in some shape or form, albeit with a variety of different terms being used, ranging from 'rapport management', 'relational practice' through to 'relational work' and 'relating'. Relating and relationality occur in various approaches to politeness, such as Helen Spencer-Oatey's ([2000] 2008) *rapport management theory* (dealing with 'rapport management'), Janet Holmes and colleagues' (e.g. Holmes et al. 2011) *neo-politeness theory* (dealing with 'relational practices'), Miriam Locher and Richard Watts' (2005) theory of *relational work*, or Robert Arundale's (2006, 2010) *face-constituting theory* (dealing with 'relating').[1] As Helen Spencer-Oatey (2011) notes in a useful overview, these approaches all have in common "a central focus on interpersonal relations, rather than, as with traditional models of politeness, a central focus on the individual performing 'politeness', which is then correlated with interpersonal relations as variables" (p. 3565). It is clear, then, that politeness is conceptualised as part of a much broader interpersonal tapestry, albeit an important part of that tapestry.

In spite of the fact that ritual – and schematic language in general – and (im)politeness often collide, the present book refers to ritual by using the collective term 'relational' (see also Chapter 1) instead of '(im)polite', for two reasons (and in what follows (im)politeness will be shortened to 'politeness', for the sake of simplicity). Firstly, not only are there relational ritual practices which are only loosely related, even in a wider sense, to politeness, but also many areas of politeness are not ritualistic, or even schematic. In terms of time (cf. Kádár and Haugh 2013), schematic language usage represents a certain, albeit pivotal, temporal aspect of politeness. Politeness often emerges and develops in a given interaction, and in many cases understandings of politeness come into existence 'on the spot', as the interactants draw from certain sets of expectancies in co-constructing interaction in localised, situated contexts. If we put politeness on a timescale, it can be argued that evaluative moments of politeness in the here and now represent a cycle of participant actions and reactions, which come into existence in either the punctuated or emergent sense of the present moment. However, and this is why there is an important interface between schematic (ritual) acts and politeness, understandings of politeness are not always completely localised in this way. A certain interaction is often the continuation of a previous one, and so the interactants construct politeness in light of understandings formed in prior interactions. Even more importantly, many contexts do not necessitate such localised understandings. In many settings, understandings of politeness are arguably less localised in the here and now given that the interactants are expected to follow certain 'scripts'. In such contexts, politeness tends to follow underlying *schemata*, that is, pre-existing patterns of behaviour used in recurrent ways that are readily recognisable to members. These schemata reduce uncertainty in the formation and interpretation of linguistic politeness for the simple reason that by relying on them, the interactants can follow pre-existing ways of understanding politeness. It can be argued that if localised understandings of politeness arise in the here and now of interaction, such schemata represent a pre-existing (potentially ritualised) frame for understanding politeness in the here and now.

Secondly, the interface between ritual and politeness does not mean that ritual and (im)politeness can and should be *approached* from a similar angle, even though some studies clearly do this.[2] The main difference between ritual and politeness resides, in my view, in their realisation, that is, politeness is primarily related to *interpretation and evaluation*, as various discursive politeness researchers such as Eelen (2001), Watts (2003) and Mills (2003b) argue,[3] whilst relational ritual should be approached first of all from the perspective of *action*, primarily because of its symbolic mimetic value. In order to illustrate this difference, let us refer to the following interactions, which represent a standard schema of a ritual of challenge from the perspective of a ritual researcher. The first one is a medieval knightly challenge, drawn from a paper by Marcel Bax (2010b), and the second one is an extract from the film *Bridget Jones: The Edge of Reason* (2004):

(2.1)

Sprac hi te lancelote saen:	He spoke to Lancelot right away:
"Riddere, nv doet mi verstaen	"Knight, enlighten me now
Van ere dinc die ic begere,	On a matter that I desire to know about,
Oft wacht v iegen min spere	Or beware of my lance.
[...]	
Bericht mi, ridder, bi vwer trouwen,	Tell me, knight, upon your honour,
Anders maget v wel berouwen,	Or otherwise you will regret it,
Die beste waerheit die gi wet	As truthfully as you can
Dat ic v sal vragen ende nine let."	What I will ask you, and do not fail to respond."
Doe seide min her lanceloet:	Then said Sir Lancelot:
"Ic ware mi vele liuer doet	"I would fain be dead,
Dan mi een ridder dwingen soude	Than suffer a knight to force me
Van dies ic doen nine woude."	To do something against my will."

[...]
Die swarte hi en hilt niet stille,	*The black [knight] did not remain standing still,*
Die op lancelote was erre;	*He who was angry at Lancelot.*
Hi omhaelde sinen loep verre	*He made his horse take a good run-up*
Ende verrechte sijn spere	*And couched his lance*
Alse die te vechtene heuet gere.	*Like one who enjoys combat.*

(Bax 2010b: 70–1)

(2.2)

Mark Darcy   Would you step outside please?
Daniel Cleaver   I'm afraid it's not possible.
Mark Darcy   Look, are you gonna step outside or do I have to drag you?
Daniel Cleaver   I think you're gonna have to drag me.

(*Bridget Jones: The Edge of Reason*, 2004)

The first conversation represents a ritual schema, which was associated with the knightly code of appropriate behaviour in many parts of medieval Europe. That is, the knight Moriaen challenges the knight Lancelot by using a schematic practice, i.e. a pre-existing pattern of behaviour consisting of making an inquiry to his interlocutor. This is not a 'harmless' inquiry: according to the knightly custom, upon challenging the other, instead of directly stating 'We will fight to death, Knight' one was expected to make the challenge indirectly, by 'forcing' the other to answer a question, who in turn is expected to decline this request, which gives a green light to the fight. The second interaction represents a contemporary British gentlemanly challenge made by Mark Darcy for the honour of a 'lady', the protagonist Bridget Jones. The source of humour in (2.2) is that this challenge is refused in a clearly cowardly tone by Daniel Cleaver who knows that Darcy is stronger than him. Just as we saw in Sir Moriaen's inquiry, Darcy's question 'Would you step outside please?' is not a neutral question or proposal: in a similar way with (2.1), there is an expected (or 'preferred', to use a technical term) response to this turn, that is, acceptance of the challenge. When, however, an unexpected answer is given by Daniel Cleaver, the schematic and ritualistic nature of Darcy's question becomes clear, as he makes it clear that Cleaver is not being given a real choice. In other words, while Cleaver makes an indirect response ('I am afraid it's not possible'), which could be understood as appropriate in other settings, it is definitely not acceptable here from Darcy's participant perspective.

From the perspective of politeness these interactions are ambiguous to some extent: although they follow a certain 'script' and the researcher can define them as 'appropriate' (or 'politic', to use a term from Watts 2003), due to their covert aggression it in fact depends on the interactants' evaluation as to whether they perceive these acts as 'polite', 'simply appropriate' or 'impolite', and how they refer to them in metadiscourse. However, in terms of rituality, there is probably no (or, at least, significantly less) ambiguity in these acts from the observer's or the participants' perspectives: since these schematic actions of challenge are *performed* normatively in both examples, the rituals tend to accord with contextual expectations. This relative lack of ambiguity can be illustrated by Daniel Cleaver's reaction in example (2.2): it is clear that Cleaver understands the ritual threat behind Mark Darcy's symbolic question, despite the fact that it could be understood in many other ways in non-ritualistic contexts. Ambiguity, of course, can occur in terms of rituality, and schematic behaviour in general, but it is perhaps more likely to step on stage when something goes 'amiss' in an interaction, as example (2.4) below and various examples in Chapter 5 will illustrate.

Although Chapter 5 will bring the interactants' understandings into the present analytic framework, and Chapter 6 will argue that evaluations can become significant in certain ritual actions, the examples above illustrate that in the relational approach to ritual somewhat more focus has to be put on action than on evaluation. To sum up, relational rituals are defined by putting a strong focus on the interface between ritual and politeness, without claiming similarity between these phenomena.

2.1.3 Structure 结构

In Section 2.2 I will set out to position relational ritual by first examining the collective category of schematic acts from a pragmatic perspective, and then narrowing the analysis down to the schematic relational phenomenon of conventions. The chapter will represent the concept of 'convention' from a specific, discursive angle (see also Chapter 5). Section 2.3 will examine relational rituals in a comparative way, i.e. by showing how they differ from the wider category of conventions. That is, the analysis follows a from broad-to-narrow approach, as is illustrated by Figure 2.1.

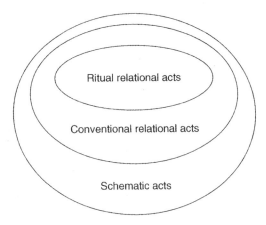

Figure 2.1 The position of relational rituals

Convention is a broader schematic category than ritual, i.e. every ritual act is conventionalised but not every conventional act has ritual nature. However, Section 2.3 will show that ritual is not the 'little brother' of conventions: whilst there is a blurred border between these phenomena, their realisations presuppose different discursive behaviours, due to which conventions per se and ritualised conventions need to be regarded as different phenomena.

2.2 Schematic acts and conventions 图式行为与规约

2.2.1 Schematic acts in relating 人际关系沟通中的图式行为

In order to position relational rituals, we need first to examine the broader category of schematic acts. 'Schematic' has to be defined because it can have various meanings. For example, in linguistics 'schematic' can refer to languages such as Esperanto, in which natural (or partly natural) vocabulary is altered to fit pre-established rules (see e.g. Tonkin 1987); in pragmatics 'schemata' can be used in a cognitive sense to describe associative processes, i.e. phenomena that provide "structure to license inferential effects without any appeal to genuine inferential process" (Mazzone 2011: 2148); in discourse analysis 'schemata' describes a sequenced group of text elements that is categorised by the genre of the text (see e.g. van Dijk 1985).

In the present book 'schemata' is approached from the perspective of sociology and organisation studies, as it is interlinked with the notion of 'routine' practice (see below). I argue that schematically organised language comes into operation due to its *recurrent* nature (which characterises various subtypes of schematic language use as well, including rituals). That is, a certain linguistic form or behaviour becomes schematic for a group of people if it is used again and again, and so in this sense it also becomes a practice of a relational network; and through the interaction of relational networks certain relational practices can also potentially become accepted on a social level. Recurrence is an important mechanism through which humans structure both information and pragmatic meaning. Although utterances come into existence in the course of the discursive co-construction of interaction, there is a likelihood for them to be formed according to certain recurrent forms and practices, for the simple reason that it is economic to rely on schemata. As Harold Garfinkel (1964) notes, a great deal of our everyday activities are recurrent, and it is recurrence that provides the 'routine' practice behind linguistic (and other behavioural) schemata. According to Garfinkel, schematic language activities have the following representative properties:

- They are often left unspoken.
- They involve continuous references to the biography and prospects of an ongoing interaction.
- They are often hidden from the external observer.

To provide a simple example, when a mother habitually asks her child after school 'How was it today?', she can use the anaphoric 'it' because both she and the child knows, from a context created by a series of (often similar) previous interactions, that the topic here is 'school'.

To sum up, routines by their nature operate with "basic schematic forms that constitute the organizational building blocks of coordinated action" (see Fairhurst and Cooren 2004: 143), i.e. 'a schematic form' (cf. van Dijk 1985) is the manifestation of an action rooted in routine practice.[4] Importantly, routine does not mean 'robotic'. It is not surprising that schematic acts play an important role in communication, as (a) they provide a pre-existing frame for understanding a communicative act in the here and now, and (b) because their use is economic. Indeed, if we observe various interactional data sets it becomes evident that we are often less original than we would normally think. There are certain situations and acts, which seem to 'speak for themselves', in a sense that they evoke relatively little ambiguity, due to the fact that the interactants, unwittingly or not, organise what they want to say in a schematic way, according to routine practices. However, a reliance on schemata should not be imagined as a robotic process of copying of models: pre-existing patterns can be made use of by members as 'discursive resources' (see e.g. Joanna Thornborrow's 2002 study for a detailed analysis, as well as Taylor 2007), i.e. as resources to be utilised in interactional struggles for power.[5] To draw upon schemata in projecting understandings of communicative acts is an inherently social practice, which can be utilised to cope with difficult situations, or even to politely gain the upper hand in a conflict, as the interaction in excerpt (2.3) below illustrates.

(2.3)

Sheriff	"We are looking for a man who might be around here."
	...
Colonel Ludlow	"What is he wanted for, sheriff?"
Sheriff	"That would be of a private nature."
Colonel Ludlow	"A private nature? That's a public office you hold, isn't it, Sheriff?"
[awkward silence]	
Colonel Ludlow	"Gentlemen..."

(*Legends of the Fall*, 1994)

Extract (2.3) takes place between a retired colonel who works on his land, and a company led by a corrupt sheriff who is pursuing a fugitive, who is in fact hiding at the colonel's property. The interaction above represents a case when a recurrent social practice, namely, the use of the form of address *Gentlemen* to address others 'politely', is utilised to conceal aggression. In other words, a particular schema is being drawn upon here as a discursive resource to accomplish a particular end. The noteworthy element in this interaction is that the colonel's final utterance, which follows a long and awkward silence and is made with a rising pitch, does not leave any doubt with regard to its meaning, that is, it politely but very determinedly signals the end of the interaction. That this is understood is evident from the pursuers indignantly leaving at that point. The form of address *Gentlemen* could have various readings in the present context. For example, it could function as a polite imperative for the sheriff to answer the colonel's question. However, as *Gentlemen* sets up the schematic interpretation of a marker of leave-taking in this particular social setting, the sheriff and his companion can have little doubt with regard to the meaning of the colonel's utterance.

As a matter of course, the interaction in excerpt (2.3) above represents a default situation where a schema is being deployed and understood according to what appears to be the speaker's intention. However, ambiguity is always potentially present in relational acts (cf. Kádár and Haugh 2013), and even those understandings that draw from schemata are never completely exempt from it. This claim has been confirmed by anthropological research (see e.g. Rasmussen 1992), which claims that schematic behaviour and ambiguity are not contradictory phenomena. One could argue that a particular schema tends to generate a default understanding, but then it depends on various factors whether this understanding actually arises in a particular communicative interaction or not. There are cases, for instance, when seemingly simple patterns just do not seem to function as such, as we can see illustrated in the following example. This interaction takes place between Veek, an alcoholic French nobleman, and his friend 'Packy', an American millionaire, at a train station, while Packy's high-class English fiancée, Beatrice, who is known for being a prude, stands next to them.

(2.4)

He chuckled amusedly and turned to Beatrice, all smiles, as one imparting delightful news.

"When last I see this old *farceur* it is in New York, and he is jumping out of the window of a speakeasy with two policemen after him. Great fun. Great good fun. Do you remember, my Packy, that night when..."

"Are you off somewhere, Veek? " asked Packy hastily.

"Oh yes. But do you remember...?"

"Where? "

(P. G. Wodehouse, *Hot Water*, Chapter 2, 1963)

When Veek begins to retell stories from Packy's stormy past the latter attempts to silence him by changing topic and enquiring about the other's plans, which is often interpreted as a sign of discomfort. However, Veek does not seem to get the hint, and after perfunctorily answering Packy's question, restarts the telling of the story, and so Packy needs to interrupt him yet again. While the schema used by Packy here is not understood by the vicomte in the way it would normally be, and it is this that creates the comical situation here, this humour could not come into existence should the reader not perceive the failure of this schema in the first place.

The above examples illustrate that there are certain pre-existing patterns which are understood by most people. This would imply that these patterns operate according to rather simple principles, that is, they are generally understood by all members of a society, having been learnt by everyone through socialisation, and thus only socially incompetent people like the vicomte in example (2.4) fail to understand them properly. However, as the following Section 2.2.2 will illustrate, the situation is considerably more complex than this, because patterns of relating are often not socially but locally constituted, and so they can remain invisible, and thus are often a source of ambiguity and confusion for the external observer.

2.2.2 Convention 规约

There are certain routine practices which specifically regulate social interaction: the ways in which people negotiate, maintain and, in some cases, renegotiate their relationships. Those forms of recurrent schematic behaviour which follow patterns associated with interpersonal relating – including, for example, understandings of 'politeness', 'humour', 'sarcasm', 'irony' and so on – are defined in the present work as 'conventional'.

The definition of convention

'Convention(al)' is a widely used term in pragmatics, but this book utilises it in a specific way, by describing convention as a practice constructed within relational networks. This accords with the discursive conceptualisation proposed in the present book (cf. Chapter 1): it can be argued that phenomena like convention and ritual are tools which facilitate "the emerging construction of face and identity in interaction" (Locher 2011: 189) in relational networks, and so in order to capture these phenomena we need to describe them in an interactionally situated way. The implications of the discursive understanding of conventions will be exploited in Chapter 5, and it is enough to note here in passing that convention as described here differs somewhat from its definition in some pragmatic studies, such as Marina Terkourafi's (2001) work, where convention is described as a social-level phenomenon. Here, the association of convention with social norms is an implicit rather than an explicit claim, which comes from a quantitative and second-order approach to relational language usage. The approach to conventional practices proposed in the present work does not contradict

Terkourafi's: I agree with the claim that many conventional relational practices operate on the social level. For instance, examples (2.3) and (2.4) above are manifestations of conventional relational practices, which are meant to be understood by everyone (i.e. they are social-level ones). As Terkourafi (2001) explains, such conventional relational acts are understood by everyone because they "encode particular illocutionary forces" (Copestake and Terkourafi 2010). For instance, the indirect utterance "I was wondering if you could open some windows?" is a conventionally encoded request to open the window, and this interpretation, just as that of *Gentlemen* in example (2.3), would be clear to almost everyone, even if strictly speaking, the request is somewhat indirect. However, as this section will illustrate, not every conventional act operates on a social level; besides, conventional practices can be understood differently and contested across relational networks.

The notion of 'convention' as it is represented here is relatively close to the definition by Richard Watts, who in his 2003 book on linguistic politeness examines the ways in which conventionalised utterances convey politeness in schematic ways. In order to capture this phenomenon, Watts uses the label EPM (expression of procedural meaning), which describes "a linguistic or paralinguistic expression that is focused on instructing the addressee how to process the propositional content of the utterance" (2003: 274). As Watts argues, EPMs are conventionalised expressions, many of which are regarded as normative (or 'politic', as Watts defines it) behaviour. An important argument in Watts (2003) is that what counts as normative or 'politic' differs across relational networks; this implies that EPMs are also subject to some socio-pragmatic variation.

As Watts' description illustrates, conventional practices manifest themselves via predetermined, formally fixed language. This relationship between conventional relational practices and form has been described by Searle (1975: 76) who argues that

> I am suggesting that *can you, could you, I want you to*, and numerous other forms are conventional requests, [...] but at the same time they do not have an imperative meaning.

Importantly, 'form' in my understanding does not necessarily cover a dictionary lexeme, or in other words it is not simply a word which is 'polite', 'impolite', 'sarcastic', 'humorous' and so on (in fact, I would argue that no word in itself has predetermined value). In order for a form to gain a certain conventional relational function, it must involve social actions and pragmatic meanings that are regularly associated with evaluations of the given action. For example, once a certain form occurs and recurs in social action which regularly occasions evaluations of politeness, it becomes a 'polite form', but of course only as long as the convention is recognised as such within a society or a relational network.

The relationship between a certain form and the relational function associated with it can be complex. As we could see in the case of *Gentlemen* in example (2.3), the interpretation of this schema as a polite convention for leave-taking not only depends on lexical meaning but also, for example, on prosodic properties. Some other, written, conventional 'forms of politeness' are represented in elaborate, graphic ways, as is illustrated in the following example (sections of interest will be circled in the Chinese text and underlined in the English translation).

(2.5)

This is a schematic Chinese invitation card (for a detailed analysis of such cards, see Kádár 2011a), the text of which reads as follows:

Our first son Guo'en

and our third daughter Meiling

will have their engagement ceremony on March 29th, 1980 in Taipei. We would like to notify about this matter, with sincere respect all our relatives and friends.

Chen Wen-kuo, Chen Mei-ling, Li Yang and Li Ao

respectfully report this.

According to the traditional Chinese conventions for invitations, one needs to denigrate oneself and elevate the other (cf. Kádár 2011a). Notably, this convention is actually represented by the graphic characteristics of traditional Chinese invitation cards. That is, in the above text the reference to others (诸亲友 i.e. "all our relatives and friends") and an honorific form which elevates the recipients (启敬 "respectfully report this") are written in large characters, which thus expresses elevation, while the senders' names are written in small characters, which thus expresses self-denigration. Such graphic conventions can become considerably more elaborate than we observe in the above example (see Kádár 2010a), but the main point here is that the conventionalised relationship between form and the relational function is not necessarily a simple one.

Whilst many of the examples studied represent conventions that are by default associated with 'politeness', conventions include practices that occasion all types of relational phenomena, including for example impoliteness (e.g. certain swear words function by default as conventionalised forms of impoliteness, see e.g. Labov 1972). Conventions come into existence through *conventionalisation*, that is, the process during which a form recurs until what it implies becomes accepted as a 'standard' meaning. Conventionalisation can be captured perhaps most clearly in historical contexts where its evolution can be traced through the years. As Jonathan Culpeper and Jane Demmen (2011) argue, certain stereotypical conventional relational forms, such as indirect requests in Anglo-Englishes,[6] actually came into existence through a long process of conventionalisation. Conventionalisation is often not an arbitrary procedure because it tends to follow social needs, as well as changes in social values. For example, the rise of conventionally indirect requests reflects a strong emphasis on individualism, which grew in significance during Victorian times, or even earlier (cf. Wierzbicka 2006).

Convention and diversity

According to the discursive framework adopted here, conventions can be more societal or 'local' in scope. Cultural norms and changes in

2 Defining Ritual from a Relational Perspective 37

such norms, which give rise to new conventions, are always constituted within a distinct group. Various groups within a society orient to different cultural values, and so it can be argued that a given culture is constituted by an aggregation of subcultures (cf. Kádár and Haugh 2013). Approaching this claim from a different perspective, a society is constituted through multiple intersecting and overlapping relational networks within which different values can develop (cf. Chapter 3). Although conventions often reflect dominant social values, as in the case of conventional indirectness noted above, they can reflect subcultural values as well. To provide an example, many Hungarian teenagers have adopted a conventional form of thanking, *köszike*. This word counts as 'cute' to many in Hungarian because it is doubly diminutive (in a rather ungrammatical way): that is, the standard form *köszönöm* (thank you) is modified with the diminutive suffix -*i* (*köszi*), which is then modified with the diminutive suffix -*ke*. This form has supposedly developed amongst female teenagers, and so it reflects a certain subcultural convention, that is, a convention of relational networks of a certain age group (i.e. teenagers) and gender (i.e. females).[7] Such conventions, which can gain popularity as in the case of *köszike*, often become the subject of social debates and criticisms, as they do not fit into the normative interpretation of 'appropriateness'. In other words, societal conventions are usually regarded as normative, and conventions particular to relational networks, insofar as they significantly differ from societal ones, are often disregarded and criticised by those who do not identify as members of that given network.

What, however, makes convention a complex phenomenon is that even the seemingly non-controversial category of societal conventions may also have different interpretations across relational networks within that society. For example, in 2004, a British author, Charles Purdy, wrote a popular book entitled *Urban Etiquette*, in which he argued:

> When I tell nice people that I write about etiquette, I can see from their faces that I am metamorphosing into Great Aunt Vivian before their very eyes: I have brought etiquette to a perfectly pleasant cocktail party. I am there to stop the fun; impose meaningless, archaic rules; and worst of all; to strongly disapprove.
>
> But I would like you to forget about Great Aunt Vivian's misinterpretation of etiquette (although the dear lady does have her uses as a disciplinarian, and she knows many things we would be wise to keep

in mind). Let's leave her to her sugary sherry and her often incorrect interpretation of *etiquette*. (Purdy 2004: 2)

This folk (and interestingly gendered) description of conventional etiquette is rather illustrative with regard to the interpretation of societal conventions. While 'etiquette' is generally understood as a collective term for normative social conventions – or, more precisely, social conventions comprise the norms of etiquette (cf. Brody 1970) – the above discussion shows that such relational conventions are perceived differently. The author, by positioning Great Aunt Vivian's 'version' of etiquette as being 'incorrect' and 'old-fashioned', makes it clear that he (and the readers he presumes to speak for) have different interpretations of what counts as socially conventional relational behaviour in modern times. However, such differences cannot be attributed to changes over time. For example, as Purdy notes about business etiquette:

> Some people automatically practice social manners at the office – but, for example, a gentleman's racing to a table to hold a woman's chair for her is generally incorrect at a strictly business lunch.... If they so desire, ladies can greatly help confused gentlemen and set a proper professional tone by saying something like: "Please don't get up" if someone does so when she leaves the conference-room table, for example. (Purdy 2004: 83)

That is, there are different understandings of societal conventions constituted across different relational networks and groups,[8] and the way in which these societal conventions are held to differ intersects, in part, with the ways in which individuals, and groups of individuals, are identifying themselves in terms of age, gender and professional status, for instance. And, as the above-cited extract illustrates, there are even conventional linguistic and non-linguistic means of handling situations in which different understandings of 'societal convention' conflict with each other, thus leaving evaluations of conventional relational practices open to contestation.

It should also be noted that societal and network conventions coexist, and the choice as well as the interpretation of a given convention depends on one's 'footing' in a given context. For example, one could refer to the case of many workplaces, which Etienne Wenger (1998) argues can involve one or more 'communities of practice' where a group within the workplace (or sometimes the whole workplace) is focused on some common task. A larger workplace is constituted by different communities of practice, which have their own, potentially different, conventions, but when members of different communities of practice interact with each other, they may invoke societal conventions.

Every convention has a specific history of development. As we saw in the case of the Anglo-English convention of indirectness (cf. Culpeper and Demmen 2011), major social changes can give birth to certain – in fact, often a set of – societal conventions, as social changes transform the ways in which people negotiate relationships with each other. Since such changes take place at the societal level, the conventions which they evoke reflect dominant societal values which are perpetuated through socialisation (and sometimes even through education). Such conventions are thus often *transparent* to anyone who observes a conventional interaction, even though they are subject to challenge and variation as we saw in Charles Purdy's examples (see Chapter 4 for more detail on 'transparency'). However, in relational networks that tend to be closed, conventions are often evoked by 'local histories'. These local histories, which should be defined as 'relational history', refer to the historicity of the way in which members of the given relational network recurrently interact with each other in ways that are both constrained and afforded by localised, network-specific schematic relational practices. Network conventions thus evolve through relational histories that reflect both the biography and evolving prospects of the network, which can be somewhat hidden from the external, or non-member, observer (cf. Garfinkel 1964). More precisely, conventions developed in a distinct group may not be intentionally hidden, but simply constituted in ways that make sense to network members. Although some conventions, like the Hungarian teenager greeting *köszike* above, are noticeable to the researcher and make sense to anyone irrespective of age, there are some other conventions, created by smaller networks – often a group of few or just two people – which can be understood only after prior explanation.

The following extract, cited from Gaëlle Planchenault's (2010: 99) study on a French language transvestite website, illustrates this point.

(2.6)

Bonjour à vous toutes, je suis très émue à la pensée de me trouver parmi vous et d'être la copine de la semaine je ne l'aurais jamais imaginé. [. . .] Merci de vos témoignages à toutes qui me donnent aussi la force d'être et un merci tout particulier à Isabelle pour son site.

Hello to all⁽ᶠ⁾ of you⁽ᶠ⁾, I am very moved⁽ᶠ⁾ to be among you and to be the girlfriend of the week. I would never have expected it. [...] Thanks to all⁽ᶠ⁾ of you for your life stories; they give me the strength to be myself and a special thank to Isabelle for her website.

According to Planchenault, the posters at this website conventionally use feminine French grammatical forms (marked with 'f'),[9] and also apply markedly polite forms and avoid any rudeness in their interactions. These strict behavioural schemata are considered somewhat unusual in the setting of discussion boards where conflict tends to be present (cf. Locher 2010 on the normativity of rudeness in certain online settings), and so may appear unusual from the etic perspective of a non-member of the network. The localised conventions for this relational network become understandable, however, if one reads the webmaster's description for newcomers, which prescribes conflict avoidance and a 'soft' style for posters, in order to generate a harmonious style, which is needed by many in the socially disadvantaged group of transvestites. In other words, what we can see here is a particular convention vis-à-vis politeness being 'codified' by a network, in a somewhat similar way to etiquette manuals that codify social conventions. However, unlike social conventions, the codified conventions applying to the website in question are acquired only by those who join the network.

The above example represents a network convention, which is somewhat hidden but which can be 'decoded' by the observer because (a) it is codified in writing, and (b) because the above-mentioned 'soft' behaviour is a stereotypical marker of femininity, which is then associated with transvestism. There are, however, some other relational conventions, which are not formally codified and, even more importantly, do not make any sense to outsiders (i.e. from an etic perspective) unless one clearly understands the specific relational history of a network. As a simple representative example, I will relate a personal story. When I lived in China I used to go to martial art exercises on a daily basis and during the training I made friends with a young Chinese who attended a Chinese chef school. This person was eager to speak about the new recipes he learnt and also frequently gave me advice as to which Chinese dishes I should try – treating me as a foreigner who needed educating in the local culture. Whenever we met, I would ask him the following schematic question:

(2.7)

今天该吃什么?

Lit. What do we need to eat today?

This question became an in-group convention, which functioned as a greeting. From a participant perspective it was associated with politeness as it appealed to the Chinese person's professional identity as a chef (despite the fact that he was a student at that time). For network outsiders, and in isolation (i.e. without knowing the interactants' relational history and their identities in the given network), this utterance does not make much sense because it differs from greeting conventions in Chinese. In other words, this convention is not transparent to the observer.

As we have seen, convention has different degrees of hiddenness – or, perhaps, we should say 'transparency' as it is not intentionally hidden – and social 'normativity' depending on the size and type of the network. This difference also determines the life cycle of conventions: social conventions are likely to last for a very long time, until major social changes invalidate them, while network conventions cease to exist when a network dissolves. Semi-transparent conventions of larger networks like the Hungarian teenagers' form *köszike* are more likely to survive for a longer period than non-transparent ones, simply because they are more likely to be 'inherited' by new networks. For example, while new groups of teenagers have developed their own conventions, *köszike* continues to be in use as a pragmatic 'heritage' from previous generations of teenagers. Also, *köszike* has been adopted by other network types such as males who often use this form in a new sense, i.e. as a source of gendered humour.

Conformance to expectations

The discussion on the degree of transparency of recurrent behaviour is related to *expectations*. As already noted, members of a network do not usually hide their conventions (although there are also intentionally hidden forms of recurrent behaviour, cf. Chapter 4), but simply take them for granted as they constitute expected linguistic behaviour within their circle.

Expectations do not only differ across societal and relational networks. There is also an important distinction that can be drawn between recurrent forms or practices (a) which network members regard as *likely* to happen (sometimes called 'empirical norms'), based on their personal experiences and relational histories, and others (b) which they consider *ought to* happen (sometimes called 'moral norms'); see Eelen (2001), Haugh (2003) and Culpeper (2008). In other words, there are conventions which we simply expect to 'be there', and we tend to regard a breach of these expectations as grounds for evaluations of 'impoliteness', 'rudeness', 'improperness' and so on. For example, an utterance which does not use feminine French grammatical forms in the aforementioned transvestite website (see example 2.6) is open to being interpreted as impolite, irrespective of whether the person who has produced it intends to be impolite or not. There is, however, another type of overtly moralistic expectation. This expectation occurs when conventions, in particular societal ones, are not followed in the way in which and the extent to which one would prefer them to be followed, as we saw in the case of Mr Purdy's claim, and which translates into the criticism of a generation's manners. The British writer Thomas Blaikie has written books and articles about the lack of civility among the younger generations. In an article published in the *Telegraph* he argued,

> Young people have always been rude, far ruder than anybody else. It goes back at least as far as Jane Austen. [...] Even the Queen, aged 19, knocked off a policeman's helmet on VE [Victory in Europe] Day, so she once told the writer Hammond Innes.
>
> But the young of today are worse than preceding generations. This is the depressing conclusion of a survey by the Left-wing think tank Demos. (Retrieved from: <http://www.telegraph.co.uk/culture/3653126/Why-are-the-youth-of-today-so-rude.html#>)

As this example illustrates, moral expectations inevitably involve contestation. Thus, it can be argued that conventions, in particular those which are more societal in scope, are open to being challenged by certain social networks. My data suggests that such challenges are less likely to emerge in the case of more local conventions. Conventions which are societal in scope are accessible to various networks with potentially different values, and this is obviously a source of different understandings of a given convention as 'in/appropriate', as well as debates that arise from such different understandings. This implies that there is always some potential for several (competing) social conventions to coexist.

To sum up, the operation of conventions is bound up with expectations, both empirical and moral. The current description has overviewed the main properties of conventionalised relational acts. It has been argued that convention operates at an in-group level, just as the in-group ritual practices studied in this book; although there are plenty of conventional relational practices that count as socially normative, they are subject to changes across social networks (similarly to social-level rituals, cf. Chapter 4). Practically all of the phenomena studied here such as diversity, differences between the 'transparency' and life cycle of certain schematic relational practices and so on, also manifest themselves in the specific conventionalised practice of rituality, as the following chapters of this book will argue.

In what follows, let us focus on the specific issue as to how ritual, which is a conventionalised form of behaviour, comes into operation, and how it differs from other conventional relational practices.

2.3 Relational rituals 人际关系仪式

Occasionally in my data, there is a blurred boundary between conventional and ritual actions, due to the fact that every ritual is conventionalised. But usually these forms of behaviour can be clearly distinguished from an interpersonal perspective, as there is a divide between the roles convention and ritual play in relating. As the discussion above has illustrated, conventional behaviour implies a particular emphasis on *conformance*, i.e. the need to conform to network expectations. Ritual, on the other hand, represents another important way in which recurrent schemata operate in interaction, vis-à-vis mimetic *performance*. Thus, whilst ritual performance presupposes conformance to network norms, it also provides something else in terms of relational behaviour. It depends on the interactants' understanding (which the analyst can, for example, attempt to capture in longer stretches of interaction) and behaviour whether an utterance functions as a convention or a ritual. For example, extract (2.7) above used to have a strong performance (ritual) value, which however was lost with the passing of time and this form became a 'plain' (conventional) greeting, which was responded to with a standard 'Hi' and which was normatively expected to occur. Note that distinguishing convention and ritual on the basis of the interactants' perspectives implies diversity in the understanding and interactional effect of conventional and ritual utterances. That is, it might be that an utterance has an 'additional' performance value for some interactants but not for others.

2.3.1 Mimesis 模仿

Mimetic ritual performance has received various definitions in anthropology. It appears in the work of the anthropologist Émile Durkheim (1912[1954]) who regarded mimesis as a phenomenon limited to certain religious ritual practices (see Chapter 4 on Durkheim's view on rituals as sacred practices), in which a phenomenon is repeated in order to magically create something new. As Durkheim notes,

> They [i.e. mimetic rituals] presuppose not only the shift of a given state or quality from one object to another, but the creation of something entirely new. The mere fact of repeating the animal generates that animal and creates it; by imitating the sound of wind or falling water, the clouds are made to form and dissolve in rain, and so on. [...] resemblance acts by itself and is directly efficacious. (Durkheim [1912] 1954: 263–4)

Furthermore, Durkheim claims that mimetic ritual acts are predominantly tribal phenomena, and although mimesis continues to exist in the ritual practices of our day, it often becomes a meaningless practice:

> [A]mong cultivated peoples and societies, believers are often encountered who, while having doubts about the special efficacy that dogma attributes to each rite taken separately, continue none the less to practice their religion. They are not sure that the prescribed observances are justifiable in detail, but they feel that they could not dispense with them without falling into an undesired moral confusion. (Durkheim 1912 [1954]: 265)

Durkheim's definition is echoed in contemporary research by McClenon (1997). Others, such as Turner (1967) and van Gennep (1909 [1960]), argue that mimesis is present in every ritual action, and they use this term to describe the performance value of rituals in general. The present work follows this latter conceptualisation, by describing all types of relational rituals as mimetic.

Why is mimesis so important from the perspective of relating? A joint concept in anthropological theories, irrespective of their definition of the scope of mimesis, is that mimesis operates vis-à-vis (re-)enactment. As Gruenwald (2003) notes,

> Mimetic representation [...] refers to an event that is condensed into a time span, or space, that achieves complete realisation in the process, not of being repeated, but of being enacted as ritual. (Gruenwald 2003: 125)

By performing the symbolic act of ritual we enact and re-enact certain beliefs and values. As anthropological theories argue, (re-)enactment is important because through this process ritual has aided, and continues to aid, humans to form social or relational networks, as it provides a powerful way in which people's social dependence can be expressed (this, of course, includes dependence on the realm of the sacred in the case of religious rituals).

For example, a tribal religious ritual of dancing has an important role in reinforcing the bonds of the tribe, as it provides a joint experience which is recurrent (usually ritual events take place at prescribed times), and also it symbolically codifies and, what is more important, re-enacts the roles of the dancers with the relational network, as well as their relationship with the performance. That is, to stick to the example of the ritual act of dancing, it codifies certain roles like 'chief dancer', 'subordinate dancer', 'leading musician' and so on, as well as the relationship between the performance and the external world (for example, the group performs particular dances in order to commemorate a deity). Thus, the act of dancing symbolically 'encodes' and practically re-enacts the social order of the community, as well as the community's values (respect towards that deity).

The re-enactment of community values can be observed even in fairly trivial, or 'everyday' ritual practices; for example, *Welcome on board!* (acknowledgement of one's acceptance in a relational network; cf. Ch. 1) is a form widely associated with the rite of passage (see more on such rites in van Gennep 1909 [1960]), which signals acceptance into a network. It is more than a convention, because in terms of relationality a ritual like *Welcome on board!* does not simply conform to expectations. By uttering these words the speaker symbolically *changes* the addressee's status, by providing her or him membership to the network. Uttering these words in a specific institutional setting is a powerful mimetic act because the speaker does not speak for him or herself, but instead (s)he animates the voice of the network or institution and re-enacts the network's values – in a way, this is not so different from the leader of a tribe who confers adult membership on a young warrior through a rite of passage.

It is pertinent to note that certain social theories argue that mimesis constitutes an interface between rituals and other social phenomena. Most importantly, experts of the sociology and history of play[10] and game such as Johan Huizinga in his book *Homo Ludens* ([1938] 1955), and some other theorists such as Caillois ([1958] 1961), claim that mimesis is an important form of play; in fact, Caillois distinguishes mimicry (mimesis) as one of the four major forms of play. These theorists argue that not only can game and play be ritualistic, but, vice versa; ritual is a form of game in a wider sense. It is not a coincidence that game/play and ritual share certain characteristics such as strict sequential order (cf. Chapter 3).

2.3.2 Mimesis in operation 模仿的运作

So how does ritual come into existence and how is it related to convention? Ritual practices come into existence through *ritualisation*. In anthropological theories ritualisation is described as a direct process, i.e. when a group of people who animate the voice of an institution create a certain ritual practice.[11] For example, Bell (1992) in her seminal study describes the process of ritualisation as follows:

> I will use the term 'ritualization' to draw attention to the way in which certain social actions strategically distinguish themselves in relation to other actions. In a very preliminary sense, ritualization is the way of acting that is designed and orchestrated to distinguish and privilege what is being done in comparison to other, usually more quotidian activities. As such, ritualization is a matter of various culturally specific strategies for setting some activities off from others, for creating and privileging a qualitative distinction between 'sacred' and 'profane', and for ascribing such distinctions to realities thought to transcend the powers of human actors. (Bell 1992: 74)[12]

However, the relational approach adopted in this book suggests that there is also an indirect source of rituals: once a convention is adopted by a social network, and when it takes on mimetic functions/value from a participant perspective, it becomes ritual. It is interesting to examine indirect ritualisation – which plays an important role in the data I have studied thus far – as it illustrates the role of mimesis as a phenomenon which separates ritual from convention.

In principle, my data suggests that any conventional practice of a network can become a ritual if it is recognisably performed. In order to illustrate this point, let us analyse the following excerpt.

(2.8)

Queen Gorgo	Spartan!
King Leonidas	Yes, my lady?
Queen Gorgo	Come back with your shield, or on it.
King Leonidas	Yes, my lady.

(*300*, 2006)

2 Defining Ritual from a Relational Perspective

This interaction is cited from the action film *300*, which retells the Battle of Thermopylae. In this interaction Queen Gorgo – wife of the Spartan King Leonidas – bid farewell to the King, leader of 300 Spartans who set off on a suicidal mission to protect their kingdom from the Persian army.

The Queen's farewell includes two ritual acts, which neatly represent the difference between ritual and convention. First, Queen Gorgo addresses her husband in the third person as "Spartan!", and then she utters "Come back with your shield, or on it" – this latter utterance refers to the habit that it was a symbol of defeat if a Spartan lost his shield in war. With the context in mind, it is obvious that these utterances are more than simply conventional acts, as the Queen goes beyond conforming with contextually situated expectancies. While it would be proper for the Queen to address a Spartan commoner as "Spartan" and remind him of his duties, and in such a context this would be regarded as conventional, she interacts here with a superior husband-king to whom she bids farewell forever. The rationale behind this seeming discrepancy resides in the mimetic ritual nature of these utterances. That is, by addressing the King as "Spartan" (i.e. a rather puritanical) convention, instead of choosing a more emotional form of greeting, the Queen seems to emphasise – more precisely, mimetically re-evoke – the heroic (stereotypically Spartan) spirit of their relationship. This is reinforced by the King's brief and seemingly emotionless responses to the Queen, as they co-construct the ritual. In other words, the Queen plays a certain role here and convention becomes a ritual through this situated performance.

The reason why mimetic performance, such as the one in example (2.8), functions effectively is supposedly due to its affective and emotive value (see Chapter 1, as well as a detailed analysis in Chapter 5). Mimesis is formed in a way that reflects the given network's history (and prospects), which is referred to as network 'ethos' in this book. For example, the interactional rituals of farewell in example (2.8) come into operation through the pathos of the utterances, that is, the seemingly emotionless heroism of the greeting, which reflects the Queen and King's in-group ethos of being representative of the Spartans. This seeming emotionless performance is what appears to generate emotions in both participants and observers and, importantly, relational affection between the participants.

The affective function of ritual should not be understood as autotelic (i.e. having within itself the purpose of its existence or happening), and it is not a coincidence that it is referred to as 'function'. Emotions and relational affection often address interactional needs, as they have a psychological effect on those who participate in the ritual. As noted by Manfred Kienpointner (1997: 262), ritual acts create an atmosphere in which states of mind alter, an atmosphere which "cannot be endangered even by seemingly rude utterances". This state of mind is often referred to in the field as the 'ritual moment'. As Jan Koster (2003: 219) notes, the ritual moment has a key communicational function because it creates "a temporary destruction of awareness of the wider meaningful relations of one's individuality and the reduction of the self to the immediate physical experience of the here and now" (see Chapter 5). This physical experience is a 'recurrent here and now', in the sense that ritual language use ties one into all of the other times such a ritual schema has been used. That is, the moment is experienced through looking into and relying on a series of events; the utterance is connected to another time and place and potentially another context altogether. In the case of example (2.8) above, speaking in a ritual heroic way supposedly results in a state of mind in which saying goodbye becomes easier. It is pertinent to note that the ritual moment neatly illustrates the interface between ritual and game; as Huizinga ([1938] 1955) observes, in the sphere of game the rules and habits of 'ordinary life' are no longer valid. The transformation of 'ordinary life' into this altered state, according to Huizinga, characterises any kind of game, including children's play, tribal cultures, sport events and so on.

2.3.3 The visibility of mimesis 模仿的可视性

Although mimetic performance is present in every relational ritual practice, its visibility (from the observer's perspective) is subject to variation. As Chapter 4 will illustrate, relational rituals – just as conventions – include, for example, socially conventionalised and thus widely known, relational practices such as the above-discussed *Welcome on board!*, in which mimesis is relatively obscure, as well as more localised in-group practices which can be more clearly mimetic (cf. Reijnders 2007). Locally constructed rituals can also differ in terms of mimetic visibility. In order to illustrate differences in the visibility of mimesis, let us refer to two cases of in-group ritual practices; in both of these cases mimetic performance is relatively visible, yet differences apply in terms of visibility.

The first case is an anecdotal reference to a ritual practice which was popular in the 1980s and 1990s in schools across Budapest, adopted by groups of young males: at parties and other social gatherings when a male broke wind in an audible way he was meant to shout *cakes*, a word of unrecognisable etymology.[13] This not only served as an important ritual way of saving 'face', considering that flatulence and references to it are face-threatening (see e.g. Culpeper 1996). It was also an important means to strengthen in-group solidarity – as my retrospective, informal interviews with five informants indicate; it was actually 'trendy' to break wind by using this ritual. Obviously, such a ritual act is clearly theatrical, and so the mimetic performance in them is obvious.

In the second case, which is an extract from the film *Charlie's Angels* (2000), mimetic performance is more elusive:

(2.9)

(Conversation between lovers)
Chad   Is it the eggs?
Dylan   It's not the eggs.
Chad   Is it the boat?
Dylan   No, it's not the boat, I have to go though.
Chad   Is it the Chad?
Dylan   It might be the Chad.
Chad   The Chad... It's the Chad!
[*Chad falls into the water*]
...
Chad   Starfish [a form of endearment for Dylan], I would just like to say that I'm honored, honored to see you taking an interest in my work and I also think you're very pretty and... (sees girls getting scuba gear on) Starfish? Where are you going? Starfish are you going swimming? Where are you going? Where are you going again Starfish? Was it the Chad?
Dylan   No, the Chad was great.
Chad   The Chad was great.

(*Charlie's Angels*, 2000)

What the reader can observe here is an indirect, step-by-step ritual confirmation of love. This confirmation takes place through an unusual, romantic and playful performance, which makes sense if one knows that in the network of Dylan and Chad it is a ritual to talk about Chad in the third person ("*the* Chad"), as an adored entity. What happens in these two interactions is that Chad wants Dylan to confirm that she loves him, and so he involves her in a ritual game of talking about him. In the first interaction Dylan has to leave and Chad enquires as to the reason for her departure. While Dylan obviously loves Chad, she teases him and she hints that "It might be the Chad" as the reason why she is leaving. However, she makes this utterance vague, hence minimising the face threat (and keeping the door open for Chad to continue courting). In the next interaction, Dylan and Chad continue to talk about "the Chad", this time in a very flattering way. What these interactions illustrate is that rituals are often jointly co-constructed in localised relational networks (see also Chapter 3), due to which mimetic performance can be relatively complex and somewhat less visible to the external observer than in the case of the Hungarian *cakes* above.

2.4 Summary 结语

The present chapter has positioned ritual practices from a relational perspective, and filled a gap by contextualising ritual. It has argued that ritual belongs to the category of schematic acts, and, in a narrower sense, to conventions. As the following chapters will illustrate, convention and ritual have many common properties, such as recurrence, differences between socially and more locally coded practices, and so on. I have proposed that there is a major difference between convention and ritual: utilisation of the former presupposes a particular emphasis on conformance, i.e. the need to conform to network expectancies, and that of the latter presupposes performance.

In the following Chapter 3 I focus the analysis on in-group relational rituals, by discussing their representative features.

3

In-Group Ritual in Operation: Two Case Studies

群内仪式的运作：两则个案研究

3.1 Introduction 引言

The present chapter will explore how interactionally co-constructed in-group ritual practices operate within relational networks.

In Section 3.2 I will first overview the major formal and functional (interactional) properties of in-group rituals. Capturing these features is challenging due to the interactionally constructed nature of many in-group ritual practices. Socially 'standardised' normative ritual acts such as diplomatic rituals and child rhymes have prescribed vocabulary, organisation, function, etc., and these features are often clearly visible to the external observer. In order to illustrate this point, let us refer to a ritual child rhyme in Hungary (and let us recall here the claim made in Chapter 2 that there is an important interface between game and ritual):

(3.1)

Group 1	Adj király katonát!
Group 2	Nem adok!
Group 1	Akkor szakítok!
Group 2	Szakíts, ha tudsz!
Group 1	Give me a soldier, king!
Group 2	I won't give you one!
Group 1	Then I'll take one!
Group 2	Take one if you can!

This is the script of a popular game (similar to the English game 'Capture the Flag' or 'British Bulldog'), which is quite like medieval knightly challenges (see Bax 2004 and examples 2.1 and 2.2 in Chapter 2), played between two groups of children. According to the rules of this game, players in each group hold the hands of their neighbours and the groups form two lines facing each other. At each turn, one of the groups threatens the other by requesting a 'soldier'; once this has been refused in accordance with the above 'script', a member of the challenging group darts against the enemy line, and if (s)he can break through (s)he can select a 'captive' whom (s)he brings to her or his 'camp'; if the attack fails, i.e. the line cannot be broken, the attacker will be a captive. The game is to be continued until there is only one person remaining in each 'camp'.

The above text is a typical manifestation of a ritual act which is codified above the level of individual relational networks, with a vocabulary and a sequential organisation which are strictly regulated and have been unchanged (as far as I am aware) for decades. It is pertinent to note that such social-level child rituals clearly illustrate the basic anthropological function of relational rituals. Strictly defined wording and other formalised ritualistic features are important in games of (symbolic) violence like this, as they are for contact sports. Considering that ritual codification prevents the game from developing into a real fight, it indirectly facilitates conflict avoidance (cf. Chapter 2).

Although interactionally constructed in-group ritual practices seem to be less clearly and strictly 'codified' than, for example, the ritual represented by example (3.1) above, Section 3.2 will argue that they also have clearly distinguishable and relatively strict formal and functional properties, which show noteworthy resemblances to those of various socially normative rituals. Whilst interactionally situated in-group ritual practices are more difficult to observe, they also operate with predetermined vocabulary, and certain sequencing roles, etc. on the formal level, and they create the 'ritual moment' (cf. Chapter 2 and also Section 3.2) on the functional level.

In Section 3.3 I will examine the constructive relational function of in-group rituals in a wider discursive sense, by analysing their role in creating network identity. In fact, every in-group relational ritual practice contributes to the formation of a network identity, due to the fact that it facilitates in-group ethos (cf. Section 3.2). However, there are ritual practices which boost group identity formation specifically, and in Section 3.3 I aim to describe these particular practices. Relying on the framework of Mary Bucholtz (1999), I will argue that ritual practices by means of which network identity is constructed not only include strict-sense pragmatic actions such as the choice of ritualistic forms, but also discursive actions such as the recurrent ritualistic performance of certain schematic topics which are significant from an in-group perspective. Furthermore, it will be shown that relational networks do in certain cases intentionally form specific 'unusual' ritual practices in order to distinguish themselves from other networks (even though there are similarities between such distinctive practices across groups).

3.1.1 Scope 范围

When examining a topic like in-group ritual, one needs to be self-reflexively aware that perhaps a single study cannot capture the whole range of relational functions which in-group ritual can fulfil; neither can one describe each and every one of its manifestation types (cf. Chapter 5). Accordingly, I do not claim that this chapter, or even the present book, offers a comprehensive description; instead of this, this chapter simply aims to summarise what I regard as the most significant relational properties and functions of in-group ritual practices. In order to attain this aim, I will analyse two case studies of in-group ritual, which have been published as research papers (see Kádár and Bax 2013, Kádár 2012a), and which represent in-group ritual in two spatially/culturally and diachronically distant contexts. The first case study (Section 3.2) includes a corpus of e-mails written by a group of Hungarian friends, and the second (Section 3.3) includes an epistolary interaction by a group of scholars in historical China.

3.2 Formal and functional features of in-group ritual: a case study of Hungarian e-mails
群内仪式的形式与功能特征：关于匈牙利语电邮的个案研究

Let us begin the exploration of in-group rituals by looking at their major formal and functional properties, as represented in a corpus of e-mails.

3.2.1 Data 语料

The corpus studied consists of 203 e-mail messages in Hungarian from 8 major threads. These e-mails were written between 2007 and 2009 and represent the interaction of a group of three friends, all males in their early thirties. The materials were obtained from personal acquaintances who were asked to comment on the threads in the form of interviews so as to help me understand the relational history behind certain interactional moves, and also to confirm whether my understanding of particular discursive motivations was appropriate; in the extracts given below the interactants are indicated as X, Y and Z.

E-mails provide suitable material for our present analysis because e-mail is a mode of computer-mediated communication (CMC) that is "text-based, asynchronous, and involves message-by-message transmission" (Herring 2002: 114). The asynchronous nature of e-mail correspondence allows users to take time over carefully composing and editing their messages (Herring 1997). What is more, in the context of e-correspondence, in-group rituals may well occur, and can be readily discerned, for the following reasons:

- E-mails are edited to some extent; the inherent asynchronicity of the communication makes it possible for the authors to design their messages in keeping with the in-group's (sometimes quite elaborate) ritual habits;
- E-mails are private; the messages are usually accessible to a restricted relational network only, consequently it seems that in-group e-mails are likely to exhibit in-group features such as ritual communication, even though my evidence is limited to the data set in my possession; besides, previous research (see e.g. the case of transvestite websites in Planchenault's 2010 study cited as example 2.6 in Chapter 2) seems to indicate that – unlike private modes – open access modes of CMC are more likely to accommodate socially conventional ritual practices that are localised ('semi-transparent') in relational networks, for example locally interpreted and redesigned social norms which are often codified by webmasters.

Another important feature of e-mails is multimodality. It is worth noting that multimodal features play an important role in the conveyance of ritual messages, for example via emoticons that imitate gestures associated with ritualistic behaviour (e.g. ∧0∧ 'bowing' in online apologies, in particular in East Asian cultures) or through spellings that 'imitate' verbal actions (e.g. shouting; cf. extract 3.2 below).

The data set studied here has been selected because it represents a noteworthy relational function of in-group ritual: it parallels with archaic "flyting" or "the ritual enactment of conflict" (Bax 2010a: 493). Ritual contestation is an important form of human behaviour: not only do numerous cultures have a long history of ritualised aggression (Ong 1981), but also recent research such as Locke (2011) shows that ritualised aggression has always been part of both female and male (linguistic) behaviour. Historically, the ritual enactment of conflict played an important part in the avoidance/settlement of actual conflicts, and it has manifested itself in various forms of ritual language use. The practice is also present in contemporary forms such as sounding, i.e. the competitive exchange of ritual insults in African American in-groups

(Labov 1972, Garner 1983). Another interesting contemporary example is provided by Goodwin (2006: 94–6) who, upon discussing social dimensions of popular girls' cliques, notes that ritual in-group insult creates a relaxed atmosphere, and consequently plays an important role in overcoming difficult interpersonal situations. As Goodwin (2006: 96) argues, "Ritual insult typically functions to transform a potentially dangerous contest or conflict into a bout of wit, where the contest involves statements that are known by the players not to be true."

The ritual (mimetic) enactment of conflict practised by the group under study is different from socially 'coded' manifestations (cf. social ritual in Chapter 4) such as sounding, in that it reflects in-group specific practices of rituality, as the following extract illustrates:

(3.2)

Z oké, öcsisajt, örülök hg minden okééééééééjjj,
   tessék csak kunfuzni... aztán majd nyáron megküzdünk.
   vasárnap indulok new yorkba. ... beszerveztem egy csomó phd-s találkozót, yeaaaaaahhhhhh!

Z ok, little bro [lit. younger brother cheese, a diminutive term of address which counts as clearly outdated in contemporary Hungarian slang], I am glad t't all is okeeeeeee [intentional typo, mimicking Hungarian low-class spelling of the English word 'ok', as well as a shouting sound],
   just practice kunfu [intentional typo, mimicking Hungarian uneducated spelling of 'kung-fu', which is a reference to the fact that the recipient practices martial arts]... and we shall fight in the summer. I depart to new york on sunday... I organised plenty of phd meetings, yeaaaaaahhhhhh!

(E # 21)

This fragment is representative of the ritual style of this in-group, and differs from socially conventionalised forms of ritual conflict. While socially conventionalised rituals of sounding, such as those recorded by Labov (1972), can have 'local' uses, such ritual practices usually make perfect sense to outsiders, too; although supposedly not always in the ritually conditioned 'harmless' way, but as real insults (cf. Chapter 6, which discusses the opposite case, when a ritual practice that attacks in-group members is potentially seen as 'harmless' to network outsiders). Contrariwise, the mimetic insults (e.g. the opening form of address) exchanged in example (3.2) are manifestations of in-group ritual practice because they cannot be straightforwardly taken as sensible challenges by outsiders; this phenomenon is connected with the group's relational history and the concomitant in-group ethos.

The analysis of the corpus, as well as feedback from the participants, reveals that what happens in these ritual interactions boils down to a mimetic *parody* of imagined insults – which exemplifies the potential complexity of in-group ritual. Thus, a markedly harmless or mild 'bantering' (Culpeper 1996) imbues the in-group's ritual behaviour. For example, as the following analysis illustrates, upon playfully challenging each other, the members of the community studied – who belong to the Hungarian upper-middle class – apply out of context (low-class) and misspelled forms, in order to express humour on the one hand, and to keep the interaction 'harmless', on the other. It seems that taking up the (potentially insulting) 'voices' of other groups is a general practice across cultures (see e.g. Rampton 2006), and in this sense the interactions studied here are representative of ritual practices existing across cultures.

3.2.2 Formal properties: forms, sequences and activations
形式特征：形式、序列与激活

As the previous chapters have already illustrated, rituals are more often than not formally fixed: they are expressed with institutionalised lexical items, they can have certain predetermined prosodic properties, and so on. Formal fixity also applies to in-group rituals, even though it is challenging to capture it in the case of these interactionally constructed, relatively non-codified relational practices (cf. Section 3.1). In-group ritual forms and their sequential organisation count as normative for network insiders but from a network outsider/observer perspective they tend to differ from traditional, socially normative representations of ritualised language. In what follows, let us examine how formal fixity manifests itself in the corpus studied.

As example (3.2) illustrates, in-group ritual mimetically deploys lexical items that are conventionalised in the given relational network, such as intentionally outdated forms of address that serve as sources of in-group humour (cf. *öcsisajt* 'younger brother cheese'). However, ritualised forms are not merely conventional lexical items because they tend to be utilised in in-group interactions that are ritual (mimetic) by nature (cf. Chapter 2). The mimetic relationship between forms and ritual acts can be well illustrated by the sequential properties of in-group ritual.

As Bax (2004: 164) has demonstrated, socially conventionalised ritual acts (cf. Chapter 4) are governed by formulation and/or sequencing principles (see also Rothenbuhler 1998). Inquiry into interactionally

3 In-Group Ritual in Operation: Two Case Studies

(co-)constructed in-group ritual practices reveals that they follow various sequencing rules as well. Sequencing rules differ across rituals. Yet, a noteworthy principle that seems to characterise many (co-)constructed in-group rituals, in particular written interactions, and which could also be observed in seven of the eight threads in the data set, is turn-by-turn 'activation'.[1] The majority of in-group interactions in the data studied begin in a non-ritual way, and the interactants only gradually co-construct a style that represents the in-group's ritual. This process of co-construction – which is a tendency in my data rather than a rule – is an important link between in-group rituals and socially conventional rituals (Collins 2004; see also Chapter 4).

Such an 'activation' of in-group ritual is illustrated by the following extract:

(3.3)

Z X, mi újság dubaiban? megettek már a helyi majmok?...
Y épp nálam járt... megállapítottuk, h már mindkettőnknek nagyon hiányzol. siess haza, mert nem bírjuk sokáig!
csá, Z
ps: jaaaa és igénybe szeretném venni a X Tanácsadó Bt. szolgáltatásait is...

Z X, what's the news in dubai? have you been eaten by the monkeys there?
Y [the third friend] just visited me... we found that both of us miss you very much already. come back soon as we won't be able to endure [missing you] for long!
bye [slang form], Z
ps: ahhhhha and I would like to make use of X Consultation Ltd.'s service, as well...

X Szia Ubul!
Minden OK Dubaiban, a majmok nem ettek meg, en ettem meg oket, vazzze....
Rendesek vagytok, hogy hianyoltok, ezt jo hallani. Egyebkent minden ok velem,. most eppen 28 fok van es 90%-os para...
Csa, X

ps: Barmikor szivesen adok tanacsot, csak be ne szopppjad, hohohohohoho (Beavises rohoges)

X   Hi Ubul!
    All is OK in Dubai, the monkeys didn't eat me, I ate them, fuccck [intentionally misspelled variant of a spoken swear word preferred by lower-class Hungarians] ...
    I'm glad you are missing me, its good to hear this. Anyway, all is ok with me, now here it is just 28 degree Celsius and the humidity rate is 90% ...
    Bye [slang form], X
    ps: I would happily give you advice anytime, just take care that it won't scrrrew you [intentional typo], hehehehehehe (Beavis-like laughter [Beavis is a popular cartoon figure known for his low mental ability])

Z   kedves Apuka!
    elore is elnezest, de olvasva a leveledet az jutott eszembe h "Bazd meg a 28 fokodat!" (bocs!)
    ...

Z   dear Daddy!
    please let me apologise in advance, but reading your letter it has just come into my mind t't "you should fukk [intentionally misspelled variant of one of the most widely used Hungarian swear words] your 28 degrees Celsius!" (sorry!) ...

(E # 14–16)

At the beginning of this interaction, Z inquires about X's trip to Dubai. While the tone is bantering (e.g. Z states that he and the other friend Y miss X "very much", which is intentionally excessively emotional in this interpersonal relation), the first e-mail is still relatively exempt from formal elements of in-group ritual. In his response, however, X moves the interactional tone towards in-group rituality. Firstly, he playfully challenges Z by calling him *Ubul*, a rare Hungarian name which, similar to certain other rare names such as *Jenő*, can be deployed as a playful reference to the addressee's stupidity in contemporary Hungarian language use.[2] Along with this playful mimetic challenge, and the humorous way in which X accepts Z's request to give advice on a certain matter, the most important practice of in-group ritual applied by X is swearing; that is, X uses the intentionally misspelled swear words and swearing expressions *vazzze* 'fuccck' (correctly: *vazze*) and *be...szopppjad* 'screw you' (correctly: *be...szopjad*), hence utilising an important ritual practice of the in-group, i.e. recurrent swearing by misspelled expressions which are mostly used by members of the lower classes, as a discourse resource of friendly challenge and humour. Along with expressing humour by mimetically animating the voice of others, the misspelling of swear words has another important role in the ritual practice of the network studied: it formally *disarms* swearing.[3] Such disarming is not so obviously needed in some cases, for example *vazze* is a relatively 'harmless' swear word which can potentially act as a solidarity marker (cf. Rákosi 2008: 421); its use is mostly very reasonable in other cases, like when *baszd meg* (fuck, misspelled as *bazd meg*) is used.[4] The necessity of this device is further accentuated by the computer-mediated medium, in which one cannot utilise certain traditional non-verbal mitigating devices like prosody, by means of which swear words could be disarmed in certain spoken interactional contexts.

Finally, in the third e-mail, Z concludes the co-construction of the ritual style by phrasing his message in a contesting way that accords with the in-group's ritual practice. Z addresses X as *Apuka* 'Daddy', a form used by young children towards their fathers, thereby referring to the fact that X has a child. This form, as my informant confirmed, is meant to mimetically express a mocking challenge because it 'frames' (cf. Goffman 1974) X as a harmless enough personality. Further, Z uses the above-mentioned misspelled swear word *bazd meg* in this e-mail.

In sum, on the formal level, in-group ritual resembles its social counterpart, since it is manifested via both ritualised forms and sequential rules. The fact that members of the in-group studied make repeated use of different types of conventionalised ritual formal practices such as misspelling reinforces the similarity between socially conventionalised rituals and in-group rituals – as Kertzer (1988: 9) argues, ritual is a "symbolic behavior that is socially standardized and repetitive". It is pertinent to add that the reason why rituality was co-constructed in only seven of the eight threads is related to time lag between the threads: the thread in which rituals were applied without re- and co-construction (# 4) occurred very soon after the previous one (# 3), and although they are topically different the network members might have perceived their interaction as ongoing.

It should also be noted that in-group ritual, as every ritual practice, tends to reflect a somewhat intensified emotional (and affective) state (cf. Chapter 2 and Section 3.2.3), due to which the time span of in-group ritual is potentially limited in any given interaction. In other words, the interactants tend to switch back to a less ritual form at some point in the interaction, i.e. to deactivate the ritual, as the following extract (the continuation of extract 3.3 above) illustrates:

(3.4)

Z ...errol jut eszembe: mikor jossz? annak azert orulok h jol erzed magad. nem mintha itthon olyan szar dolgod lenne, nemdebar?? :)
na csa...a tanacskerest majd eloben

Z ...this reminds me: when do you come [back]? I am happy though that you feel well. not that you are having a shitty life here, right?? :)
well, see ye [slang form]...will ask your advice when we meet

(E # 19)

In this closing e-mail Z makes it clear that he is about to close the thread. He switches back to a relatively neutral tone, which thus signals a virtual leave-taking on the level of metacommunication.[5]

3.2.3 Functional properties 功能特征

As Grimes (1990: 13) argues, ritual "is not a 'what', not a 'thing'. It is a 'how'." Indeed, in order to compare the more locally conventionalised in-group ritualistic practices of relational networks with socially conventionalised rituals, it is necessary to go beyond their formal similarities, that is, to examine whether in-group ritual fits into the wider pragmatic understanding of rituality (Bax 2010a) in terms of interactional function.

As already noted in Chapter 2, perhaps most importantly in-group ritual fulfils a Durkheimian socio-relational function (see also Burke 1987: 75), that is, it functions as a theatrical mimetic performance that regulates relations and creates solidarity (cf. Section 3.3). Ritual acts are performances from both the participants' and the analyst's perspectives (although they are *experienced* only by the interactants), in the sense that they make it necessary for the performers to take part in a (relational) practice which differs from the practices of 'ordinary' life. The performance of in-group rituals also helps in-group members to successfully cope with potentially problematic situations. This relational problem-solving function can also be observed in my data: in a seemingly contradictory way, the enactment of mock conflict has a conflict-resolving function, and in this sense these rituals are potentially both "earnest and playful" (Turner 1982: 35). In order to illustrate this point, let us analyse the following extract:

(3.5)

Y Kedves Barátaim!
   Ezt a címet kérlek, most rögtön töröljétek a levelező programjaitokból, ha csak nem szeretnétek vele hivatalosan levelezni.
   Az y@index.hu él csak.
   Erre a levelemre, erre a címre ne válaszoljatok már
   Y

Y Dear Friends!
   I would like to ask you to delete this [e-mail] address from your mailing programs immediately, unless you intend to send official messages here.
   Only y@index.hu is alive.
   Do not send any answers to this e-mail, to the present address
   Y

Z Hehe, Y nagyon kiffffinomultan ir... Ilyen muveltek a fonokok?

Z Haha, Y writes in a very reffffined way... Bosses are that well educated?

X MILLYEN "KEDVES BARÁTAIM!!!!! Ki a fahhom kedveeees?

X WHHAT "DEAR FRIENDS"!!!!! Who the fucck [intentional typo] is niiiice?

(E # 37–39)

Example (3.5) shows similarities to workplace banter studied by Yedes (1996). Prior to this interaction, X and Z, by accident, had sent in-group messages to Y's new office e-mail address. Y, who works in a managerial position in a company, and who perceives that these e-mails might be viewed by the company's web administrator, reminds X and Z to avoid sending e-mails to this address, in an official tone that reflects his awareness of the 'outsider' webmaster's presence. In turn, Z, this time sending his message to Y's private address, switches to sarcasm, and finally X clearly switches to the in-group ritual challenging style. By responding in a style that gradually becomes ritual, Z and X seem to react to the fact that (a) it might have been rather unpleasant for Y to receive their very informal e-mails at his office address, and also that (b) the official tone in which Y had to answer is a source of potential tension as it is markedly different from the in-group style. That is, X and Y's mimetic co-construction of symbolic conflict (instead of apologising) not only reinforces in-group identity but also potentially functions to prevent the formation of any real conflict.

To sum up, the mimetic re-enactment of acts – in the present case, the theatrical performance of an imagined conflict – is a common functional feature of in-group ritual and social ritual. As with every ritual act of mimetic re-enactment, in-group ritual operates with related framing devices (cf. Goffman 1974; see also Bax 2004), which provide clues for interpretation, hence minimising the chance of ritual moves being interpreted as non-ritual.

As a functional property relevant to the relational function discussed above, in-group ritual, like socially conventional ritual, has a psychological effect which has been defined as the ritual moment. As noted in Chapter 2, the ritual moment creates an atmosphere in which states of mind alter; as Koster (2003: 219) argues, ritual activity produces "a temporary destruction of awareness of the wider meaningful relations of one's individuality and the reduction of the self to the immediate physical experience of the here and now". Although the 'here and now' is, of course, virtual in contexts such as the asynchronous communication mode of e-mail, the stimulating cognitive effect seems to come into play irrespective of the channel through which a ritual is enacted. Clearly, by means of ritual practice the interactants can playfully defy normal behaviour, that is, act beyond societal conventions. In the data under study, this function becomes apparent when ritual is applied to negotiate a difficult situation without offending other members of the group, as illustrated by the following extract:

(3.6)

Z   ne rinyálj, X! majd megyünk korán...lelépünk korán...de előtte zabálunk (ha gondoljátok, összedobhatnánk a menüt együtt...de felőlem akár pizza is lehet)

Z   don't rabbit, X! we will go early...nick off early...but before that we can gobble up (if you want, we can jointly put the menu together...but as for me I'm happy with pizza as well)

X   Megyünk? Valami hiba csúszott az többesszámmal, baszkikám. Ki mondta, hogy takarítani akarok pakolás lözben?

> Ha annyira fenyőfa meg minden, mér nem találkozunk Y-nál,
> úgy is meg akarom nézni a lakását.

X *We* [my emphasis] go? There is an error here with the plural, old
prick [playful swear word]. Who said that I want to clean up [our
flat for guests] while I pack [for a forthcoming journey].
If [you want] a Christmas tree and everything [i.e. Christmas
celebration] all that much, whhy [intentional typo] don't we
meet at Y, I want to see his [new] flat anyway.

(E # 108–109)

In this interaction, Z and X negotiate who is to host the Christmas party for the three friends and their spouses/partners. Z wants X to host the party, and X declines – which amounts to a 'face-threatening situation' (cf. Brown and Levinson 1987) even among close friends, not only in Hungary but arguably in many cultural settings. In order to cope with this precarious situation, both X and Z make use of the in-group ritual of mocking challenge, which seems to allow them to perform this negotiation directly, without concerns about immediate face needs. In other words, by playing their part in the theatrical mimetic performance of their ritual, X and Z become members of a community with a unique in-group ethos rather than acting purely as individuals, and so they can afford to interact outside social convention.

To conclude, the present section has discussed the formal and functional properties of in-group ritual, with special focus on interactionally (co)-constructed relational practices. In terms of formal/behavioural aspects, interactionally (co)-constructed in-group ritual comes down to a relatively flexible form of ritual behaviour, even if flexibility is a matter of degree and may vary across in-groups. Engaging in in-group ritual can require a fair share of creativity from the interactants, considering that it is often not formally codified. In-group ritual can operate with an ad hoc interactional structure, in the sense that certain in-group ritual acts are realised through the co-construction of interaction, and such acts are dynamic, too (see e.g. extract 3.5). Furthermore, in-group ritual is processual by its very nature: new in-groups form new in-group rituals, although there are in-group rituals that are 'inherited', potentially via urban legends, from other relational networks without becoming social rituals (see Chapter 4 on the lifespan of different ritual types). We may refer here to the example of the Hungarian ritual *cakes* (cf. Chapter 2), which was adopted by groups of young males, as a ritual utterance when one passed wind in an audible way. As the informal interviews mentioned in Chapter 2 revealed, the noteworthy aspect of this ritual is that several groups practised it as an in-group ritual, often without realising how widespread it was, and there were also different 'local' variants of the ritual. On the other hand, all the groups interviewed referred to the origin of *cakes* as 'inherited' from older brothers and friends, which suggests that the ritual was not created by their groups.

In spite of these differences between locally conventionalised ritual practices and their social-level counterparts (see also Chapter 4) both the formal and the functional approach suggest that they share various essential relational properties of social ritual. Mimesis seems to be a strong binding factor behind these similarities. With the development of relational history, and under the influence of in-group ethos, in-group ritual is often abstract and has lost its mimetic relationship with its original model, as the data examined illustrate. Consequently, in-group ritual as represented here is performative, since more often than not 'truth conditions' scarcely play a role in such rituals, in a similar way to many socially 'coded' ritual practices. For example, the ritual challenges studied are so very different from 'real-life' challenges that they are unlikely to be taken as challenges; besides, there are formal framing devices to prevent this possibility (e.g. intentionally misspelled swear words). An anecdotal case may serve to illustrate that occasionally in-group rituals can even contradict reality: I used to address my daughter as *tömör baba* 'bonny baby' as part of an affective in-group ritual to express solidarity (and the child had a ritual answer to this form). This ritual was 'historically motivated' in that my young daughter was in truth a bonny baby; but the ritual went on after she was no longer a baby, thus operating in the face of the altered physical reality.

3.3 In-group ritual and the construction of network identity: a case study of historical Chinese letters
群内仪式与社交网络身份的构建：关于汉语古代信函的个案研究

The present section will examine the wider, discursive function of in-group relational ritual practices, by focusing on how they contribute to the construction of the identities of the relational networks within which they are performed.

It can be argued that a relational network is an entity constituted by practices (cf. Bourdieu 1978), rather than a spatially located group (even though it can as well be one). Through joint activities (cf. Clarke 2008, Angouri and Marra 2011), common language and dialect (cf. Eckert 2000), religious exercises (cf. Oberoi 1994) and various other practices individuals tend to form groups; physical proximity is not a precondition for joint practices to operate: relational networks come into existence, for example, in online settings (cf. Aouragh 2011). All common linguistic and behavioural practices of a relational network contribute to the formation of its identity, and also there are relational practices that specifically serve the construction of network identity; these include relational practices by means of which individuals shape their relationship with, and role within, a group, and represent and position the relational network towards out-group people. As my data suggest, relational ritual practices play a key role in the formation of network identity, and among ritual practices, in-group ones are particularly important in this respect. This is for the reason discussed in Section 3.2: they are formed within the network, and so they represent the in-group ethos.

As noted in Section 3.1, every relational ritual act contributes to the formation of network identity; the present analysis is limited to in-group ritual actions that primarily serve this specific purpose. In terms of methodology, this study relies on Mary Bucholtz's (1999) work. Bucholtz argues that identity-forming practices manifest themselves in two ways at the level of language use:

> Negative identity practices are those that individuals employ to distance themselves from a rejected identity, while positive identity practices are those in which individuals engage in order actively to construct a chosen identity. In other words, negative identity practices define what their users are not, and hence emphasize identity as an intergroup phenomenon; positive identity practices define what their users are, and thus emphasize the intragroup aspects of social identity. (Bucholtz 1999: 211–12)

Following Bucholtz's definition, the present section approaches *positive* identity formation practices, that is, cases when individuals engage in ritual practices in order to construct their identities as group members, by reflecting on their network's ethos. In-group relational ritual practices which formulate network identity can be divided into two major categories, namely (a) ritual actions that formulate a specific network identity implicitly, without distinguishing the given group from other networks, and (b) ritual actions which are distinctive, i.e. which form network identity by explicitly distinguishing one relational network from others. Our focus is on the way in which ritual practices form network identity vis-à-vis (a) lexical and (b) discursive topics.

After introducing the data of the case study (Section 3.3.1), in Section 3.3.2 I will examine the formation of identity vis-à-vis the first category of ritual actions, which formulate network identity without explicitly positioning it against other groups or society at large. These practices, which in the present analysis include the discursive choice and ritual performance of schematic topics, are present in the ritualistic interactions of every relational group I have encountered thus far. By their nature, they reflect the group's specific circumstances, and as they are not intentionally distinctive they more often overlap with the normative practices of various other relational networks.

In Section 3.3.3 I will explore the second ritual category by means of which network identity is formulated: the creative practice when a relational network intentionally adopts in-group ritual practices which contradict wider social norms, in order to position itself against other networks or society, hence creating its distinctive identity.

3.3.1 Data 语料

This section explores the discursive identity formation practices of a historical southern[6] Chinese group: inhabitants of the Shaoxing 绍兴 area in Zhejiang Province who moved to northern China. This southern Chinese group was chosen because in China there has been a long-standing southern vs northern nationalistic and ideological opposition (see Eberhard 1965, Friedman 1995). This opposition originates in Chinese history: there were significant linguistic and social differences between the southern and northern regions of the Chinese Empire, and these areas were ruled by different dynasties during extended periods. As a result of sociocultural barriers, the populations of the southern and northern areas developed different stereotypes. Inhabitants of the north regarded, and often continue to regard, southern Chinese as 'feminine', 'profit-oriented', and 'improper/non-standard speakers' (in reference to the fact that most of the southern Chinese are 'dialect' speakers and speak standard Chinese with a 'heavy' accent; cf. Chan 1998). Southerners are often referred to by northern Chinese as the 'barbaric southerners', or *nanman(zi)*南蛮子. On the other hand, the southern Chinese consider their northern compatriots 'provincial' and 'servile' (in reference to the northerners' inclination to follow the central government, traditionally located in Peking). Southerners often describe the people of the north as 'country bumpkins', using degrading terms such as *tubaozi* 土包子 (bumpkin).

Because of this opposition, contexts in which southern Chinese form their identities in contrast to their northern counterparts, and vice versa, provide noteworthy data with which to study identity formation. This section analyses the correspondence of a closed circle of expatriate Shaoxing scribes who lived in the north: a corpus of 60 letters (see Kádár 2009), selected from the epistolary collection *Xuehongxuan- chidu* 雪鸿轩尺牍(*Letters from Snow Swan Retreat*), written between *c.*1758 and 1811[7] by the office clerk Gong Weizhai 龚未斋(1738–1811).[8] The present corpus has a special significance from the perspective of identity formation because along with their particular concrete goals (such as request, apology, invitation), many letters by Gong Weizhai fulfil an important major social function, namely, the formation of camaraderie among a group of Shaoxing clerks who lived in the north.[9] As becomes evident from the correspondence of Gong Weizhai, as well as that of his friend Xu Jiacun 许葭村 (his exact dates are unknown), these scribes formed a closed relational network in the capital: although they made connections with 'out-group' (*wai* 外) people, including for instance business partners, northern colleagues and courtesans, they primarily relied on their own network, and aided each other by means of favours and gifts.[10]

A theoretical and methodological issue that should be addressed here is the present chapter's reliance on a corpus that was written by a single author. Since the letters were produced by one individual, their reliability as representing the style of a relational network is questionable. In order to address this problem, the data studied was compared with the other most important epistolary corpus of the Shaoxing group, namely Xu Jiacun's (see above) *Qiushuixuan-chidu* 秋水轩尺牍(*Letters from Autumn Water Retreat*; cf. Kádár 2010a); particular attention was devoted to the aforementioned group of letters that represent the correspondence between Gong and Xu. This comparative research has shown that most unique features of the letters studied are not Gong's individual preferences or idiosyncrasies but rather they represent the group's style.

3.3.2 The first category: non-contrastive identity formation
第一类: 非对比性身份的形成

Let us first examine ritual practices that form a network's identity without positioning the network against others. Although this category includes a wide variety of practices, the current analysis focuses on ritual acts which primarily serve this goal: ritual discourse on topics that concern the group. The data I have studied thus far reveals that relational networks, perhaps without exception, undertake discussions on topics which are salient for their members; recurrent discourse on these topics can become a ritual practice by itself.

For example, if we survey the present corpus of socialising letters, it becomes evident that the correspondents undertake recurrent mimetic – i.e. ritualistic – discourse on certain schematic topics. As the analysis below will illustrate, these discursive rituals tend to coincide with the discursive practices of various other groups I have encountered thus far; this accords with the claim made in Section 3.3.1 that identity-forming rituals which belong to the first category (non-contrastive identity formation) only reflect the group's situation, i.e. issues that concern those who belong to a relational network, rather than being intentionally distinctive. Yet, the practices studied here have a somewhat unique characteristic, at least from the contemporary reader's perspective, which adds to their value for the present case study. The way in which the schematic topics are performed occasionally represents 'ritual extravagance', to use Bax's (2004) term, i.e. these stereotypical identity-constructing topics are situated in performances which are sometimes overtly theatrical. This is supposedly due to the historically situated characteristic of the correspondence studied.

In the corpus we can identify the following major ritual themes, in 36 of the 60 letters (in more or less indirect form):

1. Difficulties in the author's and his addressee's lives as office assistants
2. Southern literati in the north
3. Letter writing

In 28 of the 36 letters these topics occur jointly, which explains their high frequency in the corpus. In what follows, let us analyse how these discursive topics operate in identity formation.

Difficulties in the author's and his addressee's lives as office assistants

In Gong Weizhai's correspondence, a popular theme is lamentation over the difficulty of his life as an office assistant, as well as the expression of sympathy for addressees who struggle with the same problems. Complaining functions as an in-group ritual in many cultures (cf. Alemán 2001), and so this discursive ritual represents a somewhat stereotypical in-group ritual practice.

For example, in the following extract (3.7) (cited from letter no. VIII. 4[11]) Gong laments over their difficulties to cover even their fundamental needs, due to their low salaries as office clerks:

(3.7)

孟浪棲枝，徒留笑柄。为今之计，只好借乡试名色，决意旋归，惟是行李萧条，不独旅人减色，还祈毋忘季布一诺，践省城传述之言，使不至流落地方，得以老死牖下。是皆居子周急之赐也。

And now, if I were to linger here in my current predicament I would be a laughing-stock. For this reason I can do naught but use the triennial province examination as a pretext to leave and return home. However, I have faced difficulties in covering my travel expenses, and, apart from the journey, have had the additional worry of being forced to respectfully ask you to remember my need and recall the promise you made to me in the provincial capital to aid my return home.

Supposedly, these laments reflected some personal disappointment with the author's and his peers' lives in the north (see a philological analysis of this issue in Kádár 2012a). Yet, it is pertinent to note that such complaints are somewhat theatrical (mimetic), considering that office clerks were relatively well-paid people in historical China, compared with the majority of the population. The obvious reason for this recurrent complaint is that it must have fulfilled a positive identity-forming function, for individuals who see themselves as 'poor' compared with their masters, the civil officials.

The symbolic and ritual nature of this discursive topic becomes even more visible in the following extract (letter XV. 3), in which the author laments over his own difficulties in order to admonish his nephew, i.e. the ritual topic functions as a discursive resource (Thornborrow 2002). In order to understand the indirect admonishment message here, one needs to know that this letter is a response to the author's nephew who is worried about some financial matters:

(3.8)

余惟以碌碌终生，不能自立为愧。吾侄当求其所以自立者，贫不足为忧，且断不可忧焉！

I have spent my life carrying out menial tasks and I am ashamed that I was unable to achieve independence. My nephew should seek to stand on his own two feet, and not be held back by the fear of poverty, which itself is nothing to fear.

Southern literati in the north

As previously noted, opposition between the southern and northern parts of China is one of the central discursive topics in the correspondence studied. Similarly to laments, this ritual practice covers the relational phenomena which Presthus et al. (1976) defined as "nationalistic ritual", and which is present in various forms in the interaction of many other relational networks.

In fact, this discourse reflects to some extent a traditional ritual literary practice in China: many literati from both the south and the north wrote disparagingly about each other (see Eberhard 1965). However, what gives a somewhat specific, in-group character to Gong Weizhai's discourse on this topic is that he often seems to go beyond the conventional ways in which this topic is discussed, by recurrently addressing it from various angles. For example, a typical discursive topic is the author's 'cultural' difficulties in the north, as well as his expression of sympathy for the addressees' similar struggles, as represented by the following excerpt from letter no. XV. 4:

(3.9)

西人之子，竟为吾辈意计所不能料。行路之难，真难于上青天矣，可怜哉！长安居大不易，有就须曲就之。即如仆逗留此间，亦非得已，然终无可如何耳。

It is indeed hard for us to understand the mind of the people of Peking. Thus, for strangers like us attaining our goals is as difficult as ascending into the blue sky and this is a dreadful matter! It is very difficult to live in the capital: even if one manages to find a post here he must force himself to undertake it, no matter what it is. One need but look at my humble self: I remain here as I have no alternative and am unable to find a better path.

It is obvious that people from all parts of China migrated to the capital city of Peking, and so just as in the case of example (3.7) above the author's lamentation seems to be somewhat symbolic and mimetic.

Another related discursive topic is the author's description of his yearning to return to the south, as illustrated by the following excerpts cited from letter no. VI. 2:

(3.10)

惟足下先赋归与，弟须三四年后始能践约。耕山钓水之乐，请先独得之。

You, sir, decided to return home first, and this younger brother of yours must wait three or four years before being able to do the same. Hence I beg you, sir, to enjoy the pleasure of ploughing the land and fishing the rivers yourself till my return.

The expression of emotions is in fact an important part of the network-identity-forming ritual performance, as it seems to boost the affective value of the ritual act (cf. Chapter 5). The theatrical performance of emotions is present in various forms in the ritual practice of contrasting the north with the south. For example, the following excerpt cited from letter no. VIII. 1 represents the author's melancholy when he, having managed to leave his office in order to return south, had to say farewell to his friends who would continue to work in the north:

(3.11)

兹已决意南旋，腊初买车起程。惟与知已远达，未免怅快。

Now, at last I am resolved to return to the South, and at the beginning of the Twelfth Month I will prepare my carriage and embark on my journey. All that troubles me is the distance that shall stand between us, my friend, and I cannot suppress feelings of melancholia at this prospect.

As the final goal of the members of the Shaoxing group was to return home after they built a career in the capital, discourse on this aspiration – as well as the expression of sorrow when a group member finally attained this goal and had to leave the others behind – fulfilled a group-identity-forming ritual function, similar to the discursive topic of the antipathy towards northern life.

A further recurrent and ritualistic discursive topic related to the south vs north dichotomy is the clearly nationalistic comparison between these areas, to the advantage of the south, as illustrated by the following citation:

(3.12)

松竹梅为岁寒三友。而北地松竹不多见，梅更无之。惟夭桃秾李，每灿烂于丰台芍乐之间。
然转眼而成为黄土矣，增花落春残之感。南冠而北游者，亦往往为习俗所移，
贵春花而忘秋实。致岁寒之盟，与松竹梅同其廖落，殊为唧叹。

The pine, the bamboo and the sour plum are the three friends of winter. However, here in the North there are very few pines and bamboos, and the sour plum is even rarer. It is only the beautiful peach and plum tree blossoms amongst the peonies of Fengtai that attract the eye during winter. Yet, in the twinkle of an eye they fall to the earth and the sorrow at their passing and the longing for spring becomes even stronger. The men of the South who come hither are gradually changed by the land – just like the peach and plum which bloom beautifully once a year, but lose their flowers in an instant, they tend to value appearance and not intrinsic worth. Thus, it is as difficult here to find lasting friendship as it is to behold the pines, the bamboo, and the sour plum, and this is deeply regretful.

As this excerpt, cited from letter no. I. 3 illustrates, there is an explicit evaluative description of the south vs north dichotomy in Gong's correspondence, southern culture and identity appearing to be more valuable than their northern counterparts.

Letter writing

The office assistants of the Shaoxing group were expert letter writers: they were regarded as a distinguished group of epistolary experts, or Shaoxing-shiye 绍兴师爷 (lit. Revered Masters from Shaoxing). Therefore, recurrent, ritualistic discourse on epistolary activity fulfilled a fundamental group-identity-forming function in the correspondence of Gong Weizhai, as illustrated by the next excerpt cited from letter no. XII. 3:

(3.13)

惟三十余年，客窗酬应之札，自据胸臆，畅所欲言。虽于尺牍之道，去之千里，而性情所寄，似有不忍弃者，遂于病后录而集之。内中惟仆与足下酬答为独多。惜足下鸿篇短制，为爱者揣去，仅存四六一函，录之于集。借美玉之光，以辉燕石，并欲使后之览者，知仆与足下乃文字之交，非势利交也。

Nevertheless, for more than thirty years, in service far from home, I have written extensive correspondence in which I narrated my feelings with artless words. Although these writings are a thousand miles distant from what one would call the art of letter writing, they record my various dispositions and I feel reluctant to throw them away. Therefore, after recovering from my illness I have copied and collected my correspondence. Amongst my letters, those which this humble servant wrote to you, sir, are by far the most numerous. It is regretful to me however, that most of your outstanding letters of various length are no longer in my possession, my friend, and I have only one letter of forty six sentences left, which I have copied into my collection. Thus, I would like to ask you, sir, to lend me your refined works and let them illuminate my worthless collection, like shiny jades enlightening worthless stones. In this way the readers of my work will know that the relationship between you, sir, and my humble self was a true friendship between men of letters and not the snobbish and greedy connection of some of the literati.

The mimetic nature of this discussion becomes evident if one considers the message of this letter. The present letter serves the purpose of socialisation, which is proved by the fact that the author requests the recipient to lend him his letters. Edited collections of historical Chinese letters were single authored (Kádár 2010a), and so the author's request is symbolic and it primarily serves to elevate the other interlocutor and hence reinforce the relationship. The social function of this letter is 'wrapped' in discourse on letter writing. Quite understandably, discourse on an activity in which a group has special skill (see e.g. Bucholtz's 1999 discussion on the intellectual discourse of female nerds) fulfils a strong positive identity formation function. Psychologically, emphasis of a group's strength reinforces myths (cf. Bourdieu 1991 above) of group identity, which aid members to regard their group as a distinct one.

Like other discourses examined in this section, this ritual discourse of letter writing does not have a distinctive nature, in that discourses on the 'state of art' are adopted by a wide range of relational networks. For example, Redding and Ng (1982) found a somewhat similar behaviour in Hong Kong Chinese companies, and Cova and Salle (2000) described ritual discourses resembling this in Western workplace settings.

The present section has examined the ritual practice of reflecting on a relational network's circumstances by recurrently performing schematic discussions on topics which are significant for the members as group-identity-formation devices. In what follows, let us examine the second case of network-identity-formation vis-à-vis ritual practices.

3.3.3 The second category: contrastive (counter-social conventional) ritual practice 第二类：对比性（反社会规约）仪式实践

Non-contrastive identity-forming (first category) practices, including those studied in Section 3.3.2, operate as a default means of ritual identity formation. However, occasionally members of relational networks intentionally adopt distinctive ritual mimetic practices to make their group saliently different from other groups, as well as 'society' per se. Nevertheless, as my data suggests, the distinctive practices of different groups show similarities, i.e. 'distinctiveness' should be regarded as an aspiration rather than an outcome. These practices tend to contradict what counts as socially conventional and normative. We could observe the operation of these practices, for example, in the case of the Hungarian friends in Section 3.2, who adopted a distinctive style.

The Shaoxing corpus includes a noteworthy manifestation of this phenomenon, namely, the application of 'unusual', or more precisely distinctive, forms that trigger politeness (cf. Chapter 2 on the interrelation between politeness and rituality). Many of these forms have been analysed in Kádár (2010b), and so the present analysis is restricted to the exploration of their role in group identity formation.

In the Gong Weizhai corpus there are some cases when the author, by using certain linguistic forms, symbolically defies the norms of deference but in fact expresses a polite meaning. Such utterances work in a similar way to 'mock impoliteness', as defined in Culpeper (1996: 352):

> Mock impoliteness, or banter, is impoliteness that remains on the surface, since it is understood that it is not intended to cause offence.

Such mimetic performances seem to have a strong group-identity-forming function. As the corpus studied demonstrates, members of the Shaoxing group made use of tools of politeness that were somewhat unconventional in order to differentiate themselves from the inhabitants of Peking. In a sense, these linguistic practices show some similarity to the intellectual "word coinage" of a group of female nerds examined by Bucholtz (1999: 212): exactly as female nerds coin new terms as part of their identity work, Shaoxing clerks made innovations in traditional forms that occasion deference.

Importantly, when focusing on second case contrastive ritual practices I do not intend to suggest that the interactants' choice of a polite (mock impolite) ritual register was always intentional. I agree with Mills (2003b) who notes that the choice of interactional style is often not an explicitly intentional process. Yet, it could be argued that the application of innovative style requires some intentionality,[12] and in such marked cases it aims to reconstruct the group ethos shared by members of the network. The Shaoxing clerks probably used new literary forms as they shared the belief that they were a distinguished group of expert letter writers who led lives beyond conventions.

There is indirect evidence indicating that members of the network studied shared a heroic group ethos. This ethos can be observed, for example, in the way in which Gong represents his recipient in letter no. VIII. 2:

(3.14)

曾忆云雨寺前，坐柳阴而听黄鸟，足下纵酒肆谈，解衣磅礴，有不可一世之概，今尚得如当年豪迈否？

3 In-Group Ritual in Operation: Two Case Studies 75

I recall the old times when we were sitting in front of the Yunyu Temple in the shadow of the willows listening to the song of the orioles: you, sir, drank plenty of wine and spoke openly, loosening your jacket and talking without ceremony, and your spirit indeed surpassed our whole generation. Do you still preserve the heroic spirit you possessed in those days?

The piquancy of this heroic description of the recipient as a blunt and brave person is that it is accomplished in a deferential and highly sophisticated way: it would be difficult to imagine the recipient or the author talking in a truly blunt and heroic manner. In other words, this claimed bluntness was mimetic and ritual, and was in fact meant to be the in-group manifestation of the Shaoxing network's cultural superiority.

This ethos manifests itself in the ritual practice of 'mock impoliteness' (cf. Culpeper 1996): 'sophisticated bluntness' appeals to the addressee's interactional expectations on the one hand, and also serves as a form of self-representation, on the other. On the level of linguistic forms, the members of the Shaoxing group apply several types of 'irregular' manifestations of mock impoliteness, including idioms and historical references, as well as humour. In order to illustrate the function of the mimetic usage of 'mock impoliteness', which contradicts socially normative ('polite') conventions, let us look at the following extracts:

(3.15)

陈遵尺牍，名震当时。然高自位置，惜墨如金，不肯轻投一札，足下殆亦有此癖！

Chen Zun [of old] gained a great reputation amongst his generation for [his expertise in] letter writing. However, he formed an overly high opinion of himself and he spared his ink as if it was gold, not willing to send a letter to anyone [if it were not necessary]. [I wonder,] sir, whether you are not on the edge of falling into the error of his conceit? (letter no. XIII.1)

(3.16)

岂可以牛溲马勃，滥充其数？想亦足下阿其所好，而观察公谬采虚声也。

Now, why should he invite a useless fellow like me to fill a position [when I hold not the merits to do so]? I am afraid that you, sir, are partial to me due to our friendship and [that you have unintentionally misled] His Excellency to form a false image of this person. (letter no. XII.2)

(3.17)

先录此文，顺马递上，作莲幕之传单何如？呵呵！

[Yet,] first I record this poem and entrust a courier to respectfully present it to you. Is it fit even to be used as [an artless and functional] note [to keep you abreast of my experiences here]? Hah-hah! (letter no. VI.1)

In extract (3.15), written to a close friend, the author makes an analogy between the behaviour of Chen Zun 陈遵 (his exact dates are unknown), a renowned Han Dynasty (206 BC–AD 220) man of letters, and that of the addressee. This historical reference expresses a seemingly 'negative' (impolite) meaning. The author – longing for the correspondent's letter – mimetically reprimands him for sparing his ink like Chen Zun, and wonders whether his correspondent does not "fall into the error of Chen's conceit" (*yi you ci pi* 亦有此癖, lit. also has this craving). However, at the same time the author emphasises the great expertise of Chen in epistolary art by using the conventional expression *ming zhen dang shi* 名震当时 (lit. one's name shakes his age), and so by ritually scolding the addressee for behaviour that resembles that of Chen Zun, he conveys a secondary elevating meaning by comparing the correspondent's talent to Chen's.

Extract (3.16) is excerpted from a letter written to a colleague and friend who recommended the author to the Chief Provincial Judge, who decided to employ him, but the author had to decline the offer. In the present extract the author ritually reprimands the correspondent, by using the idiomatic expressions *e-qi-suo-hao* 阿其所好 (lit. flattering one's favourite) and *miucai-xusheng* 谬采虚声 (lit. erroneously building false reputation, trans. form a false image of this person). However, this mimetic ritual reprimand – another manifestation of mock impoliteness – conveys a self-denigrating meaning: it not only conveys the message that the correspondent is in fact a good friend of the author's but also denigrates the author's skill by claiming that it does not warrant the addressee's approbation.

Finally, in (3.17) the author applies the onomatopoeic word *hehe* 呵呵 (hah-hah). This lexical choice, which is clearly mimetic, would sound somewhat rude in other contexts but here it conveys a humorous self-denigrating meaning. It reinforces the discursive practice of the author who is seeking to reconfirm the group ethos of 'unconventional and heroic literati'.

It should be noted that in some cases Gong uses ritualised idioms that are semantically even ruder than the ones above. For example, in some letters the idiom *shijia-zhi-pi* 嗜痂之癖 (lit. the depraved taste of eating scabs) is applied in order to decline the correspondent's appraisal of the author's work through an act of ritualistic self-denigration. That is, in these contexts the use of *shijia-zhi-pi* symbolically claims that the correspondent who likes the author's work has depraved taste, hence the secondary self-denigrating meaning of this expression.

To sum up, the present section has illustrated the way in which contrastive (counter-social conventional) in-group ritual practices operate. It is pertinent to note that the two identity-forming practices studied in Section 3.3 tend to co-occur in the data studied.

3.4 Summary 结语

The present chapter has overviewed the way in which in-group ritual practices operate. Section 3.2 has examined the major formal and functional (interactional) properties of in-group rituals, by analysing the e-mail interactions of a group of Hungarian friends. The analysis has revealed that although it can be more challenging to describe in-group rituals than socially conventionalised ones due to their interactionally constructed nature, their formal and functional properties show similarities to social rituals (but see Chapter 4 on differences between these two categories). Section 3.3 has addressed the wider-sense constructive relational function of in-group ritual practices, by looking into how they construct network identity. It has been shown that network identity is formed through two major ritual practice types: (1) ritual discourse on topics that concern members of a relational network; and (2) ritual strategies to differentiate a relational network from other networks and/or society.

After overviewing in-group ritual, in the following Chapter 4 let us integrate this category into a typology of ritual practices based on the concept of relating.

4
Relational Ritual Typology
人际关系仪式的分类体系

4.1 Introduction 引言

The present book has so far focused on in-group relational ritual practices. As noted earlier (see Chapter 1), in-group ritual represents only a certain type of relational ritual behaviour: the current chapter will integrate relational ritual within a wider ritual typology. Such a categorisation is not only helpful because it sets in-group ritual practices in their place within the 'family' of relational rituals, but it is also needed as the relational approach to ritual acts calls for an alternative typology of rituality. Existing studies in the field tend to categorise ritual acts on the basis of their 'genre' or context of occurrence; as this chapter will argue, from a relational perspective a ritual typology should categorise rituals according to the type of relationship which evokes a given ritual practice.

4.1.1 Previous typologies of ritual behaviour
关于仪式行为的既往分类体系

Classification plays a pivotal role in anthropological studies of ritual. This interest is understandable because since the formation of modern anthropology the very notion of 'rituality' is defined as a *type* of action, which comes into existence through a practice of 'classification'. That is, in his groundbreaking study, Durkheim (1912 [1954]) argues that the object of ritual is the belief system of a society, which is constituted by a classification of everything into the two realms of the 'sacred' and 'profane'. As Durkheim notes,

> All known religious beliefs, whether simple or complex, present a common quality: they presuppose a classification of things – the real or ideal things that men represent for themselves – into two classes,

two opposite kinds, generally designated by two distinct terms effectively translated by the words *profane* and *sacred*. The division of the world into two comprehensive domains, one sacred, the other profane, is the hallmark of religious thought. Beliefs, myths, gnomic spirits, and legends are either representations or systems of representation that express the nature of sacred things, the virtues and powers attributed to them, their history, their relations with each other and with profane things. [...] A rite can have this sacred character as well; in fact, no rite exists that does not have it to some degree. There are words, speeches, and formulas that can be spoken only by consecrated persons; there are gestures and movements that cannot be executed by everyone. (Durkheim [1912] 1954: 36–7)

Durkheim's dual categorisation has been thoroughly criticised in various later studies (cf. e.g. Bell 1992), partly because it associates ritual and sacredness. Researchers such as Bax (2010a) have demonstrated that certain ritual practices (and these include the bulk of rituals studied in this book) are inherently mundane, and so it can be argued that Durkheim's definition represents a specific, religious understanding of 'ritual'.[1] Nevertheless, Durkheim's definition has a component which, in my view, remains very accurate: it shows that the right to access certain ritual practices is unequally distributed, which divides ritual acts from 'ordinary' ones. If one ignores the religious claim in the definition above and approaches in-group rituals studied in the previous chapters from the access angle, it becomes evident that in-group rituals fit into Durkheim's theory, as access to them is limited, i.e. only network members can perform them in a limited number of settings (the present chapter will revisit this issue).

Although the development and features of ritual typologies have been addressed in various works such as Bell (1992), Turbott (1997) and Penner (2012), it is pertinent to provide here a brief summary of some of the most representative studies that systematise ritual behaviour. Apart from the aforementioned classification, Durkheim (1912 [1954]) categorised ritual practices as 'positive' and 'negative', the former being attempts to bring the realms of the sacred and human into contact, while the latter include ritual behaviour that separates these realms. The Durkheimian typology is fairly practical, and there are some other typologies that follow this pragmatic approach, although they apply to essentially different concepts. Perhaps the best example is the ritual typology of Turner (1969) who distinguishes two major types of ritual action: 'life-crisis rituals' and 'rituals of affliction'. The former category, partly based on the work of van Gennep (1909), refers to ritual acts that aid the transition from one stage in life to another, while the latter category refers to ritual acts that "redress breaches in the social structure" (Turner 1969: 272). Also there are some theories that approach ritual typology from an entirely different angle, by providing more elaborate categories of ritual behaviour. A representative example is Grimes's (1990) approach, which distinguishes as many as 16 different types of ritual behaviour. Finally, there are some other typologies that are of a 'specialised' nature, in that instead of providing a typology of rituals per se, they attempt to categorically define a certain type of rituality against other types; a good example of this approach is the typology of Hubert and Mauss (1899) who defined the rite of sacrifice against other types of rituality. Although one should refrain from evaluating ritual typologies, as they simply reflect different conceptualisations of the same phenomenon, an arguably appealing typology is that proposed by Bell (1997). Bell takes a middle course between the pragmatic and overly elaborate by proposing six categories of ritual acts, including:

> rites of passage, which are also so-called "life-cycle" rites; calendarial and commemorative rites; rites of exchange and communion; rites of affliction; rites of feasting, fasting, and festivals; and, finally, political rituals. (Bell 1997: 94)

Anthropological typologies are certainly useful, if not essential, to gain an institutional/situational insight into the function of rites in society, in that they reveal many possible settings and events in which rituality emerges. Furthermore, research outside of the domain of strict-sense anthropology has made an invaluable contribution to the institutional/situational mapping of ritual. Ritual norms and acts seem to imbue our daily lives,[2] and they occur covertly in many contexts which are not studied by mainstream anthropological theories, including academic and medical settings which are often described as being exempt from ritual practices by some of those who have institutional power (see e.g. Illich 1975, Bosk 1980, Gilmore 1990, Williams 2005). For example, Illich's (1975) illuminating monograph illustrates that the medical world is a highly ritualised context of human life, by arguing as follows:

> Once a society is so organized that medicine can transform people into patients because they are unborn, newborn, menopausal, or at some other "age of risk," the population inevitably loses some of its autonomy to its healers. The ritualization of stages in life is nothing

new; what is new is their intense medicalization. The sorcerer or medicine man—as opposed to the malevolent witch—dramatized the progress of an Azande tribesman from one stage of his health to the next. The experience may have been painful, but the ritual was short and it served society in highlighting its own regenerative powers. Lifelong medical supervision is something else. It turns life into a series of periods of risk, each calling for tutelage of a special kind. From the crib to the office and from the Club Méditerranée to the terminal ward, each age-cohort is conditioned by a milieu that defines health for those whom it segregates. Hygienic bureaucracy stops the parent in front of the school and the minor in front of the court, and takes the old out of the home. By becoming a specialized place, school, work, or home is made unfit for most people. The hospital, the modern cathedral, lords it over this hieratic environment of health devotees. From Stockholm to Wichita the towers of the medical center impress on the landscape the promise of a conspicuous final embrace. For rich and poor, life is turned into a pilgrimage through check-ups and clinics back to the ward where it started. (Illich 1975: 14)

This finding has been echoed by conversation analysts looking at language use in medical settings, such as ten Have (1991). Furthermore, people's lives are not only ritualised, often in unnoticeable ways, when they are physically located in an institution such as a hospital or a school,[3] but ritual practices are also broadcast to us covertly by the media (see e.g. Couldry 2012). For example, the genres of TV news, reality shows and soap operas all follow and transmit certain ritual practices.

As the above description illustrates, communicational ritual per se – or perhaps we should say the relational aspect of interactionally situated rituals – is hardly relevant to typological approaches to rituality, which categorise ritual acts according to their social event (i.e. context) of occurrence. The only important exception, as far as I am aware, is Bax's (2010a) framework, which classifies ritual acts according to their interactional properties. However, the framework of Bax (2010a) is designed to serve an analytic function rather than a typological purpose.[4]

4.1.2 The relational typology 基于人际关系的分类体系

Thus, it can be argued that a relational ritual typology can reasonably contribute to previous research, as it offers an alternative to the institutional/situational perspective. Such an innovative approach requires that we should look into the type of relationship which evokes a given ritual practice, and also into the type of ritual practice from the perspective of relating and relationality.

An interactional approach should depart from categorising ritual types merely according to the size of the group for which a ritual practice counts as normative. This is because a ritual practice, irrespective of whether it follows a schema which has been standardised (conventionalised) on the societal or more local level, is always adopted, (re-)interpreted and contested by and within networks of language users, i.e. its normativity is relative (on the relativity of categorisation see also Section 4.2.2). For example, 'social' relational practices can be contested across groups that implement and evaluate these acts (see also Chapter 2), and in-group practices can be contested both by group members and group outsiders. It is thus problematic to associate a certain type of ritual practice with a social formation per se because this would prescribe that the given formation has a uniform understanding of ritual practices (see Mills and Kádár 2011 on the problem of the 'normativity' of relational acts).[5] This does not imply that labels like '(sub)social' and 'in-group' should be abandoned, but instead of associating them with social formations they should be operationalised according to some alternative criteria, as this chapter will illustrate.

In order to briefly illustrate the social variability of relational ritual practices, let us refer to the following case. I once observed a group of young Hungarian intellectuals who employed the old-fashioned form of salutation *Szervusz, üdvözöllek* (At your service, my greetings) as a ritual in-group device. Greeting with this formula used to be a socially coded ritual, which was a distinctive (i.e. mimetic) practice of certain middle-class groups, but in the present day it counts as 'outdated'. Thus, this form is unlikely to be used by the average Hungarian, even though it would be recognisable to native speakers as an old-fashioned overly jovial expression. However, in spite of its connotations, *Szervusz, üdvözöllek* functioned as a membership-indicating ritual device in the particular group of young intellectuals, that is, a 'socially' conventionalised act has been reinterpreted by a relational network. Importantly, and example (4.1) illustrates the potential contestedness of 'social' ritual actions, this form as a ritualistic practice occurred recently in a different context, a blog dedicated to certain conventionalised and ritualistic workplace practices. The usage of *Szervusz, üdvözöllek* is represented by the following comic strip (Figure 4.1) (title: *Szervusz, üdvözöllek*) from a Hungarian blog:[6]

(4.1)

Frame 1 'At your service, Mr Department Chair, good morning'; 'At your service, my greetings [*Szervusz, üdvözöllek*].'
Frame 3 'Mother fucker'; 'Prick'

Figure 4.1   Example 4.1: *Szervusz, üdvözöllek*

In the first slide of the comic, which represents an imaginary workplace interaction, both interactants utilise lexical items that are generally categorised by semanticians as old-fashioned 'polite expressions' (see e.g. Sugimura 1986). This cartoon in fact ridicules the insincerity of ritualistic greetings in workplaces, as becomes apparent in Frame 3. It is obvious that there is a certain alternative perception of such Hungarian forms within certain groups, which contradicts their normative perception as traditional lexical representations of 'politeness'. If one dismisses this alternative perception on any grounds – e.g. the interactants in the cartoon cannot represent proper language usage due to the low level of civility (swear words are used here) – they will automatically dismiss various important alternative pragmatic implications of such forms, such as being interpreted as 'outdated', 'insincere' and so on (cf. Kádár and Haugh 2013). To sum up, the difference between the way in which a 'socially' conventionalised ritualistic practice is perceived across groups illustrates that it is not helpful to differentiate ritual practices on the basis of the size of the group that conventionalises a given social practice because such a view would be homogenising and would obscure differences in the perceptions of the given practice.[7]

Instead of defining on the basis of size, it seems reasonable to approach relational rituals vis-à-vis their *transparency* and *accessibility* to network outsiders, which of course also reveal information about the type of network that 'codifies' a ritual practice. The phenomenon of relational ritual includes practices that are clearly understandable to many and in which any language user can take part, as well as practices that are intentionally hidden and/or obscure and which exclude the involvement of the observer as participant. One can refer to these two practice types as the ends of a scale, and conceptualisation based on this scale results in the following, straightforward, typology of relational ritual practices, which I propose for the categorisation of relational rituals:

- Covert ritual
- Personal ritual
- In-group ritual
- Social ritual

This list represents a continuum of increasing transparency (cf. Chapter 2) and accessibility. The operation of these types of relational ritual practices will be illustrated in the following section.

Note that this is a second-order typology (cf. Chapter 1), that is, these types represent a (relationality-based) analytic point of view rather than the language users' views. In fact, not every ritual typology is clearly a second-order one – for example, various context-based approaches to ritual behaviour tend to categorise rituals in a non-strictly technical way – and so it is necessary to point out that this typology, just as the notion of 'in-group ritual' itself, represents a specific, technical perspective on rituality. Describing ritual categories from such an aspect implies that the names of ritual categories adopted in this typology do not accord with ritual categories used in popular discourse on (or folk theorisation of) rituality (see also Section 4.2.3).

An obvious advantage of the relational ritual typology is that it operates with a strict number of categories. If ritual actions are described according to the type of event, they offer a variety of categorisation possibilities; in order to illustrate this point, let us refer to the following citation from the famous Romano-Jewish historian Titus Flavius Josephus (37 – c.100):

(4.2)

In the mean time Agrippa [that is, Marcus Vipsanius Agrippa, a Roman statesman], the son of that Aristobulus who had been slain by his father Herod, came to Tiberius [the emperor of Rome], to accuse Herod the tetrarch; who not admitting of his accusation, he staid at Rome, and cultivated a friendship with others of the men of note, but principally with Caius the son of Germanicus, who was then but a private person. Now this Agrippa, at a certain time, feasted Caius; and as he was very complaisant to him on several other accounts, he at length stretched out his hands, and openly wished that Tiberius might die, and that he might quickly see him emperor of the world. This was told to Tiberius by one of Agrippa's domestics, who thereupon was very angry, and ordered Agrippa to be bound, and had him very ill-treated in the prison for six months, until Tiberius died, after he had reigned twenty-two years, six months, and three days. (*The Wars of the Jews*, Chapter 9, Section 5)

Agrippa's ritual acts can be categorised in various ways. Firstly, they can either be described as (semi-)religious or non-religious ritual actions, or maybe both, depending on their degree of symbolic value (i.e. whether they were simply meant to relate Agrippa to Caius or they had a religious nature). Secondly, these acts can be described as performative utterances (to borrow a term from Austin 1962), that is, the first act is a ritual of curse and the second a ritual of blessing. Whilst further alternative categories could be listed, the main point here is that describing ritual practices according to event types results in an abundance of categorisation possibilities, as well as some potential ambiguity (as in the above case of 'religious' vs 'non-religious'). This variety is reduced in the relational approach. Agrippa's actions, which constructed his relationship with Caius but which communicated grave offence towards Tiberius (even though it is clear from the context that Agrippa did not mean to communicate with Tiberius!) were obviously transparent to his contemporaries – otherwise Tiberius would not have imprisoned Agrippa. In other words, these relational ritual acts must have been widely (socially) normative ones, rather than being the exclusive preserve of a narrow relational network.

In what follows, let us overview the four ritual types proposed by the present work.

4.2 Types of relational ritual 人际关系仪式的类型

4.2.1 Covert ritual[8] 隐性仪式

The less transparent and less accessible type of relational ritual practice is that of covert ritual, which covers ritual acts that are 'concealed', either due to some degree of intentionality[9] or to the very nature of the given ritual practice (see below).[10] As 'covert ritual' is rarely discussed in the humanities and social sciences, it is necessary here to briefly summarise the meaning of this term by referring to psychology. Covert ritual practices include clinical (compulsive, and compulsive and delusional) cases, as well as non-clinical ('imaginary') cases. However, it is pertinent to note that compulsive clinical rituals with delusional beliefs which have imaginary counterparts (cf. practice 1 below), and imaginary rituals – i.e. non-clinical ritual practices which are kept in secret and are thus covert by nature – are not distinct categories. Instead, they are the two ends of a scale (cf. Tully and Edwards 2009): from both a psychological and a pragmatic (relational) perspective there is a narrow and blurred border that separates clinical cases from non-clinical ones, therefore in this section they are discussed jointly.

Covert ritual practices are created and performed by an individual, and they can operate in the following ways:

1. *Compulsive cases with delusional beliefs.* Relate the individual (performer) to an imaginary entity (or a group of entities), i.e. the realm of the 'imaginary';
2. *Compulsive cases.* Relate the individual (performer) to others vis-à-vis a ritual practice which is conventional and compulsive for the individual.

According to the psychological literature, both of these cases are compulsive rituals, that is, they represent an obsessive mental state.[11] However, technically speaking they are far from being the same: a person in an obsessive mental state can perceive a recurrent compulsive ritual performance as a potentially 'meaningful' one (often defined as 'delusional belief'), which represents the first case of compulsive rituals with delusional beliefs, or as a potentially 'meaningless' one, which is the second case of compulsive rituals. This difference is explicated in the following brief definition of compulsive ritual acts:

Obsessive–compulsive disorder

Compulsions are senseless, repeated rituals. Obsessions are stereotyped, purposeless words, ideas, or phrases that come into the mind. They are perceived by the patient as nonsensical (unlike delusional beliefs), and, although out of character, as originating from themselves (unlike hallucinations or thought insertion). They are often resisted by the patient, but if longstanding, the patient may have given up resisting them. (Collier and Longmore 2006: 346)

The 'senselessness' of compulsive ritual practices is an open question: the definition above represents a scholarly perspective, and as Marks (1987) and other psychologists observe, even practices that do not carry meaning often make some (relational) 'sense' from the perspective of those who perform them. But irrespective of this question, the definition above neatly captures the difference between delusional and non-delusional covert ritual practices (note that certain psychological theories categorise delusion as a feature of schizophrenia, and argue that there is an overlap between schizophrenia and obsessive–compulsive behaviour, see e.g. Poyurovsky et al. 2004).

If we depart from psychology and examine the above-discussed two ritual practices from the perspective of relating, it becomes evident that there is a certain gap between their relational operations, which can be illustrated by Figure 4.2.

As discussed later in this section, the first practice relates the individual to an imagined entity, but it may contribute to relating the performer with the visible world as well, i.e. it has a potential indirect relational function. The second practice is meant to relate the individual directly to a given (existing) relational network, but such compulsive practices do not accord in default with the expectations of others, e.g. due to the over-recurrent characteristic that comes from their compulsive nature (see e.g. example 4.6 below), and so they tend to trigger refusal, misunderstanding and other negative reactions. This situation can, of course, change if a relational network becomes accustomed

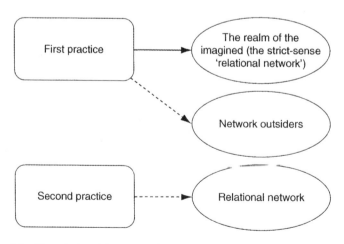

Figure 4.2 The relational function of covert ritual practices

to the presence of a person who suffers from obsessive–compulsive disorders (see Section 4.2.2).

In terms of covertness, both ritual practice types are 'codified' in the closed world of the individual, and so they tend to be non-accessible to others and occasion non-transparency. In a sense, covertness applies even to the second ritual practice type, in spite of the fact that the performer intends to communicate with others through such ritual practices. This is because these practices tend to disaccord with network norms due to their egoistic compulsive nature, and so from the non-performers' perspective these rituals can be incomprehensible by default, and they occasion negative evaluations. Furthermore, an important unifying factor behind covert ritual practices is that whilst they can be revealed to others, usually they remain intentionally hidden because they evoke shame. Because of this, the individual is likely to hide ritual practices that belong to the first case, and deny the ritual and compulsive nature of practices that belong to the second case (see an excellent overview of shame associated with compulsive rituals in Marks 1987). As a matter of course, the above-discussed two practice types have different degrees of covertness. Psychologists make a distinction between compulsive ritual practices which are 'external' and 'mental'. As Ciarocchi (1995: 89) notes,

> [E]xternal rituals are easier to monitor: An observer could verify whether or not the ritual took place. Mental or cognitive rituals take place within the person's mind, and are known only to the person.

Mental rituals tend to be unspoken, and so the only way to study them is to elicit information through psychological interviews. External rituals are easier to capture, as they manifest themselves in visible forms. The first covert practice discussed above can be either external or mental, whilst the second is inherently external, which implies that it is less covert by nature.

In the following, I illustrate the function of the two practices of covert rituals.

First case

The first type (compulsive practice with delusional beliefs) often occurs in stereotypical representations of insane hallucinations, and while I will provide a more complex, authentic case (example 4.5) below to illustrate its operation, it is interesting to look at the representation of this practice in popular works. Example (4.3) is an excerpt from the monologue in the musical adaptation of Bram Stoker's *Dracula* (2010):

(4.3)

He's coming! Master is coming to me. You are on your way! You are coming here, to London! Come to me, my life, my blood, come [...]

The speaker, Milo Renfield, is in an asylum where he recurrently speaks about, and to, his claimed master Count Dracula in a voice of utter reverence, i.e. as a performance of respect towards the dreaded one. While of course in this specific case Dracula turns out to be a 'real' entity, he is not present when Renfield addresses him, and so this utterance illustrates the way in which people who suffer from delusional obsessions utilise ritual practices, often out of fear and other negative emotions, to relate to imagined figures.

Functionally speaking, covert ritual aids social 'survival', just as any other ritual practice. For example, as extract (4.3) illustrates, since certain compulsive ritual practices with obsessive beliefs are formed to communicate with a dreaded entity, they evoke the emotions of fear and respect, by means of which they provide 'protection' for the performer. The monster that we are afraid of is less likely to hurt us, or it may even help us, if we make ritual performances of deference towards it. As a matter of course, negative relating with the imagined is not the only possible manifestation of this ritual type; as example (4.5) below illustrates, compulsive ritual practices with obsessive beliefs can also work in a positive way.

It is pertinent to note that a ritual practice is compulsive only if it creates reality for the performer. For example, relational ritual practices, as the following one which has been described in a book for parents, are *not* compulsive ones:

(4.4)

Chasing monsters out of bedrooms. "Daddy, there is a monster in my room." Here's how to get the child out of the fearful state and ease him into a sleeping one. Let him describe the monster and tell you exactly where it is. Walk around the room together, letting him share his worries. Realize that fearing monsters is a developmental stage in which the monster stands in for a frightening world. Childish fears being what they are – illogical – an explanation may not work. A more imaginative response is called for: "I'm the dad of this house and I don't allow monsters in here. He'll have to leave." Then you step into the cupboard and have a brief talk with the monster. (cited from Sears and Sears 2005: 322)

Such an interaction can become a relational ritual practice between parent and child as (a) it occurs as a mimetic performance, and perhaps also because (b) it is likely to recur until the child goes through his or her period of fear. However, it is definitely not a compulsive ritual as the performer, the parent, does not believe in monsters.

Both examples (4.3) and (4.4) above represent specific cases, in the sense that in (4.3) the ritual practice aims to communicate to the realm of the imagined, while in (4.4) it aims to relate the performer (the parent) with the real (the child). In the majority of the cases I have encountered, and this seems to be confirmed by psychological descriptions of this phenomenon (see above), compulsive ritual practices that constitute the first case communicate with the realm of the invisible *but* they also aid the performer to form a relationship with networks within the visible world. The following extract represents this twofold function:

(4.5)

I'm going to high school in one week. My life sucked in middle school; my parents divorced, I found out I was bisexual and also that I'm transgender, (which means I want to be a guy). My parents were fighting over who would get custody over me, I became suicidal and cut myself.

I had this imaginary world that I went to all the time. I created my imaginary uncle named Josh. Originally he was supposed to stay in the imaginary world (which has no name). But, eventually he came into the real world. He was there when my father was yelling at me and making me feel stupid and useless. Josh always tells me how beautiful I am every five minutes. It's good to know not everyone has betrayed me. (Retrieved from: <http://www.wisegeek.com/is-it-healthy-for-my-child-to-have-an-imaginary-friend.htm>)

The imagined (i.e. 'mental', cf. Ciarocchi 1995: 89) act of relational ritual – the recurrent words of appraisal uttered by uncle Josh – is performed here by the imagined rather than the imaginer, which illustrates that relational ritual is a mutual practice of 'networks' irrespective of whether certain members of a relational network are real or not (or, more precisely, people who suffer from a mental disorder tend to attribute 'real' mutuality to mental interactions). What takes place here is a mental performance of an imagined ritual action: the poster creates the scene of an imaginary interaction which is replayed when she encounters personal difficulties. And this is what gives rise to the indirect relational function of this practice: the poster of example (4.5), anon199615, who is an adolescent biological female, uses her imaginary conversations to successfully cope with difficulties caused by her abusive father in their relational network.

Second case

As already mentioned, compulsive ritual practices are covert (non-transparent and non-accessible), most importantly in the sense that for their performer they imply something different than they do to others, including members of the performer's physically existing relational network(s) and observers. Unlike delusional ritual practices, second case compulsive ritual practices aim to relate the individual with their physical relational network(s). However, even such 'overt' ritual practices are covert, in the sense that they are formed arbitrarily by an individual who suffers from a compulsive disorder; whilst they are conventionalised in the individual's mental world, they tend to be unconventional to others (even if members of a relational network get used to them, these practices tend to violate the standard conventional expectations of others). Thus, these practices tend to relationally separate the individual from others and to stigmatise them (cf. Chapter 6).

To illustrate this point, in example (4.6) I refer to a retrospective account (see other cases in Packer 2012); the second case ritual practice represented here triggers refusal as it differs from non-compulsive relational rituals by its over-recurrent nature:

(4.6)

I would start saying something and repeat it several times, but I wouldn't say a whole sentence, only several words at a time. That was, I guess, the most frustrating ritual I did because I was trapped within the ritual and couldn't express myself freely. I also make a ritual out of asking people questions a certain number of times – if they didn't answer me it added to my frustration.

> I had another ritual that was almost as frustrating as verbal rituals and that was touching people a certain number of times also whenever they touched me or happened to brush up against me. I would sometimes be open about it (touching them back) and then other times I would try to be subtle in my approach to touch them back – depending on if they were hostile or irritated or tried to get away from my touching them. [...]
>
> How did this affect my family? [...] Several times when I involved my mother in a verbal ritual (and we were both yelling at each other and I was fighting with her physically to get her answer to me), my brother acted like he was my dad and smacked me and picked me up and dragged me to my room [...]
>
> Dad reacted pretty much the same: hostile and irritated. He had a little more patience though. He would intervene sometimes when I would be asking my mother to answer me like I said my brother did, but he would give me a spanking and then send me to my room. This, of course, was getting out of hand and, like I said earlier, when I was fighting my mother physically to get her to answer me. Dad didn't answer me hardly when I would try to involve him in a verbal ritual.
>
> My mother, on the other hand, was affected the most; I've always been closest to her. She was caught in a bind because of our closeness. She would go along with my verbal rituals for a while to try to help, but I never could stop so she eventually had to pull out. [...]
>
> Verbal rituals made it hard to express my feelings but eventually I would accomplish something. (Rapoport 1989: 163–4)

As the author of this text makes clear, various family members reacted differently to his or her verbal and non-verbal ritual practices; here we need to recall the claim made in Chapter 1 that ritual is an action, i.e. it manifests itself in both linguistic and non-linguistic forms, which jointly realise the ritual practice, for example this person was recurrently touching others. In general, family members were not able to accept these compulsive ritual practices. Although this person attempted to relate with others via ritual practices, these practices could not operate constructively due to their compulsive nature.

It is pertinent to note here that example (4.6) interestingly illustrates the potential emotive and affective ambiguity of obsessive ritual practices which are exempt from obsessive beliefs. The narrative makes it clear that these ritual acts were disturbing also to the person who performed them, whilst being an essential relational practice to him or her ("Verbal rituals made it hard to express my feelings but eventually I would accomplish something.").

The present section has examined the category of covert rituals. In what follows, let us focus on personal ritual, which is the next ritual category in the typology based on a scale of transparency and accessibility, and which overlaps in some respects with covert ritual practices.

4.2.2 Personal ritual 个人仪式

The main difference between covert rituals and personal relational rituals is that a personal ritual act is

(a) neither a 'private' one, unlike, for example, first case covert ritual practices (cf. Section 4.2.1),
(b) nor is it saliently different from what relational networks normatively expect.

Consequently, these rituals are less likely to become stigmatised forms of behaviour within relational networks. Various personal ritual acts, like prayers, take place between the individual and the non-human realm just as their covert counterparts do, and some other practices are performed according to an individual's arbitrary ways, yet most of these ritual actions are accepted, encouraged and, importantly, discussed openly in social networks. Therefore, the main difference between covert and personal ritual acts resides in the value a network attaches to specific manifestations of 'personal'. As a matter of fact, this influences the way in which individual performers regard their ritual practice(s): personal rituals tend to be more open to network peers because they concord with network norms and thus are not seen as the 'secret' preserve of the individual.

In this sense there is an overlap between covert and personal ritual practices, or in other words the 'covertness' vs simple 'personalness' of a ritual is relative. In order to illustrate this relativity, one can refer to the fact that the notion of the 'imagined', which is present in both certain covert and personal practices, reflects relative evaluations. Following Geertz's (1973) logic, which is also echoed by van der Hart's (1983, 1988) study of compulsive rituals, ritual actions reflect and simultaneously construct reality for their performers. Stigma can be associated with any kind of ritual practice, and consequently the border between the covert and personal types of relational ritual is relative also from a diachronic perspective. For example, in the medieval world – where many people believed in the existence of monsters (cf. Bovey

2002) – certain 'imaginary' relational rituals (see e.g. example 4.3), which are stigmatised in the present day, would not have been shameful.

Furthermore, since it is a network's right to accept (normativise) or stigmatise a ritual, even some ritual practices that would count as covert may transform into a practice which is (positively) associated with a member's identity within the given network. In other words, a covert ritual practice can be accepted by network insiders, and it can become subject of in-group metadiscussions, and despite the fact that it may be the source of stigma in other settings. Once in-group discussions on personal (previously covert) rituals recur, they are in turn open to becoming relational ritual practices. In the cases I have encountered so far, such transition from covert ritual practices to personal ones (and then potentially to network rituals) occur with delusional compulsive rituals, in particular the covert (imaginary) rituals of children; see extract 4.4 from Sears and Sears (2005: 322) cited above. Extract (4.7) from the horror film *The Shining* (1980) provides a further illustration. In order to understand this conversation, one needs to know that it takes place between a young boy, Danny, and his mother Wendy. Danny has special skills and lives in his own world where his best friend is the imagined figure Tony. Wendy knows that Danny communicates, often by means of recurrent ritual practices, with Tony, and she accepts Danny's habit: consequently, the child does not hide this relationship from her, and the mother even forms and performs a specific in-group ritual with Danny. When critical topics emerge (as in the present case when an important decision is discussed with the child) she ritually involves Tony in the interaction, and Danny participates in the performance:

(4.7)

Danny Do you really want to go and live in that hotel for the winter?
Wendy Sure I do. It'll be lots of fun.
Danny Yeah, I guess so. Anyway, there's hardly anybody to play with around here.
Wendy Yeah, I know. It always takes a little time to make new friends.
Danny Yeah, I guess so.
Wendy What about Tony? He's lookin' forward to the hotel, I bet.
Danny (*He uses his index finger as a bobbing, puppet-figure to act and speak in a roughened voice like Tony.*) No, he isn't, Mrs. Torrance.

Wendy   Now come on, Tony, don't be silly.
Danny   (*as Tony*) I don't want to go there, Mrs. Torrance.
Wendy   Well, how come you don't want to go?
Danny   (*as Tony*) I just don't.
Wendy   Well, let's just wait and see. We're all going to have a real good time.

Example (4.7) shows how discourse on a delusional compulsive ritual practice becomes a relational ritual practice within a network. This transition is illustrated by Figure 4.3.

The wavy line between 'covert' and 'personal' ritual practices illustrates the aforementioned relative relationship between these categories. The arrow pointing from 'covert' to 'in-group' signals that once a ritual practice is accepted by others, because of an existing relational history or any other reason, it becomes open to becoming incorporated into the relational ritual practices of the network, as we could see in the case of example (4.7) above. The arrow pointing from 'in-group' to 'personal' indicates that in such cases the ritual performance of the individual is likely not to be regarded as 'covert' but rather as 'personal'. Finally, the dashed line of the 'in-group' illustrates that acceptance of the given practice remains a potential source of stigma in the eyes of group outsiders.

In what follows, let us examine the two major types of personal ritual practices, which show parallels with the two types of covert rituals, namely (1) personal rituals that relate the individual to the realm of invisible, and (2) other rituals that relate the individual with others in personal (arbitrary) ways.

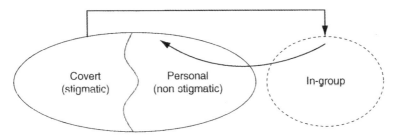

Figure 4.3 The in-group neutralisation and ritualisation of potentially covert ritual practices

First case

The following extract represents the function of the personal ritual of relating to deceased personae, in a descriptive form:

> (4.8)
>
> Several years ago, a close friend's mother died. My friend, who was very close to her mother, arranged for a wake and a memorial service. She was very grateful for all the comfort that she received from relatives and friends during that time. But after it was over, she felt empty inside, as if she needed something more.
>
> When we talked about it, she told me what she missed the most was having her morning conversations with her mother. She talked about picking up the phone on many mornings to call her mother, after her mother died, and then suddenly remembering that her mother was gone. These moments filled her with so much sadness. And yet, she felt, on some level, that her mother was still alive in a way.
>
> As we talked about it, it became clear that my friend's experience of feeling that her mother was still alive was her own internal experience of her mother, which was very strong. I suggested to her that, even though her mother was not alive any more, she could still "talk" to her mother in her mind through meditation or in a ritual that she created for herself to honor their relationship. (Retrieved from: <http://psychotherapist-nyc.blogspot.com/2011/05/power-of-creating-personal-rituals.html>)

What makes the present ritual practice a personal (non-stigmatised) one is that in many societies it is regarded as 'normal' to talk with deceased relatives, and psychologists describe it as a natural emotive reaction by those who suffer a great loss by losing a close relative (see e.g. Ollendick and Schroeder 2003: 62). Thus, such practices – unlike for example ritually talking with dreaded imaginary entities – occasion positive evaluations of 'normality'; this is illustrated by the fact that it is the narrator in example (4.8) who suggests to her or his friend to adopt this practice.

Second case

The operation of the other subtype of personal ritual practices – which relates the individual with others in personalised 'arbitrary' ways – is illustrated by the following example (4.9):

(4.9)

Sergeant Earnie Hilton, on the other hand, sought camaraderie from his *verbal ritual* [my emphasis] of recalling the war, earnestly confiding in a friend at home that 'Germany is not such a bad place to be. There is a dutchman [sic] living at our place who fought against us in the St Mihiel Drive, and now we eat at the same table, share our tobacco and laugh at each other's experiences. This may sound rather queer to you but this is the way we are treated and the way we treat the Germans.' (cited from Alexander 1998: 31–2)

This excerpt has been drawn from a text that narrates the personal histories of US veterans in wartime and post-war Germany; Sergeant Earnie Hilton developed the personal practice of recalling wartime stories in order to make friends with others. Such a practice is certainly arbitrary (cf. the discussion on this issue in Section 4.2.1) in the sense that listening to somebody else's wartime stories may not be appealing to everyone, i.e. in (4.9) it is the individual's and not the network's decision to perform this practice. However, retelling memories does not usually violate network norms, at least not in the explicit way in which arbitrarily formed compulsive practices do, such as the one represented by example (4.6). It is pertinent to note that just as with first case personal relational ritual (cf. example 4.7), second case practices can be taken up as in-group ritual practices of a relational network. The following interaction, which took place in the context of my family, illustrates this point:

(4.10)

A   Hát igen, nincs valami nagy szerencsénk ma az idővel, de talán Edinburghban jobb lesz.
D   Na persze a *te idődben* az idő is más volt.
K   Hehe.
A   Idióta.

A   Well yes, we're not having much luck with the weather today, but perhaps it will be better in Edinburgh.
D   Of course, back in your day even the weather was different.
K   Heh-heh.
A   Idiot.

This interaction took place between my father (A), me (D) and my wife (K). In order to understand what is going on here one needs to note

98 *Relational Rituals and Communication*

that my father, a Hungarian, used to work for a British company and visited England on a regular basis; upon visiting us on several occasions in England where we live, it became his ritualistic practice to tell us stories about his life in England decades ago, often by contrasting 'his time', which he perceived positively, with his recent perception of the country's fortunes. After some time, my wife and I took up this ritual of his, turning it into a form of mild bantering (along with other practices of gently teasing my father about his age), i.e. we made remarks such as 'my father's time', which thus became a relational ritual within our network, as example (4.10) also illustrates.

This section has examined the category of personal rituals. In what follows, I will examine social rituals, and their relationship with in-group rituals.

4.2.3 In-group and social ritual 群内与社会仪式

Similarly to other types of relational ritual types, the main difference between in-group and social ritual practices is a function of their transparency and accessibility. It can be argued that in practice both of these ritual types operate on the level of social networks, and as such social ritual practices just as their in-group counterparts can be challenged and altered within and across relational networks. We could observe this contestedness in the case of conventions in Chapter 2, and it is also the case of the Hungarian ritualised form of greeting *Szervusz, üdvözöllek* (see Section 4.1.2). However, whilst previous chapters in this book have illustrated that in-group ritual practices are potentially inaccessible and non-transparent to network outsiders, social ritual practices are transparent to outsiders, and they are also accessible provided that the outsiders are granted institutional right to join the ritual performance.[12]

In order to illustrate this point, let us refer to the following description of social ritual practices. This example – which is taken from a blog in which the author discusses his experiences with Midwestern Americans who are, in his view, remarkably fond of 'ritual politeness' – illustrates the metapragmatic awareness (cf. Verschueren 2000) of socially 'coded' ritual acts, which can occasion negative evaluations (e.g. 'pointless') in Western public discourse (see e.g. Chapter 1).

(4.11)

I am at the office's coffee/hot water machine. It's a Tazo tea day [the Tazo Tea Company is an American tea manufacturer and distributor].

A curly-haired woman approaches from the side and we both do a start–stop motion towards the machine.

Me	"Oh, sorry. Go ahead."
Curls	"Oh no, you go."
Me	"It's fine."
Curls	"You were here first."
Me	"Well thank you."
Curls	"You're very welcome."

I then fill my Starbucks cup with water. It feels like an *eternity* because I can sense Curls staring at my cup. I finish:

Me	"Thank you again. Have a good weekend"
Curls	"You're welcome. You have a nice weekend too!"

I think a foreigner, maybe even a New Yorker, would find this exchange ridiculous. But I've stopped questioning Midwest etiquette. Just follow the script and no one gets offended.

(Retrieved from: <http://www.dennis-jansen.com/just-sayin/ritual-politeness/>)

This interaction reflects that socially accepted rituals are open to discussion and contest in public, i.e. their contestation is not limited to members of a given relational network. It is obvious that in the case above Curls evaluates the ritual as 'appropriate', whilst the narrator evaluates it as somewhat 'inappropriate'. But the main point here is that "the script" of this ritual performance is transparent and accessible to both Curls and the narrator, irrespective of the fact that they have no relational history[13] or prospects of becoming related in the future. This social ritual act is thus relational but its relationship-forming function is temporal.

Yet, the degree of transparency and accessibility is not the only difference between in-group and social relational practices; in the rest of the section let us examine the other differences.

'In-group' vs 'social' in terms of lifespan and popular definitions

A key difference between in group and social rituals resides in their lifespan. Whilst social rituals can transform into in-group rituals, in-group rituals are somewhat more unlikely to develop into social ones. Consequently, in-group and social ritual practices have different lifespans: whereas social ritual practices are subject to modification over time (see e.g. Turner 1969), and often survive across several generations, in-group rituals tend to have a much shorter history, in that they tend to become extinct when their relational network ceases to exist (unless another network 'inherits' the given practice). Furthermore, an in-group ritual practice may disappear during the lifetime of a relational network. For example, the ritual of using the Hungarian form *Szervusz, üdvözöllek* (cf. Section 4.1.2) as a distinctive in-group ritual was active only while members of the network remained related and did not drop the practice. Yet, I do not claim that in-group rituals are inherently ephemeral; an in-group ritual can be long-lasting if, on account of increasing relational history, it becomes a more complex and neutralised practice of a group (see e.g. Kádár and Bax 2013). For an example, a discussion with members of the Hungarian group of friends studied in Chapter 3 revealed that their in-group ritual practices had been in use for nearly a decade.

Another fundamental difference between 'social' and 'in-group' rituals is related to their definitions, i.e. language users tend to refer to social and in-group ritual practices differently. If one examines the popular meaning of 'rituality' as, for example, represented by dictionaries, it becomes evident that 'ritual' implies, on the lexical level, socially prescribed practices across languages and cultures.[14] For example, the *Encyclopaedia of* defines 'ritual' as follows:

礼仪（ritual）一词源自西方，指称与象征意涵有关的一再重复的一套行为……中文（礼仪）一词的用法，是广义的礼仪范围，包括日常生活打招呼问候礼节，用餐时的餐桌礼仪，到葬礼都可以涵盖。

The word 'ritual' originates in the West, and it refers to recurrent symbolic behaviour. [...] The Chinese [equivalent] *liyi* is used to describe ritual practices in a wider sense, spanning daily acts of ritual greetings, through table etiquette, to funeral rituals.

As this description makes clear, the 'native' Chinese equivalent of 'ritual', *liyi*礼仪, includes predominantly social practices. The *Oxford Dictionary*'s[15] online definition of 'ritual' is relatively similar, at least in the sense that it describes ritual as a social-level act:[16]

a religious or solemn ceremony consisting of a series of actions performed according to a prescribed order [.]

The lack of 'in-group' in these definitions is of course unsurprising because 'in-group ritual' is a technical second-order term, which reflects a specific understanding of ritual behaviour. However, it is noteworthy that empirical analysis similarly shows that it is rare for interactants reflecting on their own ritual activity, to associate manifestations of in-group ritual behaviour with 'rituality'. This is the finding from a modest case study I undertook, by interviewing 11 Hungarian acquaintances of mine. Whilst this case study does not have any significant proof value due to the small number of participants, and quantitative research on various aspects of relational rituals is an area for future research (if it is possible at all, cf. Chapter 1), it is worth reflecting on its outcome.

I gave my respondents the following (imagined) example of an in-group ritual conversation, without informing them about my definition of in-group ritual acts:

A következő párbeszéd két fiatal barátnő között zajlik le:

- Mizujs? Találkozunk *ott*?
- *Ott*? Csak ketten, mint mindig? (vihog)
- Aha. (vihog)

Hogyan írnád le ezt a párbeszédet?

The following conversation takes place between two young female friends:

- What's up? Will we meet *there*?
- *There*? Just the two of us, as always? (giggles)
- Yep. (giggles)

How would you describe this conversation?

This simple interaction, which includes a mimetic reference to relational history, would clearly be a case of in-group ritual practice according to the present framework. However, none of the respondents defined it as such, and instead they referred to it by using various labels such as *baráti humor* (case of friendly humour), *csapat beszéd* (team talk) and so on. It is pertinent to note, however, that several of the responses made it clear that they *sensed* that a ritualistic activity was taking place. For example, one of them noted the following (the respondent's comment is edited):

Ezek a fajta beszédbeli „összekacsintások" összekötnek másokkal. A lányok nyilván egy közös emléket idéznek fel, ezért is nevetnek. Szerintem mindegyikünknek vannak hasonló beszélgetései azokkal, akik közel állnak hozzánk.

These "winks" in talk are what link us with others. Obviously, the girls recall a common memory, and this is why they laugh. I think all of us have similar conversations with those who are close to us.

To sum up, a fundamental difference between social rituals, which tend to be defined as 'rituals' (cf. example 4.11), and their in-group counterparts is the way in which they are popularly defined and reflected on. The association of social ritual with 'rituality' also manifests itself in metadiscourse that emerges in interaction; this can be illustrated by the following example, taken from the film *A Beautiful Mind* (2001):

(4.12)

Nash   I find you attractive. Your aggressive moves toward me... indicate that you feel the same way. But still, *ritual* [my emphasis] requires that we continue with a number of platonic activities... before we have sex. I am proceeding with these activities, but in point of actual fact, all I really want to do is have intercourse with you as soon as possible.
[*pause*]
Nash   Are you gonna slap me now?

This extract provides a representative example of the recognition of social ritual vs other types or relational ritual acts. The protagonist, the scholar John Nash, suffers from serious schizophrenia, and so this film not only represents certain in-group rituals but also many covert compulsive ones with delusional beliefs, which take place between Nash and his imagined interlocutor. Interestingly, the word 'ritual' is not used at all with reference to these relational rituals, and only occurs in the above-cited case, when Nash refers retrospectively to social rituals which he applied as practices of courting just before the interaction (4.12) above took place.

4.3 Summary 结语

The present chapter has integrated the category of 'in-group ritual' into a wider typology of relational rituals. After summarising the need to elaborate a relational typology in Section 4.1, the chapter has examined the four types of relational rituals in a comparative way, by approaching these categories via the notions of 'transparency' and 'accessibility'. It was found that there is no clear demarcation between these categories,

4 Relational Ritual Typology 103

as there are various potential overlaps amongst 'covert', 'personal' 'in-group' and 'social' rituals.

The alternative ritual typology elaborated in this chapter incorporates various types of ritual act into a single framework. There is a gap between the way in which relational rituals are represented in certain disciplines such as anthropology and linguistics, and in some others such as psychology; it can be argued that the present approach can help narrow the existing representational divide. Arguably, the formal and functional properties which were discussed in Chapter 3 operate in fairly similar ways in the four ritual types discussed here, even though I do not intend to claim that they always operate in similar ways. For example, all ritual types seem to follow strict formulation and/or sequencing principles (cf. Bax 2004): for example, the covert acts of talking with monsters and the personal rituals of silent discussions with deceased relatives all tend to be formulated following set rules, even though these rules are not socially conventionalised as in the case of social rituals.

This chapter has touched on the relationship between cognition and relational ritual, by examining the way in which relational networks accept, refute and define certain ritual practice types (in a similar way with conventions, see Chapter 2). The following Chapter 5 will again limit its focus to in-group ritual practices, from a more in-depth cognitive angle.

5
Recognition, Affectivity and Emotivity
识别、情感性和情绪性

5.1 Introduction 引言

This chapter aims to explore the phenomenon of relational rituals from cognitive perspectives, first by focusing on how in-group ritual practices are recognised in interaction, and then by examining their affective and emotive effect on the interactants. There is a fundamental link between these cognitive aspects due to the interactional nature of in-group rituals, and the cognitive unpredictability they imply. As the present chapter will argue, as in-group rituals tend to be interactionally (co-)constructed, it is difficult to establish (a) whether a ritual practice remains un/recognised or not, and (b) exactly how it triggers affectivity and emotions and what type of feelings it triggers specifically. Let us recall here the terminological distinction made in Chapter 1, relying on González et al. (1998): 'emotion' stands for an internal individual response and 'affection' refers to a process of social interaction.

It should be noted at this point that the questions studied in this chapter are not equally valid for every form of in-group relation rituals. It cannot be emphasised enough that in-group ritual has many varieties, spanning single utterances to interactionally constructed chains of acts, and utterances that recur occasionally in a relational network to frequently recurring ones (cf. Chapter 1). As some relational ritual acts are 'demarcated' by nature (cf. Staal 1979), they are utterances which not only have a definite 'shape' but also clear-cut pragmatic properties – for example they occur in very specific situations only – even if 'demarcatedness' is definitely a matter of degree.[1] Such highly contextualised ritual utterances can well become subject to metadiscourse, as they are potentially salient acts from a network insider perspective. As Silverstein (1981: 4) notes, "the ease or difficulty of accurate metapragmatic characterization...depend[s] on certain general semiotic properties of the use in question". Obviously, such rituals, given their formal fixity, offer clear semiotic cues, or 'frames' (cf. Goffman 1974), for the interactants, i.e. they generate awareness. The function of such ritual practices can be illustrated by the following anecdote told to me by a linguist:

(5.1)

I regularly go walking in the hills with a group of people (about 8–12 of us) and over the years it has become an 'in-joke' that I am the person who chooses when and where we will have our picnic lunch. In fact, I hardly ever choose, but there is a ritual[2] of asking me...when I am unable to go with them, they often text me to ask "Can we have lunch yet?" It's a joke, but also a ritual. If I know that they are out and I am not with them, I feel a bit odd (not exactly offended, but slightly ignored) if they don't contact me. Sometimes I try to get in first and text saying "you can have lunch now!"

Obviously, the observer can make some direct inferences with regard to the recognition of this ritual practice within this relational network, and its affective and emotive effect on participants, due to its 'demarcated' nature. The recognition and affective and emotive effect of an in-group ritual practice is arguably influenced by both the degree of the definiteness of its 'shape' and the degree of its interactional frequency. For example, there are some ritual practices which have inferable cognitive mechanisms clearly because they do not frequently recur; we could observe this phenomenon in the example of King Leonidas and Queen Gorgo in Chapter 2 (cf. example 2.8), when a normative (and recurrent) conventional practice turns into a ritual practice for one occasion. It seems that clearly 'demarcated' ritual practices like example (5.1) above, or the King Leonidas example, represent a specific case from a cognitive perspective; for example, the recognition and affective and emotive effect of utterance-level rituals become complex as soon as they recur with some frequency, as we could see in the case of the ritual practice of *The Chad* in Chapter 2 (cf. example 2.9).

5.1.1 Recognition 识别

To date, extensive research in sociology and anthropology has been undertaken on certain cognitive aspects of ritualistic behaviour, including states of mind evoked by liminal ritual practices (cf. Victor Turner's works 1969, 1974), the relationship between ritual and un/awareness (Koster 2003), ritual and intuition (cf. Lawson and McCauley 2002), and so on.[3] A common finding of many of these inquiries is that ritual creates a specific state of mind which differs from a non-ritual one. Despite the fact that various previous research works addressed ritual and cognition, as far as I am aware no interaction-based research has been undertaken on the interactants' discursive recognition of ritual practices, and so the field has remained relatively uninformed as to how the aforementioned 'ritual state of mind' manifests itself in interaction. That is, whilst previous research provides invaluable insight into the effect of ritual practice on the minds of those who perform a ritual act as *individuals*, there is little information on how ritual practices per se are *perceived in interaction with others* – which is a key question when it comes to the relational understanding of rituals. Putting it another way, in the discursive construction and maintenance of relationships it is not only the altered state of mind – triggered by ritual practices – that matters (although it cannot be neglected of course, cf. Chapter 3), but also the normativity and salience of a ritual practice to members of a relational network in a given interaction. Chapter 4 has already noted that there is some difference in the recognition of in-group and social rituals as 'rituals'. In the present section I will thus examine a different type of recognition, namely, awareness of the ritual practice in relating, irrespective of how the given practice is defined by language users.

The lack of interaction-based evidence implies that scholars approach ritual cognition from the researcher's own perspective and leave language users' and 'lay' observers' perspectives relatively untouched. As has been claimed by Kádár and Haugh (2013), any framework dedicated to relational phenomena should rely on multiple understandings, and it can be argued that a discourse-based approach to the perception of in-group relational ritual practices will add to previous research on rituality. The question which I will attempt to answer is: how are ritual practices perceived (and occasionally reflected on) by those who perform and take part in them?

Accordingly, Section 5.2 will analyse recognition in various ritualistic interactions, first examining conventional relational practices and then narrowing the focus down to in-group rituals. Conventions need to be revisited for the following reason: as has been argued in Chapter 2, all relational ritual practices are conventionalised, and as such they include practices that count as normative within a relational network (see Peregrin 2012 on the interface between conventionality and normativity).[4] The normativity of schematic relational practices,

5 Recognition, Affectivity and Emotivity 107

which can be covered by the collective term 'conventionality', implies that conventional (and conventionalised ritual) practices are perceived as 'natural' for the speaker and from the hearer's perspective they are unmarked. It is a question, however, whether this is a default case only, or if conventional and ritual practices inherently do not differ from what counts as 'purely' normative. In fact, a large body of previous research on conventionalised relational acts, such as Terkourafi's (2001, 2005) works, suggests that conventionalised relational acts are 'natural' for the speaker and unmarked for the hearer. For example, in her study on conventionalised politeness Terkourafi (2001: 16) – drawing from Escandell-Vidal's (1998) discussion of politeness – argues as follows:

> [c]onversational strategies, or conversational efforts, can only have their *raison d'être* as exploitations of a default, 'unmarked' behaviour. [...] being able to prevent undesirable results or to enhance positive effects entail having first a precise knowledge of expected courses of events (including, obviously, linguistic events and behaviour), and their social consequences. (Escandell-Vidal 1998: 46)

This is an important definition, and I do not intend to challenge its applicability for other types of research, all the more because conflating convention with unmarked behaviour is probably more a function of the methodology employed by Terkourafi and others in identifying/examining conventions than a claim which essentially relies on frequency of occurrence relative to (minimal) contexts of use. However, the present discursive framework proposes a somewhat different approach to conventionality as it takes the basic frequency of occurrence relative to contexts, and distinguishes conventionality at different social levels (cf. Chapter 2). The claims made here thus do not contradict what has been argued by Terkourafi and others – they simply describe conventional (ritualised) practices from a different perspective.

Terkourafi's methodological approach, in accordance with traditional speech act theory (e.g. Austin 1962, Searle 1969, 1975),[5] sets out from the presupposition that there is a general agreement about the normativity and meaning of certain relational practices, that is, that conventional practices are constructed and perceived similarly by every interactant; convention in this approach is a socially 'coded' phenomenon with generalised implicatures. Furthermore, this approach identifies conventionality with relative frequency (which occasions conventionalisation), i.e. forms and expressions are identified as "conventionalised for some particular use" (Terkourafi 2005: 148) once they occur frequently enough. This approach should be somewhat revised, in my view, when it comes to a discursive approach to relational practices, which calls for some critical interpretation of normativity (cf. Mills 2003b). Not only relational networks, but individuals as well, may have different perceptions of what counts as normative schemata or 'script' (i.e. convention) and different attitudes towards social-level conventions, but in fact, even socially 'coded' conventions can be rather diverse in a socio-pragmatic sense.[6] More specifically, socially 'coded' relational conventions can vary greatly in terms of frequency of occurrence, and the scope of their pragmatic usage – as well as their interactional perceptions – may also differ. For example, it is arguably the case that certain phrases that count as conventional, such as *I love you* (which here is not identical to a confession of love) in North American culture, are less widely and frequently used than others. Due to its emotionally loaded semantic value *I love you* can be ambiguous and can be contested, in spite of the fact that it is generally recognised as a positive convention, as the following extract illustrates:[7]

(5.2)

say "i love you" a lot

I have noticed that many of the white people I've known say it frequently. Women more than men, of course. Lucky me, some might say, to be around so much love.

But then, is it "love," when people say it so often, almost like a habit, or like, a duty?

And even if these expressions of love usually are genuine, is saying "I love you" the only way to express love?

Of course not.

But maybe saying it a lot is an especially white thing. Which is not necessarily to say that it's not something that some other racial or ethnic groups say a lot too.

I see white people habitually ending phone conversations this way – kind of, hurriedly.

"I love you! Bye!"

I've seen them saying it to their children as they drop them off at school, again as the last or second-to-last thing they say: "Bye! I love you, you know!"

It's sweet, I suppose, and as I was growing up, my own mother said it a lot too. I know she meant it, but I sometimes cynically wondered how sincere she really was, if she kept saying it *so often*.

My father didn't say it often. He hardly ever said it. I now realize, with gratitude, that he showed it instead.

Actually, that's how I hear it generally works in some other cultures – don't say it, *show* it.
(Retrieved from: <http://stuffwhitepeopledo.blogspot.co.uk/2009/06/say-i-love-you-lot.html>)

The convention of *I love you* is a 'proper' relational convention in that its usage can count as a normative practice for some particular use, as example (5.2) above also illustrates, i.e. the presence of this utterance can become an expectancy in a relational network and once this is the case it is its absence, rather than its presence, which might be noticed, in accordance with what Terkourafi (2001) suggests. But this does not mean that it goes unnoticed, and becoming noticed does not mean that this conventional practice fails to operate. As the blog entry above, written by a white American,[8] makes clear, language users can reflect on their own conventional practices, even rather critically, without a given practice losing its function to operate. For example, the poster, in reference to his mother's practice notes that "I know she meant it, but I sometimes cynically wondered how sincere she really was, if she kept saying it *so often*" [original emphasis]. That is, he reflects on his mother's *I love you*s critically while knowing that these conventional acts are meaningful ones. The complexity of this situation comes from different perspectives on expectancies (cf. Kádár and Haugh 2013). That is, it cannot be taken for granted that within a relational network the interactants have, or continue to have, similar expectations, while they may also be aware of the expectations of others. For example, it might be that the author of the blog entry above and his mother used to have similar views on *I love you* but the author's view has changed as their relational history developed. This, however, does not necessarily bring along the transformation of the conventional practice because members of relational networks tend to be aware of, and do occasionally reflect on, *others'* expectations, that is, they are aware that other interactants might regard a practice as expected and normative. This is why the blog's author can suppose ("know") that his mother meant this utterance, and this is why he accepted these *I love you*s (declining them could have offended his mother's normative expectations).

To sum up, due to its focus on context, in the present framework the unnoticedness of conventional practices is only a default situation, and it can be argued that the same applies to relational rituals. The interactional perception of ritual is relatively ignored in the field, and so this is a knowledge gap that the present work hopes to fill. From a discursive perspective, conventionalised acts like rituals are subject to variability and the contestations that variability implies. This entails that rituals can become non-default for the speaker and marked for the hearer. In the data studied, this happens most often when the schematic practice of ritual deviates from the expectations of the participants of an interaction, more specifically, when (a) a certain ritual practice is not in accordance with a network member's contextual expectation, and when (b) a network member's interactional situation changes for some reason. There are of course other reasons for a ritual practice to stand out, as Section 5.2 will illustrate, and the main point to argue here is that it is impossible to predict whether a ritual practice (or any other conventionalised practice) remains unnoticed or not in interaction. Once a ritual practice becomes non-default and marked, it may become subject to some evaluation and picked up in metadiscourse, that is, the interactants will tend to discuss their ritual practices.

It is pertinent to note that involving the interactants' perceptions in the analysis leads the way to Chapter 6 in which I will examine destructive relational rituals – i.e. ritual practices that corrupt a victim's relationships within a relational network – and the significance of the evaluations they trigger. While interactants' perceptions will be theorised to some extent in Section 5.2, in this chapter I focus not so much on the evaluation of ritual practices per se but rather on cases when they become non-default for the speaker and simultaneously marked for the hearer. While of course any ritual practice can occasion evaluations, in particular when these practices are non-default and marked, these evaluations tend to differ from those of destructive rituals. That is, according to the data studied, when it comes to destructive rituals, evaluations become particularly salient because destructive ritual practices openly violate the interactional and moral expectations (or "moral sentiment", to use Durkheim's 1912/1954 term) of the person(s) whom they target, as well as that of the public, and so participants and observers of a destructive ritual practice tend to evaluate it in entirely different ways. However, due to their expected scope, my data suggests that rituals of a constructive nature tend to be evaluated according to their contextual in/appropriateness by network insiders (not necessarily by network outsiders, cf. examples 5.4 and 5.12 below), i.e. not so much in explicitly positive or negative terms but rather as in/appropriate ones, as they tend to accord with network insiders' normative moral expectations.[9]

A specific terminology is adopted to describe the salience of ritual practices from both the speaker's (or 'performer's') and the hearer's (or 'participant's') perspectives. That is, from the performer's perspective a relational ritual practice implies *consciousness* when it follows normative expectations, and it evokes *awareness* when the performer is reflexively aware that the ritual practice might become/has become salient to other participants.[10] From the participant(s)' point of view, these two different cognitive states correspond to the aforementioned categories of *unmarked* and *marked* (see further Watts 2003, Locher 2004, Locher and Watts 2005, 2008 on the un/markedness of relational phenomena). Following Silverstein (1981), it should be argued that recognition is always a matter of degree, i.e. the difference between consciousness–unmarkedness and awareness–markedness is a scalar one (and a dialectic one, see below), rather than a dichotomy.

5.1.2 Affectivity and emotivity 情感性和情绪性

The affective/emotive function of ritual practices has been noted elsewhere in this book (see e.g. Chapters 2 and 3). A fundamental question to address in this chapter is how a theory can give an account of this function of a ritual act, in particular if the given act is interactionally constructed within a group. In previous research on emotions and affection triggered by relational acts, in particular politeness, emotions and affection are described in two different – but not necessarily contradictory – ways, as the present section will illustrate. According to one view, relational acts trigger emotions and affection in a means–ends pattern, that is, feelings become significant when a given act aims to arouse a particular emotive reaction and affective effect; according to the other view, emotions and affection per se are significant in relating, irrespective of the intentionality behind a given act. Considering the interface between rituality and im/politeness, which has been discussed before in this book (and which will also be raised in Chapter 6), it is necessary to briefly introduce im/politeness-related concerns, based on which it is possible to propose an understanding of affectivity/emotivity triggered by relational rituals.

A number of scholars – most representatively, Miriam Locher and Andreas Langlotz (2008) and Şükriye Ruhi (2009)[11] – claim that the emotive/affective aspect of relational acts should not be neglected. As Locher and Langlotz (2008) argue, im/politeness and feelings are interdependent because certain acts of politeness and impoliteness are meant to evoke emotions (and affection or its lack). In this interpretation, politeness and emotion become interconnected through intentionality, that is, a certain utterance generates a specific emotion as the "interactants must be aware of the relative norms of a particular practice in order to adjust the relational work accordingly" (Locher and Langlotz 2008: 173). Putting it simply, the interactants follow or violate a particular practice with the others' feelings in mind.

Locher and Langlotz's claim that emotions can come into existence through the intentional use of relational acts suggests that emotions and rationality are not contradictory aspects of human cognition. This argument seems to me to accord with recent findings in other areas of the humanities, such as social psychology, which claim that emotions evoked by the production and evaluation of social actions presuppose some degree of consciousness, and consequently they necessitate intentionality. As Schermerhorn et al. (2011: 56) explain, it is necessary to "differentiate between self-conscious emotions that arise from internal sources and *social emotions* [my emphasis] that are stimulated by external sources". Social emotions are generated by external stimuli, such as an interaction, and they are cognitively higher order than self-conscious emotions (e.g. feeling sorrow for an unknown reason) because they "require self-consciousness, a capacity that begins to emerge in the second year of life" (Goleman 2011: 131), that is, they necessitate more than simple reflexivity as they operate with "heightened social consciousness" (ibid.). In other words, when following or deviating from certain politeness norms, we are often very much aware of the emotional consequences of our deeds.

Although Locher and Langlotz's approach covers a key area of the emotive and affective aspect of relational acts such as politeness and impoliteness, it represents emotivity and affectivity as bound to intentional actions. An important departure from the intentionality-based view of emotion in relational acts has been made by Şükriye Ruhi (2009) who argues that emotions should be studied in *every* relational act. As Ruhi argues, human cognition is always in an *emotional flux*, and therefore one cannot be completely emotionless, and the researcher cannot fully describe what is going on in terms of emotions, even though one can attempt to model the emotive/affective process. While there are certain actions in which intention is salient, one simply cannot predict the presence or lack of emotions in an interaction, without examining the way in which (a) a given interaction is constructed, and/or (b) drawing from post-interaction interviews and the like to understand the affective function and effect of a certain utterance. This view claims that emotions and affection should be studied irrespective of (perceived) intentions, in order to understand the interrelation between relational acts and affectivity/emotivity.

Following Ruhi I will argue that in-group ritual practices are emotively invested acts (cf. Chapter 1), and so they are affective by their very nature (even though the 'affectivity' of a given ritual act is obviously a matter of degree, which depends on various factors). As interactionally constructed in-group rituals are 'non-codified' in the sense that they can occur without any institutionally formalised goal (e.g. unlike a ritual speech at a birthday, which is meant to trigger the emotion of happiness in a 'pre-designed' way; see below in this section), the affective and emotive effect of these ritual acts is difficult to predict, even though they follow conventionalised schemata and may have conventionalised formal elements (cf. Chapter 3). Due to their emotively invested nature rituals also tend to have an affective and emotive effect on the person who performs them, and this twofold effect boosts the relational function of ritual performances. In other words, it is difficult to systematically capture means–ends, intention–effect relationships between the performer's ritual mimesis and the participant's reaction in every interaction. Furthermore, in certain interactions, emotions fluctuate even while the given interaction is being constructed.

This claim will be integrated into previous research on ritual emotions. Collins's (2004) groundbreaking work theorises on emotions triggered by ritual practices in the following way:

> Emotion implicitly occupies a crucial position in general sociological theory. [...] Durkheim raised the central question of sociology: What holds society together? His answer is the mechanisms that produce moral solidarity; and these mechanisms, I have argued, do so by focusing, intensifying, and transforming emotions. [...] Emotional energy, in IR [i.e. interactional ritual] theory, is carried across situations by symbols that have been charged up by emotional situations. [...] The outcome of a successful buildup of emotional coordination within an interaction ritual is to produce feelings of solidarity. The emotions that are ingredients of the IR are transient; the outcome however is a long term emotion, the feelings of attachment to the group that [were] assembled at that time. Thus in the funeral ritual the short term emotion was sadness, but the main "ritual work" of the funeral was producing (or restoring) group solidarity. (Collins 2004: 102, 107, 108)

Collins' (2004) description above illustrates that emotions triggered by rituals can be categorised as short and long term (see also Rossner 2008, Scheve 2011, Huggins 2008, Berthomé and Houseman 2010);[12] long-term emotions are defined in this book as affection. The present framework follows this conceptualisation, and it argues that the observer cannot always draw clear inferences about the particular short-term emotion(s) which an interactionally constructed in-group ritual triggers. This is because of the above-discussed fact that many of these acts lack an institutionally formalised goal (apart from the very goal of relating), and consequently the anticipating intentionality seems to play a lesser role in the performance of these acts. Furthermore, due to the interactionally constructed nature of in-group ritual, its affective value is subject to variation as the interaction unfolds.

5.2 The recognition of rituals in interaction 互动中仪式的识别

Let us take up the discussion from the claim made in Section 5.1.1, that is, that conventionalised relational practices are unmarked by default, but they can become marked, and occasion awareness, in certain interactions. It is pertinent to note first that along with 'social' conventions (cf. example 5.2 above), the more localised conventional practices of a given relational network can also gain recognition, as the following example (5.3) illustrates:

(5.3)

G Akkor holnap. Remélem nem nagyon gáz neked?
D Dehogy is, simán lenyomjuk.
G Tehát akkor oké. De megoldhatjuk másképp is...
D Persze, különben szólnék. De tulajdonképpen miért is udvariaskodunk?

G Then tomorrow. But is this not too problematic [slang word] for you?
D Ah no, we'll get it done [slang word] smoothly.
G So then it's okay. But mind you, we can resolve this differently, if needed...
D Sure, otherwise I would tell you. But then why on earth do we speak so politely?

This interaction took place between me (D) and an acquaintance of mine (G). In the first four turns the interaction unfolds in a way that counts as normative and conventional in our group in terms of style. That is, G, who asked me a favour (to meet a third party on his behalf at short notice, as his schedule changed), makes use of the conventionally polite practice of enquiring as to whether this sudden request is acceptable,[13] and he also utilises a slang word (*gáz*, lit. gas [for fart], something is being problematic).[14] This stylistic mixture seems to me to accord with our conventional network expectations and in-group ethos – that is, we are relatively young professionals who collaborate on a regular basis and who are in a working relationship that necessitates socially 'coded' conventional formality on the one hand, and can afford, or even necessitates, using moderate slang words, on the other (in order to counterbalance formality). This is also illustrated by the fact that I answer in a similar tone, by (a) responding in an adjacent way, that is, by complying with G's request vis-à-vis conventionally polite practices, and (b) by making the utterance friendly with the slang word *lenyomjuk* (lit. beat it, i.e. get it done).[15] Importantly, in contemporary Hungarian *gáz* counts as a 'harmless' word in spite of its original meaning (i.e. few language users would associate it with a reference to farting), and the same can be said of *lenyomjuk*. Because of this, unlike for example swear words which are adopted by a relational network as part of a ritualised performance (cf. Chapter 3), these forms are relatively 'neutral' lexical items which conventionally convey informality and which are relatively widely used, as far as I am aware, in Hungarian society. Thus, their usage is closer to (sub-)cultural convention than strict-sense mimetic ritual, if we define conventionality vs rituality as a scalar value (cf. Chapter 2). The joint use of these forms with conventionalised politeness can rightly be regarded as a localised conventional practice.

In turn 4, our conventional practice is reflected on by me in a humorous (and somewhat conventional!) way (cf. Mey 2011 on such conventional utterances); through this utterance I wanted to 'give face' to G, by symbolically defining our conventional practice as 'overpolite'. It is pertinent to note, however, that our conventional actions were merely normative, that is, noticing them was not due to the fact that they were being 'overdone' or 'wanting' in any other sense; on the contrary, I would have felt somewhat offended had G not followed the conventional schema upon making a request. To sum up, example (5.3) illustrates that awareness is potentially ever present when the interactants follow conventional norms, and this awareness can manifest itself vis-à-vis metadiscourse, i.e. the interactants reflect on their conventional relational practices either *in actu* or *post actu*.

Example (5.3) illustrates the dialectic relationship between conscious–unmarked and aware–marked rituals in terms of conventionality. In what follows, let us narrow the analysis down to the recognition of in-group relational rituals, which as Section 5.1.1 has argued pass unnoticed at default. We need to ask the same question at this point as in the case of wider-sense conventions, namely, how can interactants be potentially attentive (conscious) to the presence of rituals without explicitly noticing them? The answer resides in the normativity, which is due to its schematic and expected nature. In other words, it is reasonable to argue that ritual is by default unnoticed because its presence merely fulfils network members' contextual expectancies.

The default (conscious and unmarked) characteristic of relational rituals becomes particularly visible when there is a contrast between the way in which a given ritual practice is perceived by relational network insiders and network outsiders. More specifically, there are some cases in my data when relational networks adopt and ritualise certain forms, such as swearing, which would certainly count as marked to many network outsiders, but they go unnoticed by network insiders. Let us illustrate this point by revisiting the Hungarian language extract which was studied in Chapter 1:

(5.4)
1. *A* belegondolva lehetséges=   anyád
   B   =lenne bun̲kókám (.) ha (.) felfogtad volna időben hogy

2. *A*   (hhh)
   B női társaságban az ember nem (.) viselkedik bun̲kó módon mint aki nem tudja

1. *A* thinking about it it might be=   your mother is
   B   =could be yo̲kel (.) should (.) you have realised in time that

2. *A*   (hhh)
   B in female company you don't(.)behave in such a yo̲kel-like way as one who doesn't know

As was noted in Chapter 1, *bunkókám* is a ritualised term; here I reflect on its application in the ritual practices of the group studied: it is a recurrent form with a specific relational function, that is, this word recurs in contexts in which A and B negotiate life strategies. Furthermore, it operates as an emotively invested affective action, which becomes obvious from its contextual usage. In an already challenging context – the other's dating skills are questioned – a deprecatory word such as *bunkókám* would normally further increase the imposition, and so the most plausible explanation for its usage resides in its affective value. The 'harmless' affective function of *bunkókám* is illustrated by its interactional effect. Although in line 1, A reacts to this word by using the mild swear word *anyád* (your mother [is a bitch]) as a counter-challenge, *bunkókám* is not visibly evaluated. And after the very short counter-challenge, A does not attempt to retake the 'floor', that is, *bunkókám* seems to create an affective ritual 'frame' (see Chapters 1 and 3, as well as Koster 2003, on this pragmatic function or rituals). The affective function of this term seems to originate in its specific relational history, i.e. it was previously a term used in banter when the interactants were secondary school students.

A key point from the perspective of the present analysis is that *bunkókám* is obviously normative to a significant extent: although both A and B are aware of its presence to some extent (otherwise this form would not operate successfully; awareness is illustrated by A's mild counter-swearing in turn 1), it is relatively unmarked here. This contradicts a network outsider's perception of this form, considering that forms that occasion rudeness are likely to be noticed[16] (and it is not a coincidence that *bunkókám* caught my attention when I analysed this data, after which I interviewed B about the way in which he and A perceived this form). Once an offensive form like *bunkókám* is being conventionalised and ritualised (in a constructive ritual, cf. Chapter 6), it tends to lose its offensive meaning; this is why it does not violate network insiders' normative moral expectations and tends to go unnoticed (but see the claim made in Section 5.1.1, that un/noticedness is always a matter of degree).

Example (5.4) represents a case when network insiders' and network outsiders' expectations, and the markedness the given ritual practice triggers, potentially clash, due to moral issues. In fact, in the data studied there is another case of potential contradiction between network insider and network outsider perspectives, namely, when network insiders apply highly mimetic rituals. It has been noted in Chapter 2 that although every (in-group) relational ritual practice is mimetic, mimesis is more visible in some ritual practices than in others. In-group rituals that are perceived as mimetic by the observer may seem to be more marked from the network outsider's point of view than those in which mimesis is less obvious. However, as the following extract (5.5) will illustrate, this is not necessarily the way in which network insiders perceive the given ritual, as once a clearly mimetic practice becomes expected in certain settings, it becomes unnoticed. Extract (5.5) is taken from a conversation recorded in an academic institution. The interactants A and B exchange opinions with regard to the possibility of an inter-institutional negotiation with delegates from a foreign educational body.

(5.5)

1. A nem hiszem ho<u>gy</u> az övék egy (1.5) alkalmas tárgyalási módszer lenne ahhoz ho:gy
B   hhh

2. A belátható idő alatt megegyezésre jussunk (.)   igen
B   valóban ezek (.) nem tanultak <u>úgy</u> (.)

3. A   nem is annyira a tárgyalás mint inkább a kulturális hozzáállás
B tárgyalni ahogy mi (0.2)   (sniff)

4. A az amiről itt szó van
B

1. A I don't think tha<u>t</u> theirs is a (1.5) suitable way to negotiate tha:t
B   hhh

2. A within a foreseeable period we could reach an agreement (.)   yes
B   indeed they (.) haven't learnt <u>those</u> (.)

3. A   not so much negotiation than rather cultural attitude
B negotiation techniques that we (0.2)   (sniff)

4. A which is in question here
B

In this interaction, A and B – two elderly academics who were in a long-lasting close collegial relationship when this interaction was recorded – make use of a distinct supportive and somewhat 'solemn' style in their interaction: they (a) tend to avoid overlaps, (b) allow for relatively long pauses and (c) support each other's views through backchannelling.[17] A post-event interview with B made it clear that he perceives this style as normative in their community of practice, in particular when professional matters are discussed, and he and A may even regard it as unusual if their formal discussion lacked these elements of ritual performance. Therefore, the style in these interactions represents a formalised, recurrent and, most importantly, mimetic – and consequently ritual – pattern. Similarly to example (5.4), this style is not explicitly reflected upon by A and B, and therefore it goes unnoticed to the interactants whilst potentially attracting the attention of the external observer.

The present discussion has so far illustrated that in-group rituals trigger consciousness and are unmarked in default, in a similar way as with other conventional relational practices. As the following examples show, in-group rituals are nevertheless open to becoming noticed (noticedness does not mean that they are defined as 'rituals', cf. Chapter 4). Consequently, the default unmarked (conscious) mode of relational in-group rituals is in a dialectical relationship with the marked (aware) mode. The marked recognition of a ritual practice can thus only ever be potential, due to the fact that ritual operates unnoticed in default.

In theory, it cannot be determined exactly when a ritual practice becomes marked, as example (5.3) above shows. However, in the data I have studied so far there are two representative interactional situations which display markedness; these are: (a) cases when a certain ritual practice is not in accordance with a network member's contextual expectance, and (b) when a network member's interactional situation changes mid-course for some reason.

The first of these cases is illustrated by the following example (5.6), an interaction that took place in my family. As this excerpt illustrates, even relatively 'hidden' mimetic performance (i.e. 'hidden' from the observer's perspective; cf. example 5.5 above) which fulfils what is simply expected can occasionally draw the network insiders' attention to itself:

(5.6)

1. *D* figyelj (.) szerintem mindenképpen át kellene gondolnuk hogy vajon a keddi

    K (inaudible)

2. *D* ingatlant nem (unlcear) lenne-e érdemes megvenni mivel egy nagyon jó darabról van szó (.)

    K

3. *D*   =tényleg nem↓ kellene tovább húznunk az időt mert már mindjárt a nyakunkon

    K igen de=

4. *D* van a bérleti időszak vége és gáz lesz ha addig nem rendeződik a lakás kérdése (.)

    K

5. *D*   hh   /én nem

    K ez rendben >van de nem szeretnék kapkodni az üggyel mert ez egy <u>nagy</u> vásárlás/

6. *D* azt mondom hogy kapkodjuk el de nem valószerű hogy ennél (.) ennél jobb=

    K   =<u>ér</u>tem

7. *D*   <u>nem</u> úgy tűnik bogárkám arany <u>csil</u>lagom hogy felfogtad

    K ↓<u>móóó</u> (.2)   ↓<u>már</u>

1. D look (.) by all means we should consider whether the Tuesday
   K   (inaudible)

2. D property is not (unclear) worth buying as that is a considerably good price (.)
   K

3. D   =really we should stop↓ stalling because the end of the tenancy
   K yes but=

4. D is on our back and we will be in trouble if the matter of property is not settled by then (.)
   K

5. D   hh   /I don't
   K this's okay >but I would not like to hurry with this matter because this is a big purchase/

6. D say to hurry but it is uncertain whether there will be better (.) better=
   K   =understood

7. D   it does not seem that you little beetle golden star [forms of endearment] that you
   K   ↓móóó (.2)   ↓már

8. D have understood
   K

This interaction took place between my wife (K), and myself (D), regarding the matter of purchasing a property, which I wished to purchase but my wife had reservations about. In order to put this interaction into context it is pertinent to note that when discussing controversial matters we recurrently make use of a distinct, seemingly objective style, in order to avoid heated debates. The strategic rituality of 'objectivity' is not a peculiarity of our group, as it characterises many institutions (see Tuchman 1972), and it manifests itself in the interaction above in different forms such as the use of impersonal tone and the representation of the idea discussed through the lenses of 'logicality'. This relational ritual unfolds uncontested from line 1 to line 6, and it is unnoticed by the participants, i.e. both K and D perform the ritual discussion without visibly evaluating it. However, the performers seem to become attentive to the relational ritual which is taking place because in line 6, K signals that she finds the ritual exchange disturbing, by markedly switching to *another* relational ritual without drawing on any marked contextual reason. That is, first she interrupts D with *értem* (understood), which signals an impatient and definitive attempt to halt the ritual of objectivity, and then she uses a word of Japanese origin *móóó* (lit. already) as well as the Hungarian *már* (lit. already), which markedly conveys frustration.[18] The ritual nature of these "emotionally loaded words" (cf. Sanguinetti and Reyes 2011) is conventionalised in their prosody: they tend to be pronounced with a strong stress, which tends to disarm them, at least within the network in question. For example, the vowel in *mō* is produced in an overarticulated way, which reflects the way in which Hungarian learners pronounce this word and which would sound strange in a native Japanese interaction. Importantly, this relational ritual is complemented by another one: D switches to an ironical tone by using certain forms of endearment such as *bogárkám* (lit. my little beetle) and *arany csillagom* (lit. my golden star) to address K. From a participant perspective these forms signal irony, due to their overtly emotional nature, but are also recurrent as we often use them in disagreements as a relational ritual to disarm situations that could potentially turn into conflicts.

To sum up, example (5.6) represents a case when the practice of a ritual becomes marked, and the performers/participants become aware of their ritual practice (even if they may not define this ritual practice as 'ritual', as was argued in Chapter 4), due to the fact that the given ritual practice is not in accordance with a network member's contextual expectance. In other words, my wife found the ritual tiresome as she did not want to enter into a negotiation on the matter in hand, and so she reflected on it *in actu*. This reflection, which indicates my wife's awareness of the ritual 'frame', halted the ongoing ritual and opened the door to other rituals, which somewhat 'disarmed' the tension created by the disruption of the relational ritual. In my data, awareness and metadiscursive comments on ritual practice often result in the abrupt termination of the ongoing practice, as example (5.8) below will also illustrate.

As noted earlier in this chapter, another representative case when in-group ritual practices become noticed by network insiders is when a network member's interactional situation changes for some reason. Let us revisit here an example which was analysed in Chapter 3; an excerpt from an e-mail trail involving a group of Hungarian friends:

(5.7)

Y   Kedves Barátaim!
    Ezt a címet kérlek, most rögtön töröljétek a levelező programjaitokból, ha csak nem szeretnétek vele hivatalosan levelezni. Az y@index.hu él csak.
    Erre a levelemre, erre a címre ne válaszoljatok már
    Y

Z   Hehe, Y nagyon kiffffinomultan ir... Ilyen muveltek a fonokok?

X   MILLYEN "KEDVES BARÁTAIM!!!!! Ki a fahhom kedveeees?

Y   Dear Friends!
    I would like to kindly ask you to delete this [e-mail] address from your mailing programs immediately, unless you intend to send official messages here.
    Only y@index.hu is alive.
    Do not send any answers to this e-mail, to the present address
    Y

Z   Haha, Y writes in a very reffffined way... Bosses are that well educated?

X   WHHAT "DEAR FRIENDS"!!!!! Who the fucck [intentional typo] is niiiice?

[E # 37–39]

As was noted in Chapter 3, this interaction occurred when a member of the group (Y) received an e-mail from his friends in his workplace mailbox. In the text above he reminds the others that their ritual language of using mock swear words is inappropriate, by switching to a network outsider style. In other words, in this interaction Y animates a non-network voice that shows awareness of the new interactional context where the system administrator may observe this correspondence.

It is pertinent to note that the markedness of a ritual practice can occasion either *in actu* or *post actu* (retrospective) awareness. That is, while in example (5.6) awareness is signalled as the interaction is being co-constructed, in example (5.7) it occurs after some time lag, due to the asynchronic nature of e-mails (cf. Herring 1997, 2002). It is pertinent to note that such a time lag can be significantly longer, as example (5.8) illustrates – which took place after two further messages were exchanged within the group following on from the e-mail in example (5.7) above.

Once a ritual practice becomes non-default and marked, it can be subject to metadiscourse, as we can see in example (5.8). This e-mail was posted by Y to his friends, this time sent out from his private mailbox, in order to 'disarm' the tension caused by the interaction in (5.7). A noteworthy point here is that on the one hand Y explains the changed circumstances, which fits normative expectations in such a situation, and on the other hand makes a reference to the group's ritual, supposedly in order to 'restore' his regular in-group status:

(5.8)
Y nagyon formában vagytok.
   Minden Y@index.hu-ra[19] bejövő levelet Anna kolléganőm is kap. Amikor az urak erősen bazmegelnek, már ahogy szoktuk, akkor azt az irodavezetőnk is élvezheti.
Y once again, you are acting as your usual selves.
   All e-mails that come to Y@undex.hu are received by my colleague Anna as well. When the gentlemen[20] actively use 'fuck you-s', as we used to, then our office head can also enjoy the event.
[E # 42]

By referring to relational history ("you are acting as your usual selves") and their joint memories ("as we used to"), Y seems to make an indirect appeal to the group to restore the normative order.

To sum up, the present section has illustrated that in-group rituals tend to trigger consciousness – i.e. they are unmarked for the interactants – but they are nevertheless open to evoke awareness and to become marked. Therefore, we should argue that their interactional application offers a potentiality – more precisely, a regularity of potentiality – in terms of gaining notice within a relational network. This is because ritual interactions form emergent systems over time; in essence, different types of ritual action are constituted through clusters of schematic mimetic interactions, and these schematic interactions are what give rise to regularities of potentialities. Relational rituals are perceived by participants as expected, unmarked forms of language use; the default mode of rituality is a kind of stasis, which provides the potentiality for participants to switch to the mode of awareness at any point in time. Such changes tend to be evoked by factors that somehow upset regularity, but this is not a rigid rule (see example 5.3 above). The static vs marked mode discussed here can be graphically represented as shown in Figure 5.1.

The uneven line between the unmarked (static) and marked modes indicates that these modes are not in a dichotomy, i.e. awareness is a matter of degree.[21] The arrows pointing at the marked mode represent the various interactional factors such as those discussed in the present chapter, which stimulate awareness within a group. It should be noted, however, that it is not claimed that awareness per se needs to be provoked directly by others: although we cannot read the interactants' minds, it can be supposed that interactants also tend to reflect on their interactional practices, sometimes not in order to deviate from ritual

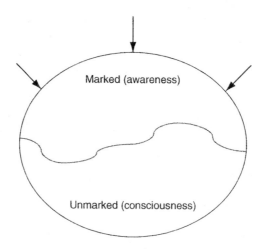

Figure 5.1 The interactional recognition of relational ritual practices

norms (see e.g. extract 5.6), but instead in order to *fit with* network expectancies. This point is illustrated by the following example:

(5.9)

1. A mondhatjuk persze azt hogy (.) igen rossz ötlet volt tőlünk bevenni őket ebbe a
   B   hhh
2. A projektbe me=rt   mert   de ahogy mondtam ez egy
   B   =azért ennyi pénzért bárkit bárkit bevennénk

3. A feltételezés (.)
   B   na igen persze nem azt mondom hogy...

1. A we could say of course that (.) it was a bad idea to invite them in this
   B   hhh

2. A project be=cause   because   but as I said this is a
   B   =well for this amount of money we would invite anyone

3. A a supposition (.)
   B   well yes of course I wouldn't say that...

This interaction is from the same recording as example (5.5) above, i.e. a conversation between two Hungarian academics who adopted a certain ritualistic performance during the negotiation of workplace matters. In turn 1, the interactants continue to discuss the inclusion in a project of an institution represented by a foreign delegation; the interaction here develops in a normative ritual way. However, in turn 2 B interrupts A with a rather practical remark, by referring to the foreign institution's financial contribution to the project. This inserted remark seems to contradict the norm of ritual performance, which presupposes longer pauses at turn-taking points and a relatively 'objective' style (cf. the 'ritual of objectivity'). In turn 2, A attempts to restore the normative order by trying to retake the floor, and in turn 3, B switches back to the ritual style by taking his turn only after a relatively brief pause. What we can observe here is an instance of self-correction, that is, B seems to become aware of his violation of the normative order of the relational ritual performed by the group and in the next turn he (supposedly vis-à-vis self-reflexive awareness) readjusts his style.

The present section has discussed the in-group recognition of relational ritual practices. In what follows, I will focus on another aspect of ritual cognition, namely, affectivity and emotivity.

5.3 The affective effect and emotivity of relational rituals 人际关系仪式的情感效应及情绪性

The present section will analyse the affective function of relational ritual acts, as well as their emotivity, from a cognitive perspective. The main question we need to answer is how the affective and emotive function of in-group ritual practices can be integrated into theoretical descriptions of relational acts, in general, and specifically, of rituals. As argued in Section 5.1.2, most ritual frameworks unanimously claim that institutionalised ritual practices such as marriages, funerals and so on evoke clearly distinguishable short-term feelings and long-term affection, according to the activity type of the given ritual.[22] This 'codified' emotion-triggering and affective function accords with how certain conceptualisations of relational acts, such as Langlotz and Locher (2013) and Langlotz (2010), describe emotions as the hearer's reaction triggered by the speaker's intentionally constructed utterance. In order to illustrate the affective and emotive function of social relational rituals, let us refer to a recent article, on the 2012 US presidential debate between Barack Obama and Mitt Romney, published on the news site *The Atlantic Wire*:

(5.10)

Obama and Romney's Ritual Pre-Debate Lovefest
If you've been craving a more uplifting tone in the presidential campaign, this is your week. President Obama and Mitt Romney have

spent much of the past year tearing each other down, but in the days before their first debate next Wednesday, they can't stop saying nice things about each other. In boxing, fighters go around trash talking like Mohammad Ali, trying to psych out their opponent by bragging. In presidential debates, candidates have to convince reporters that they are destined to lose, and if they emerge from the debate hall with most limbs still attached, they've won.
[…]

Behold, the unprecedented levels of niceness from the campaigns directed at their opponents.

Obama: Godlike Oratorical Genius

- "The president is obviously a very eloquent, gifted speaker," Romney told Fox News this week.
- Obama will "do just fine," Romney added.
- Obama "is known for his world class oratory, is a world-class debater who laid waste to Hillary Clinton, John Edwards, and John McCain," Republican National Committee spokeswoman Kirsten Kukowski said.
- "One thing that I think has been missing in some of the discussion I've heard is that Barack Obama is a very effective debater," Sen. Rob Portman, who's playing Obama in Romney's debate prep, told Politico.
- "He's articulate, he's smart," Portman added.
- "He did a great job in 2008, during that campaign as a debater," Portman continued.
- "He had some tough debates with Hillary Clinton and he performed well," Portman elaborated further.
- "He's up to speed everyday, because he deals with all these issues, federal issues everyday," Portman detailed.
- "I think Barack Obama will be formidable," Portman concluded.
[…]

Romney: Better Trained Than an Olympic Champion

- Romney has been prepping like an "Olympic decathlete" Obama spokeswoman Jen Psaki told ABC News.
- "He has been training for them like an Olympic decathlete, starting earlier than any candidate in modern history and running

5 Recognition, Affectivity and Emotivity 127

through mock debates five times in 48 hours," Psaki told the *Los Angeles Times*. [. . .]

- Romney could get a bounce in polls "just by being on the same stage as the incumbent," Obama officials told ABC.
- "Imagine if the Super Bowl was the first game you played this year," Obama super PAC adviser Paul Begala told the *Boston Globe* of Obama's unpreparedness.
- Obama "certainly hasn't participated in five mock debates in 48 hours as the Romney campaign told Politico that the governor did," an anonymous Obama aide told the *Globe*.

Of course, there are corresponding levels of unprecedented self-deprecation from two men known for their confidence in their own abilities.

Obama: Unprepared Rambler

- "But in contrast to Mitt Romney, President Obama has had to cut back some of his preparation already because of his duties as president," an anonymous Obama aide told the *Globe*.
- "The President will have a little bit of time to review and practice before the debates, but he has had to balance the management of world events, governing, time out campaigning and will have less time than we anticipated to sharpen and cut down his tendency to give long, substantive answers," Obama campaign spokeswoman Jen Psaki told ABC News.
- Obama will "have less time than we anticipated to sharpen and cut down his tendency to give long, substantive answers," Psaki told the *Los Angeles Times*, too.

Romney: A N00b Out of His League

- "I've, you know, I've never been in a presidential debate like this and it will be a new experience," Romney told Fox News.
- "Mitt Romney's a business guy and a former governor. He actually hasn't had a debate against a Democrat in over ten years I think, I guess it would be 2002 when he ran for governor," Portman told Politico.
- "People say, 'Well he's been debating with the Republicans in the primaries.' Very different debates. Being someone who prepares people for debates and having been in a bunch of debates myself – you know they have five, 10 people on the stage

all within the spectrum of the party that you're in, whether you're democrat or republican, is very different than going one-to-one with someone from the other party," Portman added. (Retrieved from: <http://www.theatlanticwire.com/politics/2012/09/obama-and-romneys-ritual-pre-debate-lovefest/57336/>)

The association of the candidates' schematic and mimetic practices with 'ritual' reflects the claim made in Chapter 4, i.e. that social rituals are more likely to be perceived as 'rituals' by language users than other forms of rituality. The 'polite' ritual practices in example (5.10) represent multidirectional relating, that is, on the surface the candidates and their teams appeal to each other's face, but in practice they aim to communicate to the public and to put in place mechanisms for saving their *own* faces, bearing in mind the potential for a negative outcome of the debate. The communicational practices which these individuals and groups utilise are relational: although they do not interact within an existing relational network, they obviously aim to relate themselves to their electors.[23] Importantly, these ritual practices are socially 'coded' ones; that is, the candidates praise the other's abilities and deprecate their own skills as these practices tend to be perceived positively in public discourse. Apart from pre-saving the candidates' faces they also accord with public moral expectations for a debate between the prospective leaders of the US, in particular in the context of a projected, very close electoral race. Although the author of the article above represents the behaviour of Obama and Romney and their circles rather ironically, by contrasting their statements with each other from the analyst's perspective, it seems that from many electors' insider perspective these ritual practices are normative. Thus, in terms of affectivity/emotivity, these practices occasion the positive appreciation of the given candidate's human and leadership values in the short term, and the feeling of relatedness with the candidate (i.e. positive and unidirectional affection) in the long term, in accordance with Collins' (2004) discussion of socially codified ritual practices.

The relationship between ritual act and affective/emotive function seems to be somewhat more complex in the case of in-group rituals, due to their interactionally constructed and 'non-codified' nature. In-group rituals often do not serve any visible interactional goal, apart from relating per se, in my data. In this sense they differ, for example, from the ritual practices of example (5.10), which have a clear goal and which follow schemata codified (institutionalised) by political norms.

Thus, although in-group ritual practice triggers short-term emotions and affection, the relationship between ritual act and emotion/affection is not necessarily a straightforward cause–effect relationship, although at times it may be so. Furthermore, the emotively invested affective actions of in-group rituals tend to trigger emotions and affection from both the performer's and the participant's perspective (even if the emotivity and affectivity of various in-group ritual practices are a matter of degree). As the following example (5.11) will illustrate, this twofold emotion/affection-triggering function of ritual boosts ritual performance within a social network. And, because of this twofold function, while it is possible to suggest whether a ritual practice evokes 'positive' or 'negative' emotions and the increase, stasis or decrease of affection, the next and more important question we need to ask is: *who* does a ritual practice evoke a certain emotion/affection for?

(5.11)

1. *D* ha (illaudible) ha kérdik az az iskolában (0.3)   hogy ki az apád=
    N   =Grievous ↑ tábornok
    K   már megint kezditek

2. *D* igen és aki= majd
    N (.)   = >mit mond Grievous tábornok a buta (.) ↑gyerekeknek
    K

3. *D* (.2) ((altered bronchial voice))²·³ bántottad a lányomat ezért megfizetsz te kis
    N
    K   (unclear)

4. *D* rohadék   ba<u>ssz</u>us   hehe (.) oké
    N   folytatnád ezt szeretem
    K   @közönségetek @van

5. *D* mutassuk meg nekik
    N
    K   ne hülyéskedjetek

1. *D* if (unclear) if they ask in the school (.3)   who your father is=
    N   =General ↑ Grievous
    K   you start it again

2. *D* <u>yes</u> and who= then
    N (.)   = >what does General Grievous say to the silly (.) ↑children
    K

3. D (.2) ((altered bronchial voice)) you've hurt my daughter and you will pay for this you little
    N
    K   (unclear)

4. D bastard   shoot   heh-heh okay
    N   would you continue I like it
    K   you are @having @audience

5. D let's show them
    N
    K   don't be silly

This interaction in Hungarian took place among my daughter (N), wife (K) and myself (D), in front of my daughter's school in England. After my daughter started to attend infant school, and following other children's regular morning remonstrations against going to school, she and I formed a fairly complex ritual practice. My daughter invented imaginary conversations between herself and her otherwise real friends who are the 'good children', and willingly attend school, and a group of imaginary 'silly children' who are being difficult and must be convinced that school is not such a bad place. Our tacit agreement was that my duty in these imaginary games was to put myself into the shoes of book and film characters and help her convince 'silly children' to attend school. In the interaction above, which took place after we watched the film *Star Wars*, I acted the evil character General Grievous who needs to teach 'silly children' a lesson because they manhandled my daughter and her friends after their attempt to convince them to go to school.

The ritual in the interaction above develops in its usual way up to turn 4 when my wife reminds me that my (rather childish) ritual performance is being watched in amazement by other parents. And this is a point where the twofold emotive and affective function of this act becomes evident: first, my daughter requested me to continue, by evaluating the ritual performance positively ("Would you continue, I like it."), and secondly while I laughed at myself (feeling somewhat ashamed) I accepted the request, and in turn 5 I positioned our ritual against the anticipated perception of others ("let's show them").

One can only speculate about what kind of short-term feelings this ritual practice triggered: for example in the case of my daughter it might have been the feeling of security, and, even more importantly, this practice aroused the mutual feeling of relatedness, potentially against other networks, vis-à-vis my anticipatory self-positioning; i.e. its emotive/affective effect was bidirectional rather than unidirectional.[25]

A difficulty behind any straightforward description of the affectivity and emotivity of an in-group ritual act is that in certain interactions, affection and emotions fluctuate whilst the given interaction is being constructed. This is apparent in the following example (5.12):

(5.12)

D Helló, Ácó!
Á Hehe, meghoztad a félkegyelmű urad, Keiko?
D Akkor megyünk a kávéházba?
K Részemről oké.
D Ácókámra amúgy is ráfér egy kis táplálék!
Á *Zotyókámra* meg nem annyira!

D Hi, Ácó [a nickname version of the Hungarian given name Ádám, see below]
Á Heh-heh, so you took along your imbecile husband, Keiko?
D So we go to the coffee shop then?
K As for me, let's go.
D My Ácó needs some food anyway!
Á And *my Zotyó* [a nickname version of my Hungarian middle name Zoltán, see below] does not need that much!

This interaction took place between my best childhood friend Ádám (Á), my wife (K) and myself (D), when we met in a square in Budapest, to proceed together to a coffee shop. In the beginning of this interaction I addressed my friend as *Ácó*, which is a nickname; using this nickname is a ritual reference to our childhood days when he particularly hated this form of address. After becoming adults I often used it jocularly, and it would be received well by my friend who would respond by counter-bantering. This happened on the occasion of the exchange recorded in example (5.12): the form seems to have been accorded normative expectations, as my friend acknowledges it by grinning, while describing me to my wife as "your imbecile husband". It is pertinent to note that here my friend activates another relational ritual, this time involving my wife: that is, while calling him *Ácó* is a ritual that involves my friend and myself, when the three of us meet, when talking to my wife, he often refers to me as *urad* (lit. your lord, i.e. your husband). This is a rather traditional form in Hungarian, which is rarely used in our age group, and the use of which is rooted in our relational history: as this form has some chauvinist connotations, and my friend knows that my wife hates chauvinism, this form is read as friendly mocking-teasing.

An emotive and affective change can be observed as the interaction unfolds: while in the beginning of the conversation the ritualised form *Ácó* obviously triggered positive emotions and boosted affection, this changed later when I repeatedly used it, and referred to the fact that my friend is slim, by stating that he "needs some food anyway". The repeated use of the nickname, perhaps along with the reference to my friend's physical shape, eventually led to the term being evaluated negatively, perhaps because of the presence of my wife – who is a network outsider from the perspective of this ritual practice. Thus, my friend reacted somewhat sharply this time, as he in turn nicknamed me by using my middle name, and claiming that unlike him I should diet; this utterance seems to indicate some frustration in this context.[26]

This section has illustrated that the affective and emotive function of in-group relational ritual practices is a complex one. Arguably in-group relational ritual acts, and their socially 'coded' counterparts, can trigger affection and emotions in accordance with the performer's intentionality. However, in some cases it is difficult to systematically capture the means–ends, intention-effect relationship between in-group ritual performance and the participant's affective and emotive reactions. Furthermore, in-group relational ritual practices are emotively invested affective actions, which potentially trigger emotive and affective responses from both the performer of the ritual and other participants. The participants' emotive and affective response may influence the performer's affection and emotions, as we observed in example (5.11) above where my daughter's reaction effected my interactional behaviour. Finally, those in-group relational ritual practices which are co-constructed (instead of 'demarcated', cf. Section 5.1) can be emotively and affectively complex, as ritual emotions and affection are often in flux as the interaction unfolds (see example 5.12).

The relationship between in-group relational ritual and affection/emotion is illustrated by Figure 5.2. As the arrows show, the ritual action influences the participant(s) but it can also influence the performer, due to its emotively invested affective nature; the arrow which points from the participant towards the performer indicates that the participant's affective/emotive reactions influence the performer's feelings. The affective and emotive value of a ritual practice comes from the relational network's history and related ethos; however, these ritual acts are interactionally (and contextually) situated, and certain contextual

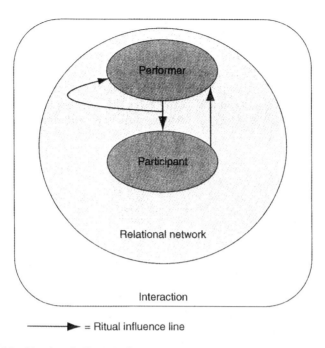

Figure 5.2 Ritual and affectivity/emotivity

expectations or preferences (cf. example 5.12) may influence how they are perceived.

The above discussion on the affectivity/emotivity of in-group relational rituals calls for a multidimensional framework, which incorporates both relational theories accounting for the affective and emotive effect of relational acts as intentional, and other theories suggesting that affection and emotions are ever present and fluctuate in relational acts. Furthermore, it calls for a warning that it is dangerous to make predictive statements with regard to the short-term emotion that a ritual practice triggers (in particular when it comes to the study of in-group ritual acts).

5.4 Summary 结语

This chapter has set out to examine the cognitive features of in-group relational rituals, in particular their recognition and emotivity/affectivity. It has been argued that it is difficult to establish whether a ritual practice remains un/recognised or not, and how it triggers emotions. These challenges accord with the understanding that many in-group ritual acts are interactionally constructed, and so their perception and affective and emotive function might vary to a large extent, in spite of the fact that ritual practices follow certain schemata.

The cognitive inquiry proposed by the present chapter paves the way for another inquiry on rituals, namely, on the evaluation of ritual practices. This is the concern of Chapter 6, which addresses destructive relational rituals.

6
Destructive Relational Rituals
破坏性人际关系仪式

6.1 Introduction 引言

6.1.1 Destructive rituals: a definition 破坏性人际关系仪式的定义

From the perspective of relating, this book has so far studied constructive rituals, i.e. in-group ritual practices that positively contribute to the formation and maintenance of interpersonal relationships. The present chapter will further elaborate upon the theory of relational rituals by exploring destructive relational ritual acts. This is a relatively unexplored area: the anthropological literature to date – as well as areas that rely on anthropological literature when it comes to rituals such as linguistics – seems to have enduring interest in the constructive aspect of ritual behaviour, and destructive ritual practices have been left behind. As the references in this chapter will indicate, it is mainly educational studies and child psychology where such ritual acts are studied, but in these fields the ritual element of these relational practices usually remains unmentioned. Therefore, the exploration of destructive rituals fills a knowledge gap in the field.

Destructive rituals can be defined as rituals that operate differently from their clearly constructive counterparts. That is, instead of boosting in-group relating,

> *destructive rituals stigmatise one in-group member (or several in-group members), that is, they have a target, and they destroy the victim's relation with, and symbolic role within, the group.*

In previous public and academic discourses, various manifestations of destructive relational rituals are aptly described as 'bullying' (see more in Section 6.4.1) or occasionally as 'harassment'. It should be noted, however, that not every type of bullying has a ritual nature, and so bullying is not a suitable technical term for the present framework.[1] As Smith et al. (1993) and Smith et al. (2008) note, bullying can be 'physical', 'verbal', 'relational' (e.g. social exclusion)[2] or 'indirect' (e.g. rumour spreading), and it can include 'single and isolated' as well as 'recurrent' cases. Destructive in-group ritual practice as it is represented here is limited to verbal and relational cases, and it excludes isolated (non-recurrent) interactions that take place outside of a relational network – that is, which might include lexical elements that conventionally occasion rudeness but which are not recurrent *practices* of a network that trigger stigma (Goffman's 1963 term; cf. the notion of 'stigma' in Section 6.2). For example, one can use conventionalised swear words in a single utterance (instead of a series of speech events), but this does not become ritual in a relational sense (unless it re-enacts a value situated within the given network's history, specifically).[3] In order to illustrate this point, it is pertinent to refer here to a recent homemade short film on Youtube,[4] *Fuck you*, which depicts an American teenager who screams *Fuck you!*s to cars from the roadside in order to show his 'braveness' to his peers, until a truck stops and the boys run away. Whilst from the performer's perspective such an act has a clear in-group ritual value (in a constructive way), from the drivers' perspectives it is not ritualistic as it is uttered by unrelated personae on a single occasion and it does not refer to a stigma associated with the addressee.

This, of course, does not mean that destructive ritual can only occur in an in-group form, even though the present chapter focuses on in-group practices. Similarly to its constructive counterpart, destructive ritual exists in out-group contexts as well; for example, the verbal representation of an unknown person's stigma (such as dispreferred racial origin) vis-à-vis a mimetic performance is potentially ritualistic. In a sense, such an act is recurrent, similarly to in-group destructive ritual practices, as from the interactants' perspectives it has historicity and it evokes social ethos related with this historicity. It is also pertinent to note that there is a degree of difference in the social recognition of certain in-group destructive ritualistic forms, i.e. the typological issues discussed in Chapter 4 also apply to destructive rituals. For example, an acquaintance of mine in Hungary retold me that in primary school he was ridiculed by others, in a recurrent ritualistic way, as *sírós* (a person who cries). Obviously, such a form is rooted in a group's relational history (this male person cried once when he was victimised, which became a source of shame picked up in the destructive ritual practice), and so it is more locally conventionalised than, for example, a term which attacks one's sexual orientation such as 'gay boy'.

To sum up the introduction of in-group destructive rituals, lexical research on swearing and foul language (see e.g. Hughes 1992), as well as more recent work on linguistic impoliteness (see e.g. Culpeper 2011b), revealed that there is a pivotal interface between convention and foul language. However, foul language in itself, as well as conventionally abusive acts, does not have ritual value without recurring and being performed within a relational network. In other words, an offence acquires ritual value through the recurrent symbolic performance element (mimesis, cf. the previous chapters), which stigmatises the victim. In order to illustrate this point, let us refer to the following online posting:

(6.1)

i was in year 4 when i started to get bullied and i am now in year 7, in year 4 i was bullied by this bunch of boys and they just constently kept saying stuff that would really hurt my feelings like saying that beacause i looked ugly they kept on calling me a RAT, it used to make me feel really upset. And now im in year 7 and im getting bullied again on facebook by this girl i dont even know because i told her to stop being horrible to my friend she kept on being horrible to me like calling me a dog and saying have u looked in the mirror lately because u look like a DOG, and just keep constantly saying stuff behind my back. I would never bully anybody easle because i no how they feel and that feeling of somebody hating you is not nice and iv bin there and i am still being bullied. SO WE SOULD FIGHT BULLING TOGETHER xxxx by and 11 year old girl called demi xx :(its a horrible feeling :(so dont do it.
(Retrieved from: <http://familyinternet.about.com/u/ua/computingsafetyprivacy/Cyberbullyua.01.htm>)

The type of bullying described here is a destructive ritual act due to its recurrent nature.[5] Notably, using animal names to describe others is a conventional form of offence in various cultures, as Bruce Fraser ([1981] 2012) argued, but in example (6.1) the conventionally offensive animal name "dog" becomes a ritual offence as (a) it refers to the targeted person's stigma, her perceived lack of beauty, because (b) it recurs, and (c) also it has a performance value (the girl referred to wraps her offensive question in the form of a staged inquiry, i.e. "have u looked in the mirror lately").

Along with conventionality, it should also be noted that not every manifestation of destructive ritual is relational, at least in the sense the present book interprets this term. As noted in Chapter 1, a secret curse that the other does not hear, or which is uttered towards an unrelated person, is not relational, despite the fact that it is ritual due to its schematic and mimetic character.

Destructive ritual reflects and reinforces the ethos of a given social network,[6] just as constructive ritual, but it represents ethos in a contrastive way, by conflicting it with one or several negatively perceived characteristics of the victim who thus becomes stigmatised. Although directly violent abuse is potentially present in destructive ritual practices, it is not a precondition for a certain act to become destructive, as Section 6.3 will illustrate.

To summarise the present definition of destructive ritual it is useful to recall the definition of relational ritual which was provided in Chapter 1:

> Ritual is a formalised/schematic, conventionalised and recurrent act, which is relationship forcing. Ritual is realised as an embedded (mini-)performance (mimesis), and this performance is bound to relational history (and related ethos), or historicity in general (and related social ethos). Ritual is an emotively invested affective action, as anthropological research has shown.

As examples in the present chapter will illustrate, destructive in-group ritual practices also fit into this model, as they are also formalised/schematic, conventionalised and recurrent acts within a social network, and also they operate through (mini-)performances. There is, however, a substantial difference between constructive and destructive in-group ritual practices, in terms of their relationship-forcing character. As was argued in earlier chapters of this book, constructive ritual is relationship forcing in the sense that its performance stimulates interpersonal relationships to develop. Destructive ritual practices function differently: their performance causes the corruption of the relationship between the performer (and the relational network) and the stigmatised person(s), and so they should be defined as 'relationship corrupting'.

It is pertinent to note that the difference between constructive and destructive ritual is relational and not moral: whilst destructive relational rituals are perceived as 'immoral' (cf. Section 6.4), we should avoid claiming that constructive rituals are inherently perceived as moral ones. Let us refer, for example, to a recent Hungarian newspaper article which introduced the in-group ritual practices of sexual slave traders, most significantly: giving the victim a new 'trade name'.[7] Technically speaking, such liminal practices count as constructive rituals as they give a certain in-group status to the victim as a prostitute (despite the fact that the forced victim may not like to have such a status at all), whilst they are clearly perceived as immoral by the public.

6.1.2 Analytic significance 分析该类仪式的意义

We must explore destructive rituals not only because they are regretfully neglected, but also because their research contributes to the theorisation of relational rituals per se. In various other linguistic areas which focus on relational studies, most significantly linguistic impoliteness research (see e.g. Culpeper 2005, 2011a), scholars have devoted more and more attention to relationally destructive phenomena in recent years. A key rationale behind this interest is that destructive relational behaviour is not merely the "evil twin" of its constructive counterpart, to use Bousfield's (2010) definition, and so its study can bring cutting-edge insight into both the constructive and destructive aspects of relational phenomena such as im/politeness. Following this train of thought, the present chapter argues that destructive rituals are worth studying for two interrelated reasons. First, as Section 6.4 will argue, examining the destructive vs constructive aspect of a ritual practice brings different perceptions and evaluations into the relational ritual theory. The importance of relying on more than just one understanding and perception of ritual acts (e.g. by conducting interviews) – according to what was suggested by Kádár and Haugh (2013) for im/politeness – has been emphasised elsewhere in this book (see e.g. Chapter 5). Yet, evaluations become particularly salient when we involve constructiveness vs destructiveness in the ritual framework. Since constructive rituals count as normative from an in-group perspective, their presence does not contradict moral expectations (cf. Section 5.2 in Chapter 5). However, destructive ritual, as the present chapter will illustrate, infringes upon whatever is regarded as normative by the public, and so participant (and non-participant) evaluations become salient as soon as one performs this type of ritual. Studying different perceptions also reveals that it is problematic to apply the notions of constructive and destructive in a dichotomic way. As Section 6.4 will illustrate, destructive ritual practice has a constructive relational value for those who perform it, that is, it is a matter of perspective whether a ritual practice is perceived as constructive or destructive. To sum up, no theory of (constructive) relational rituals can be complete without an account of destructive rituals.

Secondly, approaching rituals as relationally constructive and destructive can help us to streamline categorisation in the field. As Chapter 4 has argued, a relational approach to rituality calls for an alternative typology, and this applies to destructive rituals as well. There are a number of terms in both popular and academic discourse on rituality which describe practices that could be associated with the destructive aspect of ritual, but which in practice allow both constructive and destructive interpretations, depending on the participants' perspectives. Thus, while the categories these terms describe are certainly useful for other disciplines such as anthropology and sociology, from a relational perspective they are vague. In what follows, let us briefly overview perhaps the most representative of these terms, including 'evil ritual' in folk-theoretical/scientific discourse, and 'ritual of exclusion' in scientific research on ritual.

'Evil ritual' is a folk-theoretical term, which includes rituals of violence, as well as other ritual practices that are condemned by the public in a given society or social network. In public discourse certain rites which do not meet a given community's moral standards are likely to become evil ones (see more on morality in Section 6.1.3). For example, certain forms of what Bell (1997) describes as "political rites" are represented as evil rites if they reflect political ideals that are immoral in our eyes. These can include, for instance,

> the Nazi "Heil Hitler" salute, the public execution of a convict... [and] the cross-burnings of the Ku Klux Klan (Bell 1997: 129).

Some other political acts of rite, on the other hand, such as "the state funerals accorded John F. Kennedy" (Bell 1997: 129), are likely to be represented as 'acceptable' as they do not violate our norms.[8] Due to the interconnection between morality and ritual, ritual practices are divided into 'good' and 'bad' rites,[9] and within a certain network or society there is usually a normative public agreement about the goodness or evilness of certain rituals (even though these agreements might be contested by members of a group as well as some groups within a society). For example, the rituals of the Nazis are likely to be described as evil ones in public discourse in many societies (for such rituals see e.g. Goodrick-Clarke 1985). Rituals of violence are also often referred to, by members of 'civilised societies', as evil rituals (see Section 6.4.1 on the relationship between violence and normativity).

In a relational sense not every evil ritual is different from the rituals studied in the previous chapters: unless it has a stigmatised target and so gains a destructive function, a ritual like a secret Nazi greeting simply strengthens the bonds of a relational network, however morally unacceptable it is to certain observers. If one surveys theoretical accounts of such rituals (and it should be noted that 'evil ritual' is also used in scientific discourse, see e.g. Frankfurter 2001), it becomes evident that researchers argue for the constructive values of morally condemned and/or violent rituals. For example, as Schechner's (1995) noteworthy monograph notes, violence is usually regarded as a constructive phenomenon:

> What about the violence of ritual—human and animal sacrifice, cannibalism, flesh-piercing, initiatory ordeals [...] on through a very long list [...] Do these practices tame the violence they simultaneously actualize and represent? [...] they are homeopathic—that a little ritual violence inoculates a society against more general, and destructive anarchic violence. (Schechner 1995: 260)

That is, many scholars regard rituals of violence a 'necessary evil', which help maintain order in a given group or society. This seems to be a dangerous argument in the sense that while a little violence goes a long way in securing public order, any form of violence has potential to transform into abuse – and this also calls for the alternative approach to rituals in terms of relational de/con-structiveness proposed by the present chapter. To sum up, while in contemporary public discourse rituals of violence are associated with evil, at least in societies which regard violence as a bad thing, scholars generally agree about the constructive nature of these rituals, which includes relational constructiveness as well.

The present framework will contradict these accounts to some extent, as the main question for us is: constructive and destructive to whom? Arguably, a ritual of violence is constructive for the community but destructive for the targeted person. To sum up, the above description illustrates that 'evil ritual' is a broad term, which fails to capture the constructive and destructive aspects of ritual relating.

A somewhat similar problem emerges if one surveys scholarly terms for certain ritual actions that are destructive as default, such as the 'ritual of exclusion'. This term originates in Foucault's (1975: 231) work, in which he noted that "the leper gave rise to rituals of exclusion", as a mechanism of society to protect itself from this menacing epidemic. Accordingly, the ritual of exclusion is often associated with the ritual practices of a society that targets stigmatised individuals. However, Foucault in an interview pointed out the complexity of this term, in the following way:

> There is the first function of the university: to put students out of circulation. Its second function, however, is one of integration. Once a student has spent six or seven years of his life within this artificial society, he becomes "absorbable": society can consume him. Insidiously, he will have received the values of this society. He will have been given socially desirable models of behavior, so that this *ritual of exclusion* [my emphasis] will finally take on the value of inclusion and recuperation or reabsorption. In this sense, the university is no doubt little different from those systems in so-called primitive societies in which the young men are kept outside the village during their adolescence, undergoing rituals of initiation which separate them and sever all contact between them and real, active society. At the end of the specified time, they can be entirely recuperated and reabsorbed. (Cited from McKenzie 2004: 27–8)

That is, it is obvious that while the usual default application of rituals of exclusion is destructive (at least from the excluded person's perspective), it is not inherently a stigmatised group which becomes the subject of these ritual practices.

It is pertinent to note that vagueness in terms of relating also applies to categorical terms that refer to certain aspects of ritual behaviour which have a relationally constructive default function. For example, one can refer to a 'deconstructive ritual': this term describes rituals that reshape relationships through the ludic deconstruction and recombination of relational configurations (see e.g. Turner 1967; Deflem 1991). Thus deconstructive rites,[10] for example a marriage, tend to have a constructive default function from a relational perspective, as in traditional societies it is a ritual which deconstructs the membership of the bride in her family and at the same time constructs her membership in her husband's family.[11] However, one could argue that liminal deconstruction is also a key element in destructive rituals, which induce the corruption of the relationship between the performer (and their network) and the stigmatised person(s).

6.1.3 Data and structure 语料及结构

Unlike earlier chapters, the data studied in this chapter consists mainly of anecdotes and post-event accounts of destructive in-group rituals, as well as post-event discussions of these rituals such as example (6.1) above, rather than interactional data such as recordings. This is due to the hidden nature of destructive ritual practices.[12] While it has been argued that certain forms of in-group ritual practices tend to be 'hidden' from the observer, this seems to be even more pertinent for destructive rituals. This is due to the shame value attached to these practices in normative public moralising discourse (cf. Section 6.4.1; on ritual and shame see also Chapter 4): as destructive rituals are immoral, those who perform them prefer secrecy (irrespective of the fact that they may evaluate their ritual positively, see Section 6.4.2). Thus, apart from analysing films such as *The Bully* (2001) which display interactions that are ritualistic, and reality shows and 'roasting' shows (i.e. when well-known people are invited to ridicule a celebrity), it is difficult to record spoken data that represents destructive ritual practices. The situation is somewhat similar in the case of written and computer-mediated interaction even though there are for example open threads that represent abusive ritual in communities,[13] and extracts will be cited from such websites in this chapter. Unfortunately, it is more often than not difficult to access community websites which belong to closed relational networks with a relational history, and also reference materials on cyberbullying hardly cite abusive threads (see e.g. Kowalski et al. 2008). The present research relies on a database of 137 interactions and anecdotal descriptions of destructive rituals (see more in Section 6.3), as well as a set of 25 short (and slightly edited) interviews which I conducted in Hungary.

This chapter has the following structure: Section 6.2 will discuss the Goffmanian notion of stigma, which is key to theorising destructive ritual behaviour. Section 6.3 then explores the inventory of in-group destructive ritual – that is, its most representative practices – by drawing on some studies of impoliteness. As Chapter 2 argued, there is an important interface between im/politeness and relational rituals. Section 6.3 will illustrate that destructive rituals operate according to patterns identified by impoliteness researchers, even though there is a key difference between 'proper' impoliteness and ritual offence within relational networks, namely, that destructive in-group rituals obtain their destructive function by being performed again and again.[14] Finally, Section 6.4 will examine de/constructiveness from the perspective of participant perceptions.

6.2 Stigma 骂名

Unlike some other forms of abusive behaviour, destructive in-group ritual practices need a constant victim in order to operate. But a question to be answered when discussing a framework for ritual is how does one become a victim of the recurrent practices of destructive ritual?

144   *Relational Rituals and Communication*

Scholars engaged in organisational studies seem to be unanimous in their opinion that being perceived as 'different' from others is the most obvious *casus belli* for becoming a victim within a relational network (see a useful overview in Vartia 1996). The danger of 'difference' is illustrated by the following extract from the episode *The Bully* (2001) of the popular cartoon *SpongeBob SquarePants*:

(6.2)

Mrs Puff   [*walks in*] Good morning class. Sorry I'm late. I got caught in traffic on the way in here when that whole "I'm-going-to-be-doing-this-for-the-rest-of-my-life' thing reared its ugly head and I... [*Everyone stares at her blankly*] Anyway, we have a new student starting today, so let's all put on a happy face for Flat the flounder. [*opens the door to show a skinny flounder from the front but when he turns sideways, he's large. The entire class, except SpongeBob, has paper masks, painted with faces, on*] Tell the class something about yourself, Flats.
Flats   Well, I like to kick people's butts. [*Mrs Puff laughs*]
Mrs Puff   What a card! Now Flats, it's time to pick your seat. Just go ahead and sit anywhere you'd like. [*the class move their desks away from the middle of the room, except SpongeBob. Flats sits in the empty seat next to him*] Okay class, as you remember last week...
SpongeBob [*to Flats*] Hi, I'm SpongeBob!
Flats   Hi, SpongeBob. I'm going to kick your butt.

Although this is a humorous representation of aggression, it neatly pinpoints that SpongeBob's difficulties start from being different from others (not putting on a paper face, etc.). Yet, what happens with SpongeBob is simply abuse, which is remedied as the plot unfolds, i.e. Flats' behaviour is not clearly ritualistic.[15]

In SpongeBob's case, being different is a one-off. However, there are cases when differences from the rest of the group are perceived as long-lasting, sometimes lasting a lifetime. This phenomenon is called *stigma*, and it is defined by Goffman's (1963) illuminating study in the following way:

The Greeks, who were apparently strong on visual aids, originated the term *stigma* to refer to bodily signs designated to expose something unusual and bad about the moral status of the signifier. The signs were cut or burnt into the body and advertised that the bearer was a slave, a criminal, or a traitor – a blemished person, *ritually* [my emphasis] polluted, to be avoided, especially in public places. (Goffman 1963: 11)

That is, stigma is a ritual symbol, which excludes the individual from a relational network or society per se. It is perhaps needless to note that stigma does not necessarily entail any conscious abusive behaviour. However, as Goffman notes, stigma is an inherent source of conflict as there is a gap between non-stigmatised and stigmatised:

While a stranger is present before us, evidence can arise of his possessing an attribute that makes him different from others in the category of persons available for him to be, and of a less desirable kind – on the extreme, a person who is quite thoroughly bad, or dangerous, or weak. He is thus reduced in our minds from a whole and unusual person to a tainted, discounted one. Such an attribute is a stigma, especially when its discrediting effect is very extensive; sometimes it is also called a failing, a shortcoming, a handicap. (Goffman 1963: 12)

In terms of social psychology, this gap also implies, as Goffman argues, that being stigmatised is likely to create a perception of being abused.

Destructive ritual practice comes into operation when the person who sticks out for any reason, or who is regarded as being different or simply vulnerable, is stigmatised by the performer of a given abusive ritual (and potentially by others whose voice the performer animates). Once a markedly negative characteristic is attributed to the victim – i.e. (s)he is being stigmatised – (s)he gets a "virtual social identity" (Goffman 1963: 12), i.e. a (negative) identity attributed to her or him by other members of the network, and can be ritually and repeatedly attacked.

Stigmatisation practices are performed in many ways, but a unifying factor behind these practices is that the victim needs to have a stigma which *markedly contradicts the relational network's ethos*. While there are many people who are born with potential social-level stigmas (e.g. a physical handicap, racial or ethnic origin, sexual orientation), it does not follow that it is a social-level stigma which will be taken up in a destructive ritual. An interesting example can be found in Eglash's (2002) study, which documents the case of 'black nerds'. Eglash mentions the case of black children who were being abused – in a way that would be considered as ritual in this book – by other black children, for

146 *Relational Rituals and Communication*

speaking in an 'educated way' (i.e. by using standard American English) which contradicts the in-group ethos of being 'cool' associated with black American vernacular.

Stigma and destructive ritual practice could not come into existence if the ethos which the victim's (claimed) attributes/behaviour contradicts was not that of the *majority* of a relational network. Goffman (1963) defines this majority as "the normal", whom he describes as follows:

> We and those who do not depart negatively from the particular expectations at issue I shall call the *normal*. (Goffman 1963: 15)

In my data, "the normal" often seem to have their uncodified in-group values, and the victim becomes ritually stigmatised as a result of an unspoken agreement, i.e. as "the normal" perceive the tension between network ethos and the stigma. However, as was noted above, sometimes it is enough simply to be vulnerable to be targeted (and stigmatised), and "the normal" can negotiate as to how to stigmatise the victim who has no apparent stigma, as the following case illustrates:

(6.3)

I am an Occupational therapist in the NHS and I love my work. I am conscientious and dedicated with expertise in Brain injury. I have been qualified for 18 years and live for my work. Over the last 5 years I have been subjected to consistant bullying *where a group of managers have talked about me in their lunchbreak, joked about 'smashing my face in', made a secret agreement not to answer my questions in regard to a new computer system, making gestures behind my back and many many more nasty things* [my emphasis]. Eventually, I walked out of the building and was on sick leave for 3 months. A meeting was arranged with HR but my angry manager used it to criticise me stating things like 'look at the state of you, bursting out of your uniform. No wonder people don't respect you'. I was advised to complete bullying forms, then one of the bullies filled in a bullying form against me saying she felt harrassed that I had accused her of bullying. I was subjected to 3 hours of questions. 5 months later I have heard nothing from HR and the bullying continues. I have gained 2 stone in weight in 5 months and had a chest infection for 3 months. I despair. My wonderful career has died. I put a brave face on for the patients and nurses on the ward. I am considering sick leave again and seeking legal advice.

(Retrieved from: <http://www.nhs.uk/Livewell/workplacehealth/Pages/bullyingatwork.aspx>)

As Section 6.3 will illustrate, recurrently *not doing* something is a typical practice of destructive ritual. A noteworthy point in this description is, first, that this person becomes stigmatised without having any apparent stigma. Whilst the case might be that the narrator is simply silent about a stigma (s)he has, this is not likely, considering that prior to the five-year period mentioned in this posting (s)he was *not* stigmatised. This seems to indicate that there can be many reasons for one to become stigmatised: for example it could be that before this person worked in another unit in the NHS (National Health Service, UK), which tolerated vulnerability more than the one discussed in example (6.3), and it is due to the new community of practice's[16] different ethos that (s)he suddenly found themselves in a difficult position. Secondly, example (6.3) illustrates the above-mentioned point that there can be clear-cut agreement about the abuse of the stigmatised person. A key point here is that it was a group of managers – i.e. people who animate the voice of the community of practice and who have power to question the in-group member's right to membership – who came to this 'secret' agreement.

Example (6.3) is noteworthy also because it illustrates that some stigmas can transform as destructive in-group ritual practices develop. Although the victim was originally not stigmatised for being overweight, when the destructive ritual practice is being discussed the manager notes "look at the state of you, bursting out of your uniform. No wonder people don't respect you" – i.e. the original 'subjective' stigma (the managers seem to have decided to "smash in" this person's face) transforms into an 'objective' one (cf. the ritual practice of 'objectivity' in example 5.6 in Chapter 5).

As a matter of course, the managers' negotiation of stigmatisation in example (6.3) represents a specific case. It seems to be more often the case that stigma is interactionally co-constructed as the ritual unfolds, as the following post event interview in Hungarian which I conducted illustrates:

(6.4)

Először az egész viccesnek látszott. Nevettek a méretemen és „törpének" neveztek, én is velük nevettem, de nem vették az adást. Másnap az egyik srác már eleve bekiabált, hogy „törpe", majd lassanként már mindenfelöl jöttek a megjegyzések a szexuális éltetemre, a „gnómságomra", meg amit el tudsz képzelni. Ez már nem volt vicces, de amikor mondtam nekik, hogy állítsák le magukat, úgy látszott, csak még jobban behergelődnek. Ez így ment hetekig.

First the whole thing looked like fun. They laughed about my height and called me a "dwarf", and I laughed with them but they didn't seem to react to this. On the next day, one of the guys shouted "dwarf" at me and then gradually remarks came from everywhere about my sexual life, my "gnomely" figure, and whatever you can imagine. This was already not funny at all, but when I told them to stop, it seemed to me that this made them even worse. This went on for weeks. (#8)

In other words, stigma often comes into existence through an interactional co-construction process. As this account of the interviewee's experience in his teenage years illustrates, there can be a transition from a relatively harmless reference to the stigmatised feature and the recurrent, destructive ritual reference to the stigma.

The present section has argued for the importance of stigma in the operation of destructive rituals. As Chapter 4 has shown, certain ritual practices (in particular, covert rituals) tend to trigger stigma; however, destructive rituals are different from these in that stigma is the motor of these practices. In what follows, I will overview the most representative forms of destructive ritual practice.

6.3 Inventory 各种特点

Destructive ritual has the following practice features:

a) Recurrent non-doing (ignoring)
b) Recurrent covert offence
c) Recurrent reference to the stigma

This listing follows an increasing degree of directness. However, it must be noted that different degrees of directness do not necessarily imply differences in the perception of these practices as 'more or less destructive'. First, as Culpeper (2011a: 194) argues in his study on impoliteness, unlike what was claimed in previous research such as Leech (1983), it cannot be taken for granted that the more indirect an utterance is, the less offensive it becomes. As Culpeper notes,

> Generally, with respect to directness, it is departures from the convention, whether through using directness or non-conventional indirectness, that led to higher evaluations of impoliteness. Regarding low-power speakers commanding high-power addressees, we found that the differences between the different degrees of directness with respect to impoliteness judgments were relatively small. We suggested that the mere fact of commanding someone of relatively high power in a context where they clearly have no special right to do so is enough to lead to the evaluation of strong impoliteness, and at these higher levels of impoliteness the finer linguistic differences amongst our command items get lost in the 'white noise' of offence. We suggested that the fact that the conventionally indirect 'could you be quiet' uttered in this context does not exacerbate the impoliteness more than the other directness categories may be because of possible leakage from the conventional polite meaning associated with 'could you X' structures and the fact that the mismatch between the conventional meaning and the context is not strong. (Culpeper 2011a: 194)

While the present book uses 'conventional' somewhat differently from Culpeper (cf. Chapters 2 and 5), this description is certainly useful as it illustrates that the perception of a destructive act basically depends on the relationship between the interactants, rather than the in/directness of a given act.

Secondly, as the following Section 6.3.1 will illustrate, the recurrent nature of ritual practices renders different degrees of in/directness relatively insignificant. In other words, as a given ritual act recurs, it does not seem to matter that much whether it is indirect or not, in that recurrence itself conveys the clear message that "the normal" intend to stigmatise the victim through ritual practice(s).

In the data set of 137 interactions and anecdotal descriptions, the three practice types of destructive rituals are represented as shown in Table 6.1.

6.3.1 Recurrent non-doing 反复该做不做

An important form of destructive ritual is *not* to perform an act which is perceived and, perhaps even more importantly, anticipated as a proper (normative) convention. As Haugh argues, anticipations

Table 6.1 Different practices of ritual in the data studied

Practice of ritual	Recurrent non-doing (ignoring)	Recurrent covert offence	Recurrent reference to the stigma
Number of interactions/ anecdotal descriptions	38	47	52

involving expected behaviour are always present in the perception of the appropriateness of a given social act because "social norms are expectations in the sense of *thinking something is necessary* [emphasis in original]" (Haugh 2003: 399). Furthermore, as Kádár and Haugh (2013: 217) note, "Anticipating [...] involves presumptive forms of reasoning where inferences are grounded in experience and associative links." Thus, when a given act that is considered normative and which is anticipated to occur is not performed and intentionality is captured behind this non-performance vis-à-vis inferences grounded in experience and associative links – i.e. the hearer knows that the speaker knows that the hearer would expect him to perform the given act – this lack occasions evaluations as offensive. It is due to the recurrence of not performing that the stigma value of a given ritual act is confirmed to the victim (and also it is recurrence that seems to give power to ritual offence, as the present section will argue). In other words, recurrence occasions perceptions of "higher-order intentionality" (Haugh 2013) behind the act, that is, that the given act is *planned against* the victim.

The operation of ritual non-doing can be illustrated by the following example:

(6.5)

Isolated – staff involved would never sit with me during morning tea, lunches, meetings, courses, etc. My name was omitted from birthday acknowledgements. All other staff names on whiteboard in staff room and on work trays were in black, only mine was in red. When we were asked to bring a plate for morning teas or special lunches, no one ate any of mine. I volunteered to help on many projects only to find later that the projects had been completed without my help.
(Retrieved from: <http://www.sheilafreemanconsulting.biz/case-studies.htm>)

This description was found on a website dedicated to workplace bullying. As the author's "never" makes it clear, the sense of offensive isolation is occasioned by this ritual practice vis-à-vis repeated non-doing: he is being left out from activities in which one would normally expect to be invited.[17]

If we revisit the question of the degree of indirectness of different practices of destructive ritual it is obvious that ritual non-doing is a most indirect practice, in the sense that in the course of this social action no visible action is made against the victim – this is of course relative, as non-acting is an action when action is normative and anticipated. In this respect, ritual non-doing is a special type of relational ritual, as unlike other ritual acts it is not bound to visible forms or schematic patterns; but then of course non-doing something over a period of time is in itself a pattern.

Furthermore, ritual non-doing is an indirect practice in the sense that it is a social act which is difficult for the victim pin down. As a recent bestseller book *Bully Free at Work* (2008) notes,

> [p]erhaps the most difficult part of being excluded at work is that it's nearly impossible to pinpoint the behavior or know who to confront. Exclusion is often an act of omission rather than commission, that is, instead of doing something to the target, the difficult person at work doesn't do something, which makes the target feel confused and off-center.
> (Retrieved from: <http://www.bullyfreeatwork.com/blog/?page_id=8>)

The victim can, of course, attempt to refer to the ritual of non-doing to "the normal", but as the following thread illustrates, it is often the case that, at least in the data I studied, in the co-construction of ritual interaction such an attempt creates an opportunity for further abuse:

(6.6)

Everyone Plzz Stop Ignoring Me!!!!!

1. <u>AIRFLKISAAC</u>   (07–30–2011)

Mr. Bean ignores me pasqualina ignores me nmeade ignores me what am i not " pro" enough for them everytime i say hi they dont say anything and the next they say hi to some random person again am i not a "pro"mkwii racer do you guys want me to be 9999 vr or hack the game well first of all im all legit racing second i HATE when people ignore me... and dont put smart alec responses on this thread it will get me even more mad ind dont put this thread is in wrong section because I DONT CARE IM TRYING TO PROVE A POINT AND ITS NOT JUSt pasqualina and mr.bean its everyone!!!!!!!!!

2. Daphne   (07-30-2011)

Actually you are. Most say that people that can keep over 9000 VR are pro. And anyway, I'm ignoring you because playing with legit people is making me mad as of late (Except for Miller).

3. Wolfy   (07-30-2011)

It's because they don't feel like talking to you.
Now stop bitching.

4. ξvePorta   (07-30-2011)

Who cares? They don't have to talk to the random fanboys.
Just kidding, it's cause you're Canadian.

5. Wolfy   (07-30-2011)

Or it's probably the Canadian thing.

6. Vices   (07-30-2011)

Pats head

7. 13Stark37   (07-30-2011)

you suck soul

8. tortuga   (07-30-2011)

ignored

9. AIRFLKISAAC   (07-30-2011)

ok im sorry... i just feel bad now

10. Flying Mint Bunny   (07-30-2011)

[...]I know I would ignore him after that..

11. Γ&#Megalodon24 (07-30-2011)

xD

18. Ryan1191   (07-30-2011)

Ignores This is the wrong place to put this thread. **Now** everyone's ignoring you

(Retrieved from: <http://www.mariokartwii.com/f18/everyone-plzz-stop-ignoring-me-80655.html>)

This interaction was retrieved from an online car racing game fun site. AIRFLKISAAC sends in this post upon perceiving the higher-order intentionality behind the behaviour of other members of the online community. That is, he feels that he is being (ritually) ignored, as other community members do not respond to his postings. If one analyses the responses to his appeal to the community, it becomes clear that it is taken up by the others to further stigmatise him. In turn 2 Daphne makes a non-committal response (see more on non-committal responses in e.g. Clift 2012), by stating that he or she does not avoid AIRFLKISAAC for what the latter claimed as a potential reason for being ignored – that is, not being a professional player – but exactly because he or she is not interested in playing with professionals. By this response Daphne manages to diplomatically distance herself from AIRFLKISAAC, i.e. this is a strategy of "disaffiliation" (cf. Drew and Walker 2009), and the stigmatised person thus remains isolated. In turn 3 Wolfy animates the voice of "the normal", as he or she refers to AIRFLKISAAC's stigmatised status in an explicit manner ("It's because they don't feel like talking to you."). Furthermore, he downgrades AIRFLKISAAC's appeal to the group by designating it as "bitching", which is a frequently used word to label somebody's behaviour as deviant, i.e. different from what "the normal" would expect (cf. Zurcher 1985). In turn 4 ξvePorta makes use of what seems to be humour, by posting "Who cares? They don't have to talk to the random fanboys." While in the following sentence he designates this utterance as "kidding", this is not 'harmless' humour in the sense that (a) it represents AIRFLKISAAC's appeal as insignificant ("Who cares?"), i.e. it confirms that AIRFLKISAAC is excluded from "the normal", and (b) it reinforces the divide between the group and the victim by portraying the stigmatised person as a "random fanboy". The ritual abuse then continues, and the next turn of specific interest is 8 in which tortuga makes an explicit reference to "the normal's" stance to ignore the stigmatised by posting "*ignored*". In turn 9 AIRFLKISAAC makes a last attempt to restore his status amongst the normal by apologising for posting his enquiry and referring to his negative emotions ("ok im sorry.... i just feel bad now"). Apology could work in many other settings to restore membership; as Tavuchis (1993: 8) argues, "apology expresses itself as the exigency of painful re-membering". However, AIRFLKISAAC remains stigmatised and the destructive ritual continues: in turn 10 Flying Mint Bunny turns towards other members of "the normal" as he refers to AIRFLKISAAC in the third person, as one he will ignore, and in turn 11 Γ&# Megalodon24 supports this uptake by posting "xD", an emoticon for laughter. The ritual continues to unfold to turn 18, in which Ryan1191 addresses the victim directly again, but not with the goal to 'acknowledge' his existence. Instead of this, he animates the group's voice in the form of a verdict, by posting the utterance "*Ignores* This is the wrong place to put this thread. Now everyone's ignoring you."

The indirectness of non-doing does not decrease the destructive effect of this ritual practice, as noted above, due to its recurrence (which also gives it a clear mimetic value). Recurrence decreases the ability of the victim to mentally disarm destructive rituals as harmless ones: while an isolated occurrence of non-doing could be dismissed as an 'accident', recurrence practically forces the victim to recognise that they are being abused.[18] This point is illustrated by the following comment in an interview that I conducted:

(6.7)

Nem hívtak meg. Amikor megemlítettem a dolgot, nem reagáltak semmit, de láttam a fejükön, hogy magukban röhögnek a szemetek. Aztán újra kihagytak, és ez már magáért beszélt.

They didn't invite me. When I mentioned this matter, they didn't react, but I saw that they laughed amongst themselves, the shitbags. And then they left me out again, and it spoke for itself. (#14)

If one compares this description with example (6.4) above, it becomes evident that non-doing is clearly offensive due to its repeated nature, just as in the case of its counterpart.

It is pertinent to note that recurrence often appears as a salient issue in metadiscourse when victims recall destructive rituals such as non-doing, as in the following case:

(6.8)

Let's start from the beginning, however. Friday, was just a lazy day at work again. I finally, with the help of my boss, managed to get the man with the golfing issue to sign his settlement. And then I settled another case and made plans to settle yet another case. So, all in all, a good day on the job. So, I was in high spirits as I packed up my car and left for Vegas. The traffic was light and I made good time to my first stop to pick up two roommates. They wanted to eat, so I took them to get take out and gas up and off we went to pick up the last person. We picked the last person up and away we went. Now, the annoyance started. First, let me just point out, I don't mind driving the long distances. I don't mind if you sleep or eat in my car. I really just have two rules for these long drives – if you are going to be awake, entertain me or else go to sleep. Well, let me just say. Right from the pick ups – it was just jabber in Tagalog. Constant jabber in Tagalog. Which, let me point out, I don't speak. And the bits that were in English and I tried to join in – were ignored. And you might be thinking – well, maybe they couldn't hear me from the front, but trust me, *this was not the last time they just ignored me* [my emphasis] like I didn't just say anything. It was like I was a chauffeur. It was quite annoying. But, I thought, okay, just forget it and just listen to your music and drive these girls to Mammoth. They finally fell asleep.

...

So I gassed up (and let me point out again – the passengers had yet paid or even offered to pay for gas at this point). And away I went – slowing way down every time I got into town. Eventually we got there, and they all got out of my car – *and let me point out again* [my emphasis] – no one thanked me.

...

So, I go upstairs right away and I apologize to them very nicely. And what happens? *I get ignored again* [my emphasis].
(Retrieved from: <http://beachwhale.wordpress.com/2008/02/>)

This example is drawn from a blog, which describes the poster's bad experience with a group of female acquaintances whom she took on a snowboard tour in her car. In this case the targeted person did not let herself be victimised and the destructive ritual did not seem to have a devastating impact on her, perhaps partly because her relational history with "the normal" was short and partly because she was power equal with "the normal" (cf. Culpeper's argument on the interrelation between power difference and the effect of impoliteness in Section 6.3). However, example (6.8) neatly illustrates the importance of the practice of recurrence in metadiscourse: in this relatively brief section there are three references to the repeated nature of the abusive group's not responding; responding to the poster would have been the norm, in particular because she did a favour to the women.

6.3.2 Recurrent covert offence 反复隐性冒犯

Several researchers of impoliteness, most notably Kryk-Kastovsky (2006) in her study on Early Modern English court trials, argued that impoliteness can operate on both overt and covert levels. Overt impoliteness is direct as it is formalised (e.g. swearing), while covert impoliteness is indirect. According to Kryk-Kastovsky, in Early Modern English texts covert impoliteness is occasioned via three forms, namely various forms of address and other lexical items used in sarcastic ways, questioning strategies, and discourse markers such as *praythee*. Covert impoliteness can be captured in different settings. For example, Culpeper (2011a) cites the work of Holmes' (2000) study on workplace discourse, in which jocular abuse "often functions as a covert strategy for face-attack, a means of registering a veiled protest" (Culpeper 2011a: 215). Forms of humour seem to have an important role in covert abusive acts because, as Attardo (1994) argues, certain forms of humour inherently have some aggressive/exclusive vs cohesive/inclusive character.

Covert offence, in a similar way to some other forms of impoliteness that target the victim's identity as a member of "the normal", has the potential to become a ritual practice if it is repeatedly performed in a given group against the targeted victim, as the following extract from a newspaper illustrates:

(6.9)

WHEN does a practical joke cross the line to become bullying? This can be difficult to answer but the question should be one that businesses consider.

[...]

Greg Robertson, general counsel for Harmers Workplace Lawyers says bullying behaviour can arise when *perceivably harmless jokes* [my emphasis] get out of hand.

"What may have started as a fairly innocuous jibe, when *repeated or spread across an organisation* [my emphasis] it can wreak havoc on the targeted individual," he says.
(Retrieved from: <http://www.theaustralian.com.au/ battling-bullies-at-work/story-e6freqn6-1111117156319>)

As the solicitor interviewed in this news article explains, forms of destructive covert rituals such as jokes are dangerous because they are "perceivably harmless" (see example 6.11 below).[19] Although it is generally argued that there is a delicate balance between 'healthy' and destructive teasing (see e.g. Lytte 2007), once an action is "repeated or spread across an organization" – i.e. when it undergoes ritualisation – it gains a clear destructive function.

6 *Destructive Relational Rituals* 157

In terms of practical function, the main difference between ritual practices of non-doing and covert ritual offences is that the latter recurrently discredit the stigmatised person as one of "the normal" through making repeated soft attacks on her or him. It is again due to the recurrent performance value of the ritual practice that the victim is likely to realise their stigmatised position. In order to illustrate this point, let us refer to the following comic strip on workplace bullying:

(6.10)

Figure 6.1 Example 6.10: Ritual unrecognition

Forgetting someone's name could possibly be acceptable from a participant perspective in other contexts such as in a party at a large company where some people vaguely know each other. However, the situation is different in the case above, which represents a workplace meeting of a community of practice: in such a meeting, participants rightly suppose that their names are known by the others. Figure 6.1 represents the ritualistic nature of the practice of intentionally 'forgetting' names. First, although it is not clear whether this imaginary situation is a recurrent case or not, since it has been drawn from a website which displays examples of workplace bullying it is evident that this is a schematic – i.e. at least potentially ritualistic – way to destroy one's membership of the group of "the normal". Secondly, the practice here has a strong potential to become ritualistic because it is the boss who makes use of it, i.e. a person with the institutional right to discredit the employee as one of "the normal", as he animates the voice of the institution. Thirdly, the case above clearly reflects the performance value of the ritual. That is, instead of simply stating "Sorry, I forgot your name" the manager first makes a staged effort, by listing various possible names ("Keith,... I mean Dave, Phil, Nigel"). Making such an effort could perhaps be interpreted as a sign of goodwill in other cases, but in this interaction its destructive staged nature is clear, and it is made even more offensive by the explicitly rude utterance "whatever the heck your name is".

In terms of in/directness covert offence is in-between indirect non-doing and overt destructive rituals which will be analysed in the following section. That is, in this ritual practice there is a 'visible' act of recurrent covert offence, but this visible act is disguised as harmless, as the following example illustrates:

(6.11)

at a staff night out and after dinner we went to a bar and the Principal said, 'Come on, Trace, let's find you a man.' (Needless to say I am single);

(Retrieved from: <http://www.sheilafreemanconsulting.biz/case-studies.htm>)

Example (6.11) is drawn from an Australian schoolteacher's description of how she was bullied in her workplace. The Principal's utterance could represent 'collegial' teasing workplace humour, or jocular mockery as Haugh (2010) defines it. However, as it is part of the recurrent exclusion of the target from the group of "the normal", she perceives the destructive function, that is she contextualises this performance. Yet, there is little that this person could have done, not only because the Principal holds institutional power in an educational institution, but also because this ritual is disguised as humour and protesting against it would further weaken the victim's position, in a somewhat similar way to the phenomena studied in example (6.11) above and which will be raised again in the analysis of example (6.15). As Bloch et al. (2011) note about the act of abusive humour, jokes which disguise the hostile and punitive nature of the interaction make it difficult for the scapegoat to respond without demonstrating his or her 'lack' of humour.

6.3.3 Recurrent reference to the stigma 反复提及骂名

The most direct practice of destructive ritual is when the stigma is named. As research on this practice of destructive ritual has revealed, reference to stigma tends to operate through association, that is, there is an abstract stigmatised property which "the normal" name in the ritual act, and there is an associative relationship between this symbolic stigma and the victim's actual stigma. This is illustrated in the following example:

(6.12)

Bully Y'alright, metal mouth?

Nerd Yeah, just um... doing some homework.

Bully So you gonna do my homework as well then?

Nerd Um, I...

Bully I said, are you gonna do mine for me then?

Nerd You know I would, I've just got so much...

(*The bully grabs the nerd's chair and pushes him against the wall.*)
(Retrieved from: <http://www.scribd.com/doc/39648988/The-Bully-Script>)

This short literary text depicts an interaction between a bully and the victim who is represented as an isolated person. The bully uses "metal mouth" to address the victim; this common form of address[20] is a reference to the victim's braces. It is obvious that the stigmatised property in this case is not so much the visible physical stigma (even though according to Goffman (1963) any visible handicap can become stigma) but its symbolic implication to the relational network. That is, braces combined with the victim's 'nerdy' fondness to learn contradict the bully's (and his relational network's) ethos of 'coolness'.

As research on direct destructive ritual illustrates, in the majority of cases ritual operates vis-à-vis association: 38 out of 52 cases concern an associated stigma rather than direct stigma as in the following text, which describes Prince Harry's difficulties in the British army during his service in Iraq:

(6.13)

> Most people imagine that the life of a prince is quite privileged and pleasant, and although we're sure Prince Harry has his fair share of royal privileges, he's also gotten more than his fair share of taunting. The reason? His red hair. Although in America, red hair does not carry a stigma, in the UK, "gingers" like Harry are picked on for their colored hair and fair skin. Harry's army pals frequently call him the "Ginger Bullet Magnet," and have joked that they would buy ginger wigs to wear in Iraq, presumably to prevent insurgents from identifying the young prince.
> (Retrieved from: <http://www.onlinecolleges.net/2011/11/02/15-famous-successful-people-bullied-school/>)

This text was found on a website which describes stories of various celebrities who suffered in-group abuse. Prince Harry's situation is similar to that of a nerd in a school (cf. example 6.12): in a unit that fights on the front line his privileged social position, which is open to imply a sense of 'being spoilt', contradicts the ethos of toughness. In his case the physical stigmatised property is his red hair and fair skin, which make him a "Ginger Bullet Magnet", i.e. a soldier who is more disadvantaged and vulnerable than others (he will be fired on by Iraqis as they know he is the prince), and who has to be protected by his peers (hence the potentially offensive suggestion that the other soldiers "would buy ginger wigs to wear in Iraq"). The ritual nature of this offence is made clear by the author of this text, when they describe references to his "gingerness" as "frequent" ones.

However, association is not a precondition for direct destructive ritual practice to operate, as the remaining 14 cases in my data set illustrate. Practically any property such as racial origin – or a physical property as in example (6.4) above – can become the subject of destructive ritual practices.

The present section has overviewed the three types of destructive relational ritual practices, which have different degrees of in/directness. The discussion has so far represented these practices from the victims' perspectives, i.e. I have focused on their destructive effect. In what follows, let us examine the different perceptions from which destructive ritual practices can be described.

6.4 Different perceptions of ritual practices
对仪式实践的不同感知

As has already been commented upon in some detail, destructiveness is a relative value for two reasons. First, from a relational perspective the constructive function that destructive ritual practices potentially fulfil for "the normal" cannot be neglected. For instance, we could recall the following section of example (6.6):

4. ξvePorta   (07–30–2011)

Who cares? They don't have to talk to the random fanboys.
Just kidding, it's cause you're Canadian.

5. Wolfy   (07–30–2011)

Or it's probably the Canadian thing.

While both turns 4 and 5 function as answers to the stigmatised person's question, Wolfy also uses this response to express agreement with ξvePorta, i.e. the relationship between "the normal" is being enforced. And, relating becomes even more explicit in turns 10 and 11 of the same interaction:

10. Flying Mint Bunny (07–30–2011)

[…] I know I would ignore him after that..

11. Γ&#Megalodon24 (07–30–2011)

xD

Whilst this as a point does not need further explanation, it is pertinent to note that this constructive function also appears occasionally in metadiscourse on rituals. For example, a child who Menesini et al. (2003) interviewed about his leading role in abusive acts which are described as ritual in the present book noted that "I … feel great because I got the attention of other kids".

Secondly, destructive ritual practices seem to occasion more diverse evaluations than their constructive counterparts. As Section 6.4.1 will illustrate, destructive rituals are evaluated negatively both by the victim and also in public moral discourse. This is an important point to address here because in the anthropological literature, which does not usually concern itself with the destructive relational function of rituality (cf. Section 6.1), those ritual practices which have any potential destructive function, such as rituals of violence, are often approached from a diachronic perspective, as practices that are relationally constructive for the wider community in the long run. Although this is arguably an important point, the present study proposes a different uptake, by approaching destructive ritual practices from a 'lay' or community moral perspective, and focusing on the shame attached to these practices. Section 6.4.2 then approaches destructive ritual from the language users' perspectives, and argues that a ritual practice occasions positive or negative evaluations depending on the evaluator's relationship with the given act. It is obvious that for the stigmatised person these ritual practices are harmful, and therefore studying "the normal's" evaluations is more interesting. As the discussion thus far has shown, for members of "the normal" destructive ritual practices do not imply negative meaning, as they confirm the ethos of a relational network. However, the wider (societal) moral refusal of these practices studied in Section 6.4.1 occasions awareness that such positive evaluations are likely to be contested by others. That is, the shame value attached to destructive practices makes evaluations ambiguous, and the same ambiguity can be observed in the evaluations of those who are 'semi-participants' in a destructive ritual act.

6.4.1 Public evaluation of destructive rituals 对破坏性仪式的公众评价

Importantly, the potential constructive relational function of destructive ritual practices does not imply that they are similar to the constructive ritual practices studied in the previous chapters. In general, antisocial stigmatising is evaluated negatively by the public in various societies, as a result of which there are labels attributed to such practices such as 'bullying' in English, *ijime* in Japanese, *szivatás/csicskáztatás* in Hungarian, and so on.[21] That is, whilst destructive ritual practices can occasion different evaluations, mostly depending on one's relationship with the ritual, there is a general awareness about the moral inappropriateness of these practices. This is different from the evaluation of a constructive ritual, the practice of which is normative (it fulfils expectancies), i.e. it is unlikely that it is evaluated negatively, in particular by network insiders (see e.g. the case of 'disarmed' swear words in Chapters 2 and 5, which are potentially offensive for network outsiders but harmless to network insiders).

Historians like Muir (2005) and anthropologists like Schmidt and Schröder (2001) argue that in certain places and times certain ritual acts – which are described in the present framework as acts with potential destructive function – such as rituals of violence were and continue to be socially approved. Yet, whilst these ritual acts, such as the public humiliation of a stigmatised entity, are potentially destructive, scholars usually focus on the fact that these ritual acts were/are socially constructive. For example, Muir (2005: 33) provides the following account on the activities of the so-called 'youth abbeys', i.e. gangs of young men in medieval Europe:

> The activities of youth-abbeys could be highly ambiguous. Providing a rite of passage through the "dangerous" years that licensed rowdiness and even legitimated certain forms of violence, the abbeys also enforced community moral standards (especially with regard to sexual behavior) on others. In France they performed ritual charivaris and in Italy *mattinate* that humiliated couples whose marriages somehow failed to measure up to the community's standards...

However, previous research also makes two further points. First, destructive ritual practices were and continue to be *endured* rather than *supported* by the public, especially by those in power within a society whose voice counts as 'normative'. This is the reason behind the mechanism that certain abusive ritual practices, after some time, become prohibited and/or condemned. For example, in revisiting the history of 'youth abbeys' above, Muir also notes that after the medieval period their activities were outlawed:

> As authorities themselves abandoned ritual punishments, they became less tolerant of popular rites that led to disorder. Spaces and times that were once the priviliged place for the illicit gradually came under public regulation. The esplanades outside of town walls had been the locale for the brawls of youthful gangs and the turf of unregulated prostitutes who entertained clients in the full light of day. At night the streets of towns and cities became the dangerous territory of the young who escaped the control of adults and public authorities. [...] Throughout the early modern period governmental authorities strove to transform all open spaces into public property [...] Youth-abbeys [...] were delegitimated in town after town. (Muir 2005: 147)

Secondly, it is also important to note that those historical destructive ritual practices which are documented in historical sources seem to function against individuals and groups that are stigmatised on a social level, i.e. they did not function in an arbitrary way. It can be argued that societies imposed and continue to impose *restrictions* on destructive ritual practices.

Furthermore, it is pertinent to note that sources from various cultures suggest that people were and continue to be aware of the danger of what are defined here as destructive ritual practices in different periods and places. This is the reason why various historical educational materials give instructions to the reader as to how to avoid a certain in-group practice transforming into a destructive ritual. For example, a historical Chinese textbook for foreigners cites the following dialogue, in order to illustrate the importance of the difference between a joke and ritual abuse:

(6.14)
说：我的兄弟。你委实生得标致。果然风流。真个可爱。想杀了我。
答：你果然有心想我。你实在有心想我。你一嘴都是胡说。花言巧语。假意儿。骗别个罢了。你来骗我。
说：我果然想你。不是假话。我若是骗你。我就赌一个大大的咒。给你听么。
答：你赌来。
说：你听着我赌得明明白白的。若是糊涂。一点都不算的。
答：好好。你就赌来。
说：我若没有真心想你的。我那头发尾。登时生一个斗来大的疔疮。永世不得收口。流脓流血。烂到见骨。这个咒。大不大。狠不狠。
答：果然大。果然狠。这个咒。果然亏你赌。
说：不是。你教我赌么。我就照你嘴。赌给你听就是了。
答：你这个光棍好油嘴。我不和你讲。我要回家去了。
说：给我留留么。再坐一会儿罢。实在我真舍你不得的。
答：你舍我不得。你这一条毛巾。送我做记记。肯不肯。
说：怎么不肯呢。有更好的也肯。希在这一条毛巾。就不肯的道理。你要就拿去。
答：多谢多谢。
说：还有一句话讲。方才我有东西给了你表记。你如今有什么东西回答我呢。
答：我是没有什么给你的。你若是不愿意。你就把手巾拿回去罢了。谁要你的。
说：我的好兄弟。不要使性儿。会使性的人快老。我如今和你相量。你既没有东西回答我。你把头儿朝过来笑一笑。给我亲个嘴儿就罢了。
答：唉呀。这个人好醒醒。把口水弄得人家满嘴都是。
    得罪得罪。好朋友玩。不要生气。生气就不好玩了。
    我们后生的人。出来都是爱玩的。不曾见你这个人。玩得太刻薄了。
    是我不着了。如今赔个罪儿。不要恼了。

Statement You, young brother, are handsome, rich in talents and truly likable. I have missed your company.

Response You truly thought of me?! You are speaking nonsense, with these blandishments and hypocrisy. Fool someone else but not me!

Statement I truly was thinking of you, this is no lie. To prove that I do not try to fool you, I will take an oath in front of you!

Response Take it then!

Statement Bear witness that I make a clear oath. If it is unclear it shall not count.

Response All right, all right. Make the oath!

Statement If I did not truly think of you, let a huge furuncle grow atop my head in an instant! Let it never heal, let pus and blood flow from it, and let it rot until the bone is exposed! Is this oath big and ruthless enough?

Response It is big, it is ruthless, but, after all, this oath is made merely by *you*.

Statement But you bade me make the oath, I acted as you wished, and you were my witness!

Response You, ruffian, are a glib talker, I will not speak with you, I want to go home.

Statement Will not you stay for a while? Please remain seated. I truly loathe parting with you.

Response If you really loathe to part, give me this towel as a token of our friendship, would you?

Statement How could I refuse? If I had anything better I would also give it to you. How could I disagree to give you a towel! Take it if you wish.

Response My sincere thanks, my sincere thanks.

Statement But there is something: I just gave you a thing as a token of our friendship, so what do you give me in return?

Response I don't have anything for you! If you don't like this, take your towel back! Who wants your things!

Statement You, good brother, should not be headstrong. Those who are headstrong age quickly. Let me suggest this: if you have nothing to offer in return, turn your head and laugh at me, and give me a kiss.

Response Ha, this guy really is filthy! Wants to spit his saliva into another's mouth!

...

Do not take offence, do not take offence! When good friends mock each other you should not grow angry. If you get angry you spoil the game!

We youngsters enjoy jests, but I've never seen anyone who was as harsh in mocking as you.

I was at fault and I now apologise. Please do not be angry.
(Cited from Kádár 2011b: 82–5)

This textbook dialogue which prescribed normative behaviour makes it clear that recurrent ritualistic mocking should be disarmed by apologising, in order to prevent it developing into a destructive ritual practice.

To sum up, even though certain forms of rituals of violence were accepted in certain periods and places, we should be aware that destructive ritual practices per se were perhaps never formally endorsed in any society. Furthermore, if one observes morality books, behaviour manuals and other historical sources, as well as contemporary movements and legislation against destructive ritual practices, it becomes evident that in normative public discourse, destructive acts are condemned. Thus, we can conclude that destructive ritual, when recognised as such, attracts negative public evaluation.

6.4.2 Participant/onlooker perspectives 参与者/旁观者视角

The destructive character of a ritual becomes relative when one focuses on the perspective of participants and onlookers (i.e. people in the community who passively watch in-group ritual practices). "The normal" tend to reflect on their ritual practice positively (or, at least, non-negatively) both as the interaction is co-constructed and in retrospection, and onlookers who failed to restore the moral order by opposing the destructive practice, or who associate themselves with the ethos of the ritual practice, can also emphasise the 'harmlessness' of a given ritual practice.

6 Destructive Relational Rituals 167

In order to illustrate the interactional evaluations that a destructive ritual practice is likely to generate when it comes to "the normal", let us examine the following online thread, from the online fantasy game website League of Legends. Prior to the interaction depicted here, there was an incident (described as a 'locally coded' (in-group) racist slur by the stigmatised person, a Lithuanian, in turn 17 of example 6.15 below): the stigmatised person's acronym was changed without his consent to one that he found insulting. As becomes evident from the thread, although this person tried to protest and also requested other group members to use his proper acronym, this just led to a further destructive ritual about his name and personality. The present thread, which supposedly took place after he openly raised the possibility of taking legal advice, represents a noteworthy case. In the beginning of the interaction the destructive ritual continues, but when the stigmatised person (8 bit gunny is his new acronym, having changed it from '(31) Dogs' i.e. the acronym the player found insulting; his original acronym was DogTrainer) joins in and posts some threatening messages, most of the attackers switch to the ritual of ignoring the stigmatised (cf. Section 6.3.1) but a member of "the normal" decides to '(re)interpret' the ritual to the victim:

(6.15)

1. DD Seventh   (13–04–2011)

    I have recently seen a good DogTrainer, sadly he doesn't like it when I call him DogTrainer.
    Hence I'd like some community ideas on a name to give to my DogTrainer.
    Ideas?

2. Vektro   (13–04–2011)

    Tron Day-ner(d)

3. x1ve   (13–04–2011)

    CatCooker. very chinese tho ∧_∧

4. A Random Mop   (13–04–2011)

    PigPeddler
    RhinoRustler
    GoatGuardian

5. Pettzon   (13–04–2011)

   LiceBreeder

6. Moonwhisp   (13–04–2011)

   Master'o'lol-thread
   Or perhaps something more similar to DogTrainer:
   PuppyConductor
   And all this thread needs to win, is having a link to it's inspiration. Sadly, that might be perceived as offensive by someone... ☺

7. SHmklV   (13–04–2011)

   MrBiches

8. wlmins   (13–04–2011)

   PhallusMasseuse

9. 8 bit gunny   (13–04–2011)

   i like the last one – MrBiches

10. Moonwhisp   (13–04–2011)

    Really, well in that case.
    I hereby dub thee: PhallusMasseuse. :P

11. 8 bit gunny   (13–04–2011)

    that's not the one i liked
    [...]

12. oneFive   (13–04–2011)

    how he leaves you with the name 31 dogs this is so funny haha anyways dude calm down dont you find it funny too ? if you sue them pls make a video documentation :_)

13. 8 bit gunny   (13–04–2011)

    ill try to document as much as i can, i already sent multiple emails to different riot contact addresses and ill see witch one replies to me fastest

14. Moonwhisp   (13-04-2011)

In your search for a new glorious nickname, I came up with another suggestion.
You could be:
TheArtistFormerlyKnownAsDogTrainer.
Come on. What do you think? ☺

15. 8 bit gunny   (13-04-2011)

further mocking just provided me with further evidence, im not encouraging you, but thank you

16. Moonwhisp   (13-04-2011)

Does this mean you seriously can't see the entertainment value in this whole affair?
I sincerely hope that's not the case.
[…]

17. 8 bit gunny   (13-04-2011)

After the thread was closed, i didn't receive even single 1 reply in my ticket, they just ignore me, again. And i find as much amusement from being called "a dog", as a black guy finds from being called "a niger". Im curently discussing with my laywer, on what exactly did mister Serif meant by changing my name from DogTrainer, to 31 dogs, to me personaly it sounded like he was targeting Lithuanians as a bunch, saying that we are all dogs

(Retrieved from: <http://euw.leagueoflegends.com/board/showthread.php?t=166637&page=3>)

In turns 1–8 the ritual develops in a default manner, i.e. different members of the group post insulting comments as they play with the stigmatised person's acronym. In turn 1 DD Seventh opens the topic as he refers to the victim's recent protest ("sadly he doesn't like it when I call him DogTrainer") against changing the acronym "DogTrainer" to "(31) dogs". This opening, which is a theatric (mimetic) performance, as all in-group members seem to know about this event, is an encouragement for other members of "the normal" to engage in the ritual practice. This is also reinforced by the style of the utterance, e.g. DD Seventh refers to the victim in a patronising form as "*my* [author's emphasis]

DogTrainer". In response, various insulting proposals are suggested, perhaps most salient of which (from an analytic perspective) is that of Moonwhisp in turn 6 where he notes "And all this thread needs to win, is having a link to it's inspiration. Sadly, that might be perceived as offensive by someone... ☺". This message:

- reflects the poster's awareness that the stigmatised person openly protested previously against the stigma,
- represents the ongoing destructive ritual as a humorous one, and
- also positions the victim's *anticipated* protest as invalid.

In turn 9 the stigmatised person joins the discussion. At first he seems to accept one of the derogatory acronyms "MrBiches" (that is Mr Bitches, a person who is 'bitching', i.e. complains without any valid reason). It might be that at this point he tries to join "the normal" in a self-mocking way in order to improve his in-group situation. But irrespective of the goal of this utterance it is just oil on the fire, and in the next turn Moonwhisp offers him *another* one of the offensive acronyms proposed before, "PhallusMasseuse", i.e. he makes it clear that the stigmatised status is maintained. When the stigmatised person attempts to protest, his remark is not accepted.

The next point of particular analytic interest is what is denoted as turn 12 here: oneFive addresses the victim by proposing that he accept the offensive acronym: "how he leaves you with the name 31 dogs this is so funny haha anyways dude calm down dont you find it funny too ? ? if you sue them pls make a video documentation :_)". While this utterance seems to provide an opportunity to the stigmatised person to communicate with "the normal" and it includes an emoticon, in fact it simply encourages him to accept the stigma generated by the acronym without further protesting, and also it represents him as a person who overreacts to things – this is what Harré et al. (2009) call "negative positioning". Furthermore, it mockingly refers to the victim's previous or supposed intention to sue the gaming website, by proposing to make a "video documentation". This is obviously not possible as it is an online interaction, i.e. the stigmatised person is positioned again as someone who 'should not be taken seriously' (unlike members of "the normal"). In turn, the stigmatised person responds in a menacing way, stating that he has already started to collect documents on the abuse he suffered.

This is a turning point, as from here "the normal" ignore the stigmatised person, maybe because they sense that this matter has turned serious, but it is more likely that they switch to the ritual practice of non-doing (see Section 6.3.1 above) – or perhaps both these motivations operate jointly here. However, a member of "the normal", *Moonwhisp*, continues the interaction for a few turns. In turn 14 he attempts to disarm the in-group ritual practice, this time by proposing a less offensive acronym as in turn 10; note, however, that he continues to uphold the destructive discourse, as he represents the other's complaint as "your search for a new glorious nickname", i.e. he seems to position the other as a non-serious person. When in turn 15 the stigmatised person responds, *Moonwhisp evaluates* the group's ritual practice as a humorous one, by posting "Does this mean you seriously can't see the entertainment value in this whole affair?" Following this, after a brief exchange *Moonwhisp* joins the others as he chooses to ignore 8 bit gunny, and the stigmatised person sends in two messages, which remain unanswered. His last message, in turn 17, is of interest because it represents the victim's evaluation of the ritual practice, which, unsurprisingly, is completely different from that of *Moonwhisp* in turn 15.

To sum up, the present example illustrates that the evaluations which destructive rituals occasion, differ significantly from their constructive counterparts (see above), i.e. their performance is evaluated mainly depending on one's interactional position. Putting it simply, in terms of participant perspectives, the evaluation which a ritual occasions seems to depend on whether one is the stigmatiser or the stigmatised.[22] However, *Moonwhisp*'s evaluation in example (6.15) also illustrates that evaluations are influenced by the social shame that destructive ritual practices evoke – this awareness might be the reason behind the euphemistic labelling of the act.

It is pertinent to note that the practice of euphemistic labelling in terms of evaluation seems to be widespread. As was noted in the introduction to this chapter, destructive rituals can more often be captured in the form of retrospective accounts, than in ongoing (real-time) interactions. Therefore, the evaluations the researcher is able to retrieve often represent the observer's perspective because, in a sense, even those who originally participated in an interaction become semi-observers when they narrate and reflect on an event retrospectively. There is, however, a fundamental gap between the perspectives of those who participated in a ritual event – and who consequently represent an act from the insider's (emic) perspective – and those who evaluate a ritual event from the outsider's (etic) moral perspective (see Pike 1967 on this distinction, as well as Chapter 1). The data studied suggests that network insider evaluations do not fundamentally differ, irrespective of whether they occur in interaction or in retrospective accounts, and they are equally positive and/or euphemistic. This is also supported by psychological research: for example, Bandura's (1991) noteworthy study on aggressive children's reasoning for recurrent (i.e. potentially ritual) abusive acts shows that they often label their acts in a euphemistic way ("Just a bit of fun"), quite similarly to what we could observe in example (6.15). This euphemistic labelling reflects awareness of the fact that their practices are regarded as morally unacceptable by the public.

Furthermore, onlookers – i.e. members of the in-group who do not actively participate in the performance of destructive ritual evaluations – also tend to evaluate these rituals euphemistically, as 'harmless'. As the examples in Sections 6.3.1 and 6.3.2 illustrate, from an outsider perspective ritual stigma, especially its indirect forms, may seem to be less dramatic than, for example, swearing (although swearing itself can function as a ritual practice triggering stigma), and occasionally it requires some insider explanation to understand what is going on in a ritual act, as in the case of examples (6.7) and (6.8) above. A possible harmless event can be devastating from the stigmatised in-group member's emic (in-group) perspective. That is, it can work the other way around as, for example, in-group banter which could potentially harm the external observer but tends to be harmless for in-group members (see Culpeper 1996). Yet, despite the indirectness of these ritual practices, once outsiders understand their function they are likely to evaluate them negatively. However, the situation seems different in my data when it comes to onlookers who are passive insiders. This point can be illustrated by the following account provided by an acquaintance of mine:

(6.16)

Amikor ezek történtek nem gondoltam volna, hogy amivel a srácok poénkodtak az *ennyire* megalázó neki. Csak amikor évekkel később e-mailben elküldött mindenkit a francba egy osztálytalálkozó előtt, akkor jöttem rá, hogy baromira utálta a helyzetet. ... Pedig ezek csak kisebb szopatások voltak.

When these things happened I didn't realise that the jokes made by these guys were *so* humiliating for him. Only when years later he sent the whole class to hell before an anniversary meeting did I realise that he hated this situation like hell. ... Although these were just smallish slurs.

Such evaluations accord with that of active members of "the normal", and they seem to be motivated by the awareness and anticipation that even being a passive onlooker is problematic if an event is morally objected to by the public. That is, people in retrospect may re-evaluate their historically situated understanding of the given act, as might be the case in example (6.16). This is a tentative claim, which is only supported by the fact that outsiders react differently to such practices in retrospect.

To sum up, although members of "the normal" tend to evaluate their practices positively, these evaluations reflect some awareness of a wider negative social evaluation.

6.5 Summary 结语

The present chapter has set out to examine destructive in-group relational rituals. It has been argued that examining these ritual acts is significant, not only because they have elaborate practices, as Section 6.3 illustrated, but also because the examination of destructive ritual practices brings the interactants' perceptions and evaluations into relational ritual theory. In the case of constructive ritual acts evaluation is not so significant because in default these normative acts accord with normative moral expectations within a group (cf. Chapter 1). Evaluation seems

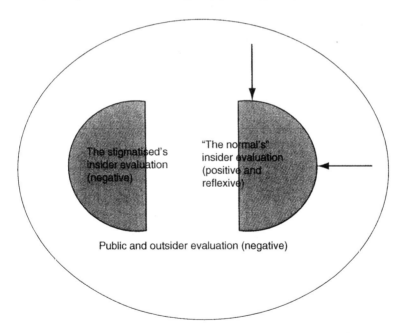

Figure 6.2 Different perceptions and evaluations of destructive rituals

to become important when it comes to destructive rituals because of their dual characteristic, i.e. they perform a constructive relational function for "the normal" (i.e. they are perceived positively) and they are generally evaluated negatively in wider public discourse. These different perceptions are illustrated in Figure 6.2.

As this chapter has argued, "the normal's" evaluation – which can include the evaluation of both active performers of a ritual act and that of passive onlookers – does not take place in a vacuum but tends to reflect awareness of wider social evaluation of the act (arrows in Figure 6.2 stand for this influence).

After having concluded the exploration of relational rituals by looking at both their constructive and destructive functions, in the following chapter I will summarise the framework elaborated in the present book, and propose some areas for future research.

7
Conclusion
结论

7.1 The framework 分析框架

The present book has proposed a discursive and relational framework of ritual, by focusing on in-group ritual and its relationship with other types of rituality. I have elaborated a relational interpretation of ritual, which approaches interpersonal relating from a discursive perspective, and thus captures ritual by focusing on different interactional practices and expectations. This approach aims to depart from describing ritual from the analyst's specific first-order outsider (etic) perspective as much as possible by proposing a broad second-order concept of rituality (cf. Chapter 1), and to evidence relational practices and expectations by analysing interactional data and interviews. Thus, the present analytic framework incorporates the interactants' understandings of rituality in a specific way: whilst it disregards popular understandings and normative definitions of rituality per se when describing relational rituals (nevertheless, such definitions are made use of to describe normative values associated with rituality, cf. Chapter 4), it examines the interactants' discursive behaviour and retrospective views on interaction. While supposedly no framework can capture all aspects of rituality, and the present one is no exception, this model has proved to be apt to describe the relationship-forming interactional effect of ritual behaviour.

Approaching ritual through this model has shown that our language use in relational networks is considerably ritualised, not only in certain institutions (cf. Chapter 4) but also in non-hierarchical settings; this questions the validity of the concept of 'deritualisation' (cf. Chapter 1). If one describes rituals using a narrow definition proposed by extant research (cf. Section 1.1.1 in Chapter 1), it may seem that language rituals have a marginal role in interpersonal relating. This accords with popular representations of ritual phenomena. In modern Western popular culture, ritual is often referred to as a 'void' phenomenon or 'formality' (cf. Chapters 1 and 4). For example, in the British newspaper *The Telegraph* actress Angelina Jolie described her marriage with Brad Pitt by stating "Usually people fall in love and everything revolves around the *ritual* [my emphasis] of marriage, children are an afterthought."[1] Even in contexts where ritual is portrayed positively it tends to be associated with certain demarked acts (cf. Chapter 1), as John Lennon's words might illustrate: "Rituals are important. Nowadays it's hip not to be married. I'm not interested in being hip." Furthermore, the situation is not significantly different in cultural contexts in which ritual tends to be regarded positively in default, like in Chinese culture. For example, a recent, somewhat nationalistic, website described Chinese rituals in the following way:

(7.1)

礼仪是一个人乃至一个民族、一个国家文化修养和道德修养的外在表现形式，是做人的基本要求。中华民族自古以来就非常崇尚礼仪，号称"礼仪之邦"。

Ritual represents the cultural and moral standing of people, nations and countries, and it is the basis of our humanity. The Chinese nation advocates ritual since ancient times, and [our land] has been called "the country of rituals".

(Retrieved from: <http://edu.pcbaby.com.cn/resource/heibanbao/wmly/1210/1146171.html>)

Whilst such descriptions differ from their Western counterparts in the importance they attribute to ritual, popular accounts seem to accord across cultures in that they represent ritual as a socially conventional phenomenon. An advantage of the relational model is that it sheds light on the operation of rituals beyond this socially conventionalised level, hence putting ritual back in its proper place in interpersonal relating.

The second-order approach proposed in this book is broad enough to accommodate theoretical insights from various disciplines. As Chapter 4 has argued, relational rituals are represented differently in certain areas such as anthropology and linguistics, and in others like psychology, and it is essential to avoid restricting the relational framework to the way in which ritual is traditionally understood in the former group of disciplines. The comparison of the four relational ritual types has illustrated that covert, personal, in-group and social rituals are types of a larger relational phenomenon, as they share many relational properties.

The relational approach can also blend historical and contemporary pragmatic inquiries. As Chapter 3 has shown by the analysis of two case studies, in-group ritual operates in considerably similar ways in spatially/culturally and diachronically distant contexts (similarity, however, does not entail any claim for diachronic or cross-cultural universality, cf. Section 7.2). Furthermore, the relational perspective is suitable for clarifying the relationship between ritual and other pragmatic phenomena – most significantly, politeness (cf. Chapter 2) and impoliteness (cf. Chapter 6). This marking of 'borders' is needed because, as Chapter 2 has argued, the ritual–politeness interface is often treated relatively vaguely in the field of politeness research (see also Section 7.2). Along with elaborating the ritual–politeness interface, the relational theory adopted in this book, drawing on sociology and organisation studies (cf. Chapter 2), has positioned ritual within the larger phenomenon of schematic/conventionalised language use, instead of describing it as an isolated phenomenon. Finally, analysis of interactionally (co-)constructed relational ritual practices brings cognitive insights into ritual research (Chapter 5), such as the bidirectional affective effect of ritual performance and the potentiality of recognition.

The present framework has implications not only for ritual research proper but also for discursive pragmatics, in particular politeness research. In various chapters of this book I have referred to politeness and impoliteness, and their interface with rituality, in order to define relational rituals. However, this relationship can be approached the other way around, by observing certain practices of politeness from a relational ritual perspective. In order to illustrate how the relational ritual framework can be operationalised in other areas, it is pertinent here to refer to an ongoing project that I have been conducting. This cross-cultural ritual research project involves the five target languages of English, Hungarian, Standard Arabic, Japanese and Chinese, and its findings will expand on the scope of the present book, which has not ventured into cross-cultural (and intercultural) research in spite of relying on multilingual data.

7.1.1 The cross-cultural (and intercultural) ritual project[2]
跨文化仪式研究课题

Following Sachiko Ide's (1989) work, an important notion in cross-cultural politeness research is the so-called 'volition' and 'discernment' dichotomy. Ide elaborated this concept as a critique of the universalistic model of Brown and Levinson (1987), by arguing that the universal model is problematic primarily because it relies on the idea that politeness comes into existence when the speaker flouts conversational maxims through the means–ends reasoning of individuals (i.e. as speakers use language in a strategic way, in order to trigger a certain inference associated with politeness). Drawing from the Japanese native notion of *wakimae* (lit. discernment), Ide (1989) argues that in Japanese one's behaviour is judged to be polite when one discerns the appropriate communal norm that applies in the situation, and this overrides individual rationality. This differs from Western practices of politeness, which operate through the means–ends reasoning of individuals, defined as 'volition' by Ide.

As Kádár and Mills (2013, forthcoming) argue, this notion raises various issues from the perspective of the critical theorisation of politeness. From the viewpoint of the present framework, the volition–discernment concept seems to be problematic because it describes cross-cultural differences in terms of politeness by implicitly mixing ritual and politeness. Ide's (1989) work – and, in fact, various other cross-cultural communication theories which adopt this concept (including recent ones such as Tao 2010 and Holmes 2012) – tends to use discernment as an umbrella term to cover socially conventionalised, and often ritualistic, language use. Volition, on the other hand, is often illustrated either by conventionalised but not ritualistic examples, or emergent non-conventionalised interactions. It is illustrative to refer to Ide's (1989) now 'classic' example of discernment:

(7.2)

> * *Sensei-wa kore-o yonda.*
> 'The professor read this'
>
> *Sensei-wa kore-o o-yomi-ni-natta.*
> 'The professor read[Hon] this'

(adapted from Ide 1989: 227)

Both sentences above are references to a lecturer's activity (i.e. that he has read some material) from students. However, the first example is claimed to be improper in Japanese communication, irrespective of context, because students are expected to use an elevating honorific inflection when referring to a lecturer, who is their superior (i.e. *oyomi-ni-natta* instead of *yonda*), as seen in the second example. In other words, in Japanese the use of honorifics and other formal forms is not necessarily bound to what universalistic frameworks of politeness describe as rational individual choices in relation to achieving certain goals or ends, but rather to patterns normatively expected in certain situations and hierarchical relationships. According to Ide, then, the Japanese tend to perceive the so-called rationality of politeness as a means to fulfil communal rather than individual strategic goals, even if these two goal types coincide.

In terms of rituality, the 'appropriate' second utterance in example (7.2) represents ritualistic talk about a respected person, in which the normative usage of honorifics displays a mimetic relational activity (theatric display of one's reverence). This, however, raises questions regarding the comparability of such data with predominantly non-ritualised interactions. It seems that Ide (1989) places the interface between social ritual and politeness under the umbrella of discernment and contrasts this interface with non-ritualistic politeness. Failing to define the relationship between politeness and ritual (cf. Chapter 2) leaves the notion of discernment open to criticisms such as Pizziconi (2011) and Kádár (2007a); critiques argue that discernmental language usage is often not intrinsically polite, as it can be utilised in various contexts such as humour, offence, etc. On the other hand, as Kádár and Mills (2013, forthcoming) note, Ide's (1989) findings cannot, and should not, be completely dismissed, as they point to an important area where cross-cultural differences manifest themselves: in certain languages such as Japanese and Arabic socially conventionalised rituals seem to be more saliently present than in other languages. The reason why Ide's framework intermixes social ritual and politeness is likely to be that social rituals are often represented as normative 'etiquette', which triggers their association with politeness. The relational ritual typology proposed in this book offers an alternative to capturing cross-cultural relational differences: instead of contrasting the interface of social ritual and politeness with non-ritualistic polite interactions, it seems to be more productive to compare the salience of different types of ritual across cultures.

As early results of the cross-cultural project seem to indicate, the relational differences that the notion of discernment and volition imply are not so much related to politeness per se[3] but rather to rituality. Furthermore, these cross-cultural differences in relational rituality seem tendentially to be more typological than functional, i.e. they reside in differences of importance devoted to various types of relational rituality. In cultures such as Arabic and Japanese, social rituals seem to count as normative in a broader range of interactional contexts than for example in English and Hungarian. Also, in the dominating ideologies of these 'discernment' cultures, social ritual practices tend to be represented as key elements of 'correct' language usage (in Japan, for example, many social ritual practices are part of general education). Thus, whilst social rituals are used in every culture – and the understanding of 'ritual' seems to be limited to social ritual, irrespective of cultural context (cf. Section 7.1) – it is likely that in certain cultures social rituals are ideologically more significant than in others (see also previous research such as Fakhr-Rohani 2005, Okamoto 1999, Byon 2012).

This ideological dimension seems to be an important reason why in 'discernment cultures' social ritual practices are used in settings which do not necessitate deference. This point is illustrated by the following extract from Standard Arabic data collected by a participant of the cross-cultural project:

(7.3)

Anwar Hathi [...] Allkhubza [...]
Here you are [...] the bread [...]

Malik Allah ebarik feek wa yarham waldaik (.) Rabna yohfdak wa ma yihrimna menak
Allah bless you and mercy be upon your parents (.) Allah protect you and keep you around us

This extract is cited from a dinner table conversation of four close friends; one of the interactants, Malik, performs a ritual blessing as a constructive social relational ritual, in order to thank his friend Anwar in an elaborate way (from the researcher's perspective), for bringing various dishes. The context of this interaction would not occasion polite discernment in Ide's (1989) sense: as no hierarchy is concerned here and the conversation is generally informal, and the interactants are not meant to be deferential to each other. This indicates that in cultures like Arabic social rituals tend to be regarded by many as an integral part of constructive in-group relational behaviour.

The ideological importance devoted to social rituals does not imply that in-group relational rituals are not important in these cultures: they are sometimes less noticeable from an observer's perspective, due to the ideological salience of social rituals (on this issue, see Pan and Kádár 2011). For example, the following extract illustrates that in cultures such as Arabic social rituals may transform into in-group rituals, in a similar way as in other cultures like Hungarian or English (cf. Chapter 4). This anecdotal account was supplied by a Libyan colleague who collected example (7.3) and it occurs here in a slightly edited form.

(7.4)
> I remember one of my friends used to address me as 'my respected lady' when we first met. Later when our friendship developed to a stronger and closer relationship, whenever we remembered this highly deferential form of address, we laughed. That is to say, this phrase became like a code which indicated our mutual understanding.

Whilst 'my respected lady' (Saidati Alfadila) is usually associated with social ritual practices, this form has a specific in-group implication here, rooted in the network's relational history.

In cultures which emphasise 'volition', relational ritual seems to be a less salient issue in normative language ideology. Note that this is a preliminary finding and further evidence will have to be collected to substantiate this claim. However, previous anthropological research such as Forand (2002) indicates that ritual and language ideology are more interrelated in cultures which Ide (1989) describes as 'discernment cultures' than in others. While people tend to be educated in 'proper' constructive ritual behaviour in every culture, in non-discernment cultures social ritual tends to be ideologically less important than in discernment ones: it is restricted to certain institutional settings which necessitate a formal style of expression, such as courtrooms (cf. Harris 1984, 1995, Archer 2011), formal business meetings (cf. Vergaro 2002) and certain political settings (cf. Bendix 1992, Bennett 1980).

The project thus suggests that contrasting cultures on the basis of the concept of discernment poses problems, and it seems fruitful to refocus research of this phenomenon on rituality. Yet, we should not simply revisit the target of research, as we also need to consider how to capture cross-cultural differences; taking a discursive pragmatic perspective implies that the analyst should avoid making prescriptive claims about culture-specific relational behaviour. Instead, in order to capture cultural socio-pragmatic diversity, we need to compare *ritual tendencies*, that is, describe a culture according to the way in which it ideologises ritual, and compare findings with the practices of a wide range of relational networks.

The operation of ritual tendencies can be illustrated by Figure 7.1. The diagonal line is meant to illustrate the claims that (a) the normative importance of social vs in-group ritual differs across cultures, and (b) this is a relative value, which a discursive theory should not attempt to impose prescriptively.

182 *Relational Rituals and Communication*

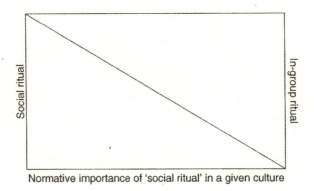

Figure 7.1 Difference of normative ritual types across cultures

7.2 Looking ahead 研究展望

To sum up, the relational approach opens up new research vistas both within and outside narrowly defined ritual research. The present book has laid the theoretical foundation for further explorations, but there is much work to be done in ritual research.

For example, although the present book has provided an interdisciplinary analytical framework, by drawing on findings of fields such as anthropology and linguistics, as well as psychology and education studies, research of relational ritual should integrate results from further disciplines, which consider ritual as significant. Disciplines such as economics (e.g. Hugh-Jones and Reinstein 2012) provide insights into rituality from perspectives that are rarely discussed in social, linguistic or anthropological inquiries.

Previous experience indicates that theories that fail to depart from culturally based conceptualisations unnecessarily limit the understanding of relational rituals. This, however, does not mean that we should not give due consideration to the ways in which historical and contemporary scholars from various cultural backgrounds have theorised and continue to theorise rituality (even though some awareness is needed in such an undertaking, as the terminological discussion in Chapter 6 has illustrated). In particular, we should extend current inquiries to historical native conceptualisations of rituality: lying somewhere between scientific and folk-theoretic understandings of rituality is what Kádár (2007b) terms "proto-scientific" research. This research arose in the work of scholars in the past where ritual behaviour was studied, not systematically in its own right, but rather as just one part of a more holistic record of customs and philosophical beliefs. In certain historical cultures such as the Chinese there is a long proto-scientific history of studying ritual (in particular ritualised politeness) for educational or moral purposes (defined as *lixue* 礼学 i.e. rituality research). Even though such theories inevitably lack the methodological and terminological systematicity of their modern counterparts, they are invaluable as sources of understanding of rituality that go beyond folk theorising. Such conceptualisations have considerably more to offer for an understanding of cross-cultural ideological differences in terms of rituality (see Section 7.1.1 above). Involving such native conceptualisations in the scope of research is in accordance with the objective of elaborating a broad theoretical view, which can accommodate various theories and perceptions of ritual (cf. Chapter 1 and Section 7.1).

There are several formal properties of ritual acts which should be revisited from relational and discursive perspectives. Such properties include, for example, ritual repetition, which has been noted briefly in the discussion of covert rituals in Chapter 4. As anthropologists such as Taylor (1994) argue, some ritual acts come into existence not only by recurrence but also through discursive repetition. A similar phenomenon has been identified in research on acts of offering in certain cultures (e.g. Gu 1990, Kádár 2012b), which gain their ritual function through repetition. An important task for future research is to describe these phenomena from a discursive angle, and to model the underlying schemata of these practices.

Along with focusing on the use of ritual within certain networks, discursive research on relational ritual should address ritual exchange *between* networks. If we return to the Durkheimian ([1912] 1954) interpretation of ritual, it is evident that its function as survival strategy is twofold: it aids the individual in shaping her or his relationship within a network, but also aids networks in avoiding conflict and working out relationships with other networks by exchanging rituals (see more e.g. in Traube 1986). Thus, cross-network ritual relating is a key area to explore, and a micro-level analysis can serve as a starting point for intercultural ritual research.

We should also aim to capture qualitative differences between the ritual practices of past and present (cf. Chapter 1). In such an undertaking we should utilise the relational framework and adopt rigorous methodological principles. Instead of simply contrasting social ritual practices in historical and contemporary times, it would be reasonable to compare both social and in-group ritual practices, in data which reflects the interactants' interactional (co)construction of ritual practices. In fact, there are various overlapping issues between cross-cultural and historical ritual research: for example, various studies such as Jucker's (2010) work represent diachronic differences in terms of relating through the discernment–volition dichotomy (cf. Section 7.1). Therefore, re-examining discernment and volition through the relational ritual theory proposed in this book could also be utilised in comparative, diachronic–synchronic research on ritual.

This pilot study has developed a roadmap by which we might more effectively and fruitfully navigate the field in the future. It has radically departed from traditional approaches to ritual, in order to integrate rituality into discursive research on language usage, hence filling an important gap in the field. Ritual research has been left behind in pragmatics, and within ritual research proper, relationality has remained largely untouched. The present book has revitalised ritual research by showing that ritual is a key relational phenomenon to study, and that in order to capture it we need to go beyond traditional paradigms, challenge theoretical understandings in a self-reflexive way, and undertake interdisciplinary research. I am not suggesting that in order to progress we entirely dispense with traditional anthropological and linguistic models of rituality: as this book has illustrated, many elements of these works can be used in the relational theory proposed in this book. The framework developed here offers, I hope, a way forward in pursuit of an ever more comprehensive and nuanced understanding of relational rituality, which is a fascinating aspect of interpersonal communication.

Notes 注释

1 Introduction

1. Note that such popular representation of ritual is not only present in literary pieces but also in other genres; for example, web search indicates that many blogs tend to represent ritual either as a religious phenomenon or a ceremony (as a representative example it is worth visiting the blogs of marriage officiants such as <http://www.elisabethcoffey.com/articles/chaotic.html>). On popular interpretations of ritual see Chapter 5.
2. Note that the present framework approaches construction of interpersonal relationships through a two-way distinction, by focusing on the construction and destruction of interpersonal relationships. This differs, to some extent, from some recent studies on relationality – most significantly, Arundale (2010) – which make a three-way distinction between supportive, threatening and stasis foms of "facework". Whilst I certainly agree with the validity of this categorisation, I distinguish between 'constructive' and 'destructive' ritual acts because I aim to relate my framework to linguistic im/politeness research; as I will argue in various chapters of this book, im/politeness and rituality have an important interface but they are not inherently related. The labels 'constructive' and 'destructive' are meant to describe this relationship, i.e. constructive is the ritual equivalent of politeness and destructive of impoliteness; in this categorisation of behaviour the maintaining/stasis mode is regarded as part of constructive behaviour.
3. I intentionally use 'relational ritual' instead of Goffman's (1967) term 'interpersonal ritual', in order to illustrate that the present framework has a post-Goffmanian scope.
4. It is illustrative to observe the frequency of metapragmatic discourse on 'empty' rituals. For example, whereas a web search as such is not suitable for quantitative research, it is remarkable to see that a Google web search on 'empty ritual' retrieves some 123,000 hits (the search was made on 28 November 2011).
5. The following chapters will provide extensive references, so it is enough here to mention a few works – which I regard as key publications – as examples: see Bell (1992, 1997), Geertz (1973) and Donald (1991) for anthropology, Bax (2004, 2010a, b) for linguistics, Goffman (1967) for sociology, Muir (2005) for history, Huizinga ([1938] 1955) for game theory and Marks (1987) for psychology.
6. See for example Eckert and Wenger (2005), in which the unit of community of practice is used in a broader sense.
7. For example, various secret societies operating in East Asia during the early twentieth century and earlier, 'borrowed' and altered overt social linguistic and non-linguistic rituals, and often continued to use these when the 'originals' had already lost their significance in public life. For example,

ter Haar's (1998: 152–6) study on secret society rituals mentions that secret societies reserved old religious ritual practices which have disappeared on the social level. Many such secret society rituals are transitional or intermediary: although they are not, strictly speaking, actual in-group rituals – since they are purposely 'codified' – they are nevertheless 'alien', in the sense of incomprehensible, to outsiders.

8. The notions of 'group' and 'grid' aim to describe social organisation across cultures. 'High group' refers to a social structure in which a high degree of collective control is practised, whereas a society with 'low group' culture values individual self-sufficiency. In a 'high grid', societal forms of stratification in roles and authority are durable, whereas a 'low grid' society values a more egalitarian ordering.
9. As Bax (2010b: 77) notes, the concept of deritualisation originates in the work of the sociologist Max Weber.
10. An exception is Kyriakidis (2007); however, this book describes these perspectives in a relatively simplistic way, by limiting their description to etic and emic (i.e. the first-order and second-order perspectives are left unmentioned).
11. Reliance on different perspectives implies that in certain analyses we need to go beyond the narrow-sense speaker–hearer dyad, by including e.g. bystanders and overhearers. While various chapters of this book will illustrate this point, we will refer here the following extract:

    D   megyünk apóka
    N   mi az az apóka
    A   hehe
    D   shall we go little old man
    N   what is old chap (lit. little old man)
    A   heh-heh

    This conversation took place between me (D), my father (A) and my daughter (N); I uttered the sentence *Megyünk apóka?* (Shall we go, little old man?) to my daughter. By using this form I re-evoked a ritual, which is rooted in our family history. That is, the father of my childhood friend, who was known for not being an authoritative parent, used to apply this sentence to attempt to persuade my friend, mostly in vain, to go home when he visited us. This form has been taken up by my father and me as a humorous relational ritual, i.e. often when my father wanted to make me go somewhere, he performed this ritual sentence, which then not only served as a request but it also humorously evoked the hopeless attempts of my friend's father to persuade my friend to leave. In the interaction above, I uttered this sentence to my daughter directly, but in fact it was more addressed to my father. It is thus understandable that while my daughter was wondering about the meaning implied here, my father grinned.
12. "[H]istoricity in general (and related social ethos)" refers to the case of social ritual acts which take place among interactants without relational history. It can be argued that in such situations a ritual practice forms a relationship between people because it re-evokes certain (in default: similar) feelings.
13. Note that such 'inventions' of relational networks can show much similarity with each other, cf. Chapter 3.

14. In accordance with the proposal of González et al. (1998), in the present book I use the terms 'affective' and 'emotive' separately. As González et al. (1998) argue, "Whereas the emotion is an internal individual response which informs of the survival probabilities that every concrete situation offers, affection is a process of social interaction between two or more organisms." The relational effect of ritual practices is thus referred to as affection rather than emotivity, and the latter term will be reserved for cases when we study the effect of ritual on the individual.
15. In Hungarian *anyád* can either function as a reference to the other's mother or as a swear word, and one needs to rely on contextual and prosodic clues to properly interpret this form.
16. Evaluation here refers to the hearer's evaluation.
17. The data also includes multilingual interactions in Hungarian and Japanese within my family (my wife is Japanese and I am a native of Hungary).
18. One may recall Voloshinov's (1986) definition that monologues are dialogues in a larger context.
19. Furthermore, in Chapter 2 (cf. Example 2.5) reference will be made to my previous research on Chinese visiting cards.
20. Along with the above-discussed observer's paradox, the most significant problem in my audio-recorded data is the weak quality of some of the recordings.
21. The transcription conventions include the following symbols:

@	laughter
↑	high pitch
↓	low pitch
(.)	turn-taking point
>	increased speed
<u>hello</u>	stress/louder sound
=	interruption
text text	overlap
/	contiguous utterances
( )	the analyst's remark

22. This issue will become particularly important in Chapters 5 and 6.
23. Cf. Pike (1967).
24. In this book cognition is used in a wider sense in that it includes emotions, in accordance with Goleman (1998) and Damasio (2006). As Chapter 5 will make clear, the present cognitive approach is limited in the sense that I focus on cognition from the perspective of relationality.
25. As noted before, in my terminology, in order to relate ritual research with politeness research, 'constructive ritual' includes both constructive and stasis forms of behaviour (cf. Arundale 2010).

2 Defining Ritual from a Relational Perspective

1. In more concrete terms, these scholars describe relating and relationality as follows (cf. Spencer-Oatey 2011 for a more detailed description; note, however, that I do not fully agree with the way in which Spencer-Oatey represents Arundale's work):

a. Locher (2004, 2010) and Watts (2008) (see also Locher and Watts 2005, 2008) adopt the term 'relational work' to refer to "all aspects of the work invested by individuals in the construction, maintenance, reproduction and transformation of interpersonal relationships among those engaged in social practice" (Locher and Watts 2008: 96). Locher and Watts examine the wider context that formulates relational work, and they use 'relational' in a wider sense, i.e. to describe both the interpersonal relationship and the interactants' states of mind.
b. Robert Arundale (2006, 2010) uses the term 'relational' in the sense of "indexing the dynamic phenomena of relating as they emerge dynamically in person-to-person communication" (2006: 202). That is, Arundale adopts a considerably narrower, conversation analysis-based approach, by means of which he primarily analyses the formation of interpersonal relationships.
c. Holmes and Marra (2004) and Holmes and Schnurr (2005) adopt the label 'relational practice' instead of relational work, and they analyse interaction in workplace contexts specifically. Relational practice describes the relational skills one needs to successfully interact in a workplace setting, and Holmes and her colleagues examine these skills broadly through the Brown and Levinsonian (1987) framework.
d. Spencer-Oatey (2005, 2008) and Spencer-Oatey and Franklin (2009) use the expression 'rapport management' to describe 'rapport', that is "people's subjective perceptions of (dis)harmony, smoothness–turbulence and warmth–antagonism in interpersonal relations" (Spencer-Oatey and Franklin 2009: 102). Spencer-Oatey's framework is not strictly discourse analytic as she approaches rapport via post-event interviews.

2. For example, researchers of the East Asian languages such as R. Ide (1998), Gu (1990) and Zhang (1999) tend to describe 'ritual' as a synonym for honorific communication. A rare positive exception in the East Asian field is Ohashi (2008), who makes it clear that his study reflects a specific, Japanese understanding of ritual. On the other hand, experts of Western and Middle Eastern languages such as Danblon et al. (2005), Gleason and Weintraub (1976) and Koutlaki (2002) associate 'ritual' with routine discursive strategies and linguistic forms of etiquette.
3. On discursive politeness research see Linguistic Politeness Research Group (ed.) *Discursive Approaches to Politeness*. Berlin: Mouton de Gruyter.
4. As Streeck's (1996) study makes clear, 'form' has to be understood in a relatively broad sense when it comes to schematic practices, which not only operate as linguistic forms but also as 'formalised structures' (such structures include longer utterances).
5. See also the interaction of the Chinese relational network analysed in Chapter 3, which illustrates that certain relational networks can create a routine of creativity.
6. 'Anglo-English' is a technical term borrowed from Wierzbicka (2006: 5) who, citing from Kachru's (1985, 1992) and Crystal's (2003) works, notes that "[w]hile there are many 'Englishes' around the world [...] there is also an 'Anglo' English – an English of the 'inner circle' [...] including the traditional bases of English, where it is the primary language: [...] the USA, UK, Ireland, Canada, Australia, and New Zealand". I argue that certain conventional relational phenomena such as indirect requests are typical Anglo-English phenomena, in the sense that they do not represent normative relational

practices in certain English-speaking countries which do not belong to the Anglo-English circle such as Singapore.
7. As far as I am aware no historical pragmatic research has been conducted on the history of this form, and the claim here is based on some interviews with Hungarian language users. This form occurs briefly in a recent study by Bodor and Barcza (2011).
8. In fact, one could argue that Purdy's account above itself feels rather old-fashioned.
9. In French there are masculine and feminine inflections, and it is grammatically incorrect for males to use female inflection, and vice versa.
10. Play and game cover different phenomena in some anthropological studies: play covers theatrical acts and game refers to acts of play in a wider sense. Note, however, that these terms are occasionally used as interchangeable ones – partly because it can be argued that play itself is a form of game. Whilst the relationship between ritual and play has been thoroughly studied (see e.g. Turner 1982), the in-depth examination of relational ritual acts of games remains an area for future research.
11. Importantly, this type of direct ritualisation functions as a discursive resource in particular institutionalised interactions. To give an anecdotal example, upon using a colloquial English example in one of my university classes in the UK, I made a playful reference to my foreignness, by saying to my students, 'You are the native speakers, so don't expect me to evaluate this utterance.' Seeing that this utterance was received very positively, I started to perform it repeatedly, hence making it a ritual, and the obvious reason behind the ritualisation process was to arouse the audience's sympathy.
12. It is pertinent to note that as recent research illustrates, direct ritualisation includes non-religious mundane practices as well (see e.g. Barnes et al. 2007).
13. I was unable to find etymological links between *cakes* and the English plural *cakes*.

3 In-Group Ritual in Operation: Two Case Studies

1. It is pertinent to note that one's attempt to activate a ritual is not necessarily responded to by other interactants in the process of discourse co-construction. A ritual act functions as an 'invitation' to participate in mimesis, and, in particular in the case of non-institutionalised rituals, it is the interlocutor's decision whether he or she engages in the ritual, as the following extract illustrates:

    1. N ez víz
       D igen ez víz
    2. N nem bor
       D nem
    3. N megszagolod
       D figyelj igyál

    1. N is this water
       D yes this is water
    2. N not wine
       D not wine
    3. N do you smell it
       D look drink it

This interaction took place between my daughter (N) and me (D). My daughter wanted to engage in a family ritual of persuasion, that is, she wanted me to persuade her to drink water. In our network this persuasion ritual often takes place in the form of repeated questions, that is, my daughter requests information that she already knows about an item (usually food or drink), which she wants to be persuaded to consume. In the above interaction we started to engage in this ritual; however, in this specific case I lost my patience as we had to hurry, and in turn 3 I refused to further co-construct the ritual.
2. Provided that the addressee has another name. As Hajdú (2003) notes, these names used to be very popular in nineteenth- and early twentieth-century Hungary, but now they convey a humorous meaning to many.
3. As regards function, these intentionally misspelled swear words bear some comparison to those recorded by Labov (1972). A notable difference is that, even to outsiders, these forms seem quite 'harmless', which is in line with the in-group's practice of enacting, and even parodying, conflicts.
4. The form *vazze* originates in *bazdmeg*. Whilst *vazze* has lost much of its offensive meaning, *bazdmeg* tends to remain highly offensive in many contexts, and this is supposedly why it is written here in an incorrect form (as part of the ritual performance).
5. It is worth mentioning that this metacommunicative function evinces another similarity between localised in-group and social ritual (cf. Handelman 1979; see also Chapter 4).
6. It should be noted that in the present discussion the expression 'south' is not applied in a strict geographical sense. In fact, from a geographical perspective Zhejiang Province, and thus Shaoxing, belongs to the middle part of China and not south China. However, in traditional Chinese thinking (see Eberhard 1965) the territory that lies south of the Yangtze River is regarded as southern China, and so from a cultural perspective the Shaoxing Group is a typically southern intellectual circle.
7. Historical Chinese epistolary collections, unlike their European counterparts (e.g. Fitzmaurice 2002), usually do not include subscriptions (nor superscriptions), and so it is usually difficult to date them.
8. This edited collection, containing 186 private letters of varying length written to various addressees by Gong, is claimed to be one of the most stylistically representative collections of late imperial Chinese letter writing (Zhao 1999). Furthermore, it is one of the most 'popular' historical Chinese letter collections (Kádár 2010a), and was used as an 'epistolary textbook' during the nineteenth and early twentieth centuries and hence is often referred to as an epistolary 'model work' (*chidu mofan*尺牍模范) by scholars of Chinese.
9. Most of the Shaoxing correspondents lived in smaller townships in the capital province of Zhili 直隶, mostly around Peking.
10. On the importance of favours and gifts in Chinese social life, see Yan (1993).
11. The extracts cited from the corpus studied are denoted with numbers such as 'V.4'; these are identical to the number of texts in the English translation of the corpus (Kádár 2009).
12. As innovative style aims to dinstinguish one relational network from others, it must be saliently different from socially normative styles. As

Notes 191

stylistics experts such as Myers Scotton (1998) and Gross (2000) note, such salience (or markedness) tends to entail intentionality; for example, Myers Scotton (1998: 4) notes that "writers or speakers choose what can be considered *marked choices* [original emphasis] to convey certain messages of intentionality".

4   Relational Ritual Typology

1. 'Mundane' here means that these practices are not related to religious sacredness, neither positively nor negatively (note, however, that 'sacredness' can have a more abstract sociological interpretation, see Collins 2004). As the present chapter argues, Durkheim's distinction is not at all simplistic, in the sense that it involves both positive and negative ritual practices (see below in the main text), and the mundane is not completely ignored in this typology, as negative practices that separate human beings from the realm of the sacred might have some mundane nature. However, I argue that negative ritual practices that have some mundane nature in the Durkheimian typology are not mundane in the sense that sacredness is present in them as a starting point.
2. And this fact in itself raises questions as regards the validity of the notion of 'deritualisation'.
3. The ritualised nature of education is reported to have been described by David P. Gardner as follows: "Much that passes for education is not education at all but ritual. The fact is that we are being educated when we know it least."
4. Another exception is Collins (2004), which distinguishes macro- and micro-level rituals. However, similarly to Bax (2010a), Collins does not provide a typological description of ritual.
5. Note that labels like 'social', when used as units of size, are also problematic because they tend to be vague. For example, in 1996 Aune and DeMarinis published a (otherwise very good) book with the title *Religious and Social Ritual*; this volume discussed a wide variety of ritual practices, including network and cross-network rituals, and the reader was left with some ambiguity as to what 'social' actually means in terms of rituality. It is pertinent to add that 'social' interpreted in this way is problematic also because it implicitly suggests that a certain aspect of ritualistic behaviour has only one social manifestation at a time. While research on this topic is beyond the limit of the present work, it can be argued that there is a potential for concurrent forms of social rituality to compete with each other.
6. See <http://udvozollek.blogspot.co.uk/>.
7. As a matter of course, it is not pre-evident that a socially 'coded' (i.e. socially standardised) practice like *Szervusz, üdvözöllek* must be changed when it is accepted (localised) by a relational network. There are practices such as children's rituals (cf. Chapter 3) which are adopted uniformly by different groups of children. That is, while the researcher cannot rule out the possibility that any ritual practice is open to having different implications in different networks (e.g. networks of different ages or social backgrounds may perceive this ritual practice differently), this is not at all a rule.
8. Section 4.2.1, unlike other parts of this book, relies partly on data collected by others, primarily psychologists. In the research that led to the authoring

of the present book I was not able to make a clinical data collection, and so upon examining covert forms of ritual actions I often had to refer to data documented in psychological literature, and the only first-hand source for me were online forums (see e.g. example 4.5) and literary sources (e.g. example 4.3).
9. As the present section will make clear, some covert ritual practices are intentionally hidden as they are associated with shame, evoked by reflective awareness of normative standards that these ritual practices violate (on the relationship between shame and normativity, see Bierbauer 2007). Intentionality to hide these practices may differ across situations, and so it is a matter of degree.
10. It is pertinent to note that the category of covert ritual does not include secret rituals. In fact, ritual has an important 'secret' type: for example, various secret societies operating in East Asia during the early twentieth century and earlier 'borrowed' and transformed linguistic and non-linguistic rituals into their own 'secret' ritual practices. For example, ter Haar's (1998: 152–6) groundbreaking study on secret society rituals mentions that secret societies reserved old religious ritual practices (e.g. in the case of blood covenants) which have disappeared on the social level. However, from a relational perspective secret rituals are not covert ones, at least as covertness is interpreted here, but instead they simply constitute a subtype of in-group rituals which is intentionally hidden from external observers.
11. Note that in psychology the category 'compulsive ritual' usually covers both non-verbal and verbal practices.
12. For example, as discourse analytic studies such as Harris (1984) and Thornborrow (2002) illustrate, certain ritualistic discursive resources are unequally distributed in institutional settings such as courtrooms. One could, however, add that the same applies to those in-group ritual practices that take place in networks where in-group hierarchy is significant.
13. However, this ritual definitely has *historicity*, as the blog's text also makes clear, because it re-enacts values situated in the Midwestern American context.
14. This illustrates that intercultural differences can be captured in terms of defining 'ritual', despite the fact that ritual is perceived in significantly different ways across certain cultures (cf. Chapter 1).
15. See <http://oxforddictionaries.com/definition/english/ritual>.
16. But these definitions are of course different in other senses. *Liyi* has a more comprehensive definition than 'ritual', as in English the connotation of 'ritual' is either religious or solemn, which would not include ordinary greetings or table manners.

5   Recognition, Affectivity and Emotivity

1. This point is important to maintain not only because every ritual practice has formally fixed properties (cf. Chapter 3), but also because the degree of 'demarcatedness' of a ritual practice can only be defined by language users.
2. As has been noted in Chapter 4, in-group ritual is rarely associated with 'ritual' in my data, and it seems that the more 'demarcated' an in-group ritual practice is the more likely that it is associated with 'rituality' by language

users, even though the detailed and quantitative examination of this topic is subject to later research. It should be noted about example (5.1) specifically that the person who gave this anecdotic description to me is a linguist who is familiar with the framework discussed in this volume, that is, the evaluation represented by this description cannot be regarded as purely a 'language user's' perspective.
3. Ritual and cognition is an area which is researched across disciplines, including for example archaeology (e.g. Rossano 2009), sociology (e.g. Das 1982), religious studies (e.g. Wuthnow 2007), and anthropology and culture studies (e.g. Donald 1991).
4. In fact, Peregrin's (2012) insightful study questions the validity of the term 'conventionality' as it is widely used in pragmatics. While I agree with Peregrin's arguments, I use 'convention' in the present work according to previous pragmatic research, in order to integrate my arguments with research on relational acts.
5. It is pertinent to note that speech act theory itself has been subject to critcisms, see e.g. Streeck (1980).
6. This point is confirmed to some extent by Terkourafi (2001) who approaches conventionally as a matter of degree.
7. It seems that *(I) Love you* is a noteworthy expression in the sense that it frequently occurs in jokes, as well as in metadiscourse on 'inappropriate' conventions. For example, the British radio celebrity Scott Mills used it to every caller and they used it back to him, in order to highlight the fact that there is a lot of inappropriate Americanised use of excess affect. See Mills' (2012) book *Love you bye: My Story* (London: Hachette Digital).
8. The author of example (5.2) makes clear his racial origin elsewhere in the blog.
9. Needless to say, this is only a matter of tendency in my data. Considering that the present research is based on a limited database, I do not intend to claim that constructive rituals are not evaluated as destructive ones by network insiders; it is simply that this is relatively unlikely and no such case occurs in my data set.
10. I am grateful to Jim O'Driscoll for his advice on this terminological choice.
11. Other important contributions have been made by Helen Spencer-Oatey (2005) and Jonathan Culpeper (2011b).
12. The question as to how short-term emotions can be categorised has been somewhat left behind in the field. While this question is beyond the scope of the present work, it is useful here to refer to the work of Helen Spencer-Oatey (2005: 116) who offers a useful categorisation of emotions triggered by relational acts, by distinguishing the following emotive categories:

> *Emotional reactions (own and other)*
> joy/contentment/pleasure
> pride
> surprise/amazement
> anger irritation/annoyance
> frustration
> disgust/disapproval
> sadness/disappointment/displeasure
> shame/guilt
> embarrassment/insult/humiliation

13. See e.g. Clark and Schunk (1980) on the conventionality of such requests.
14. See Forgács (2005: 51) on the origin of this slang word. Importantly, in contemporary Hungarian *gáz* counts as a 'harmless' word in spite of its original meaning (i.e. few language users would associate it with a reference to farting), and because of this, unlike e.g. swear words which are adopted by relational networks as part of a ritualised performance, this form is a relatively 'neutral' lexical item which conventionally conveys informality and which is widely used. Thus, its usage is closer to convention than ritual if we perceive conventionality vs rituality as a scalar value (cf. Chapter 2).
15. There are different explanations with regard to the origin and actual meaning of this slang word; see e.g. Kis (1992: 27) where *lenyomni* (the non-conjugated form of *lenyomjuk*) is represented as a word that originates in the language usage of the army.
16. See e.g. Fox et al.'s (2007) empirical analysis.
17. Previous research such as Tracy and Naughton (2009) has illustrated that various academic settings necessitate ritual performances like this one.
18. It is pertinent to note that my wife, a native speaker of Japanese, and I, tend to use this word (*mō* in Japanese) and some other emotionally loaded formulae such as the Hungarian *már* (lit. already) as a relational ritual to signal frustration in a playful inoffensive way.
19. …@index.hu is in fact a web-based (free) internet address; I adopted this address in order to keep Y's identity anonymous.
20. Supposedly, Y used this formal form to express irony.
21. This claim is reinforced by previous research on language usage and awareness in other areas such as Andrews (2001).
22. Ritual theorists like Collins (2004) claim that ritual practices tend to evoke similar short-term emotions within a relational network. From a discursive viewpoint this claim could be debated, but examination of this issue is beyond the scope of the present chapter.
23. On relating and political discourse, see Fairclough (2009).
24. This bronchial voice was meant to imitate the character General Grievous' speech style.
25. Note that I do not claim that short-term and long-term emotions regularly coincide, but this is the case at least in various interactions I studied.
26. It is pertinent to note that this case fits into the analysis of Section 5.2, where it is claimed that a ritual practice can become marked when it fails to accord with a network member's contextual expectance.

6 Destructive Relational Rituals

1. Note that although 'bullying' is a colloquial word it is used as a technical term in some fields such as educational psychology.
2. In these frameworks 'relational' is used in a more limited sense than in the present book.
3. For example, when a group member is expelled from the group by a swear word which refers to her or his stigmatic property.
4. See: http://www.youtube.com/watch?v=Si-SvrweHqk.
5. And also because it can be supposed that the girl mentioned in this posting enjoys the support of the network: as the poster makes clear, she was previously bullied by others as well.

6. And some destructive ritual practices of 'regulated' nature reinforce(d) the dominating social ethos (see Section 6.4.1).
7. *Heti Válasz* XII (46): 28–9.
8. But then they are unacceptable and consequently 'evil' for other groups and societies which have different moral values – which illustrates the relativity of 'evilness' in terms of rituality. A nice example of the relativity of this phenomenon can be drawn from Bell's book (1997: 129) who, along with Kennedy's case, notes the funeral of Stalin. This funeral is often represented in Western public discourse as a symbol of tyranny, that is, it is evaluated negatively, while in the Soviet Union it is generally represented positively. This point illustrates that 'public recognition' (cf. Norbert Elias 1994 [2000]) is a problematic notion in terms of destructive rituality, in a similar way to a constructive one, as recognitions of ritual may differ across certain groups and networks within a society, and they can also differ across cultures.
9. This, however, does not mean that groups and public discourses are unanimous in the evaluation of rituals. See e.g. Brakke (2012) on the diversity of ritual norms.
10. Note that 'deconstructive ritual' is an ambiguous term: in works such as Edmundson (1995: 91), which adopt 'deconstructive' as a broader (and radical) concept, following Jacques Derrida (1967), 'deconstructive ritual' is interpreted differently from anthropology.
11. Whilst the same applies to the husband to some extent, in traditional patriarchal families the husband does not 'leave' his family and so the ritual of marriage is more deconstructive from the wife's perspective. Note that in many modern Western/globalised societies the deconstructive function of marriage ritual is considerably less significant.
12. 'Covert' would be an even better term here, but this label is reserved for certain types of constructive relational rituals, cf. Chapter 4.
13. The most typical ones are chatrooms of online game websites. Importantly, online virtual identities are usually real ones for netizens (see e.g. Thomas 2007), and so this multimodal online data type (cf. e.g. emoticons) seems to be suitable to represent the destructive effect of ritual practices in interaction.
14. Due to the repeated and stigmatising nature of destructive ritual practices, one can argue that they tend to be intentional. It is necessary to note that in the field of impoliteness research there is some disagreement as regards the usage of impoliteness (see Paternoster 2012 for an overview). Culpeper (2008) and Bousfield (2008) claim that 'impoliteness' describes intentionally face-aggravating behaviour, while 'rudeness' refers to an unintentionally mismanaged level of politeness. However, Culpeper in a later study (2011a: 79–80) modified this stance, claiming that intentionality is relatively unimportant in terms of evaluation, due to which this terminological distinction can be eliminated. Culpeper suggests using 'impoliteness', as it is more academic than 'rudeness'. In the present chapter I will use 'impoliteness' partly following Culpeper's suggestion, and partly because in the phenomena studied intentionality is present anyway, that is, the way in which 'impoliteness' is used here also accords with Culpeper (2008) and Bousfield (2008).
15. And, importantly, it does not have the potential to become a ritualistic practice, at least in a relational sense, because the class obviously dislikes and fears Flats (others in the class move their desks away from the middle of the room). As the present chapter illustrates, a destructive practice can

become ritual only if it animates the ethos of the network, which is not the case here.
16. I intentionally use 'community of practice' here, in order to reflect on the fact that this is a workplace setting.
17. This extract also illustrates that different types of destructive ritual practices can collaborate as the social action is realised. For example, the section "All other staff names on whiteboard in staff room and on work trays were in black, only mine was in red" makes it clear that the stigmatised person was not simply being ignored through the ritual practice of non-doing but also there were visible actions made against her.
18. Cf. example (6.7) in which the first section illustrates that the stigmatised person tried to dismiss non-doing, but it was recurrence that made her realise that non-doing is a mimetic act (i.e. ritual) targeted against her.
19. Due to their 'perceivably harmless' character, these destructive covert rituals are subject to contestation (cf. Collinson 2002).
20. Arguably, this is a common abusive form, just as 'four eyes' (to refer to someone with glasses); one could argue that it is almost a cliché in some contexts.
21. Arguably, these labels describe different understandings of this phenomenon, but the analysis of this question is beyond the scope of the present work. An insightful pilot study on this topic was conducted by Smith et al. (2002).
22. It is necessary here to refer to Erving Goffman's (1979, 1981) notion of 'footing', which means that participants in an interaction can take different positions.

7 Conclusion

1. Retrieved from: <http://www.telegraph.co.uk/news/celebritynews/3248481/Angelina-Jolie-Why-Ill-marry-Brad-Pitt.html>
2. This long-term project is being carried out in the Centre for Intercultural Politeness Research of the University of Huddersfield.
3. Note that the present discussion is limited to the notion of discernment and volition, and I definitely do not intend to argue that intercultural differences do not exist in terms of (non-ritualistic) politeness. On methodologies to capture intercultural differences, see Mills and Kádár (2011).

Glossary 术语表

Accessibility The degree of right for an observer/network outsider to take part in the performance of a ritual act.

Affectivity The long-term feeling of relatedness triggered by ritual practices.

Anticipation "[P]resumptive forms of reasoning where inferences are grounded in experience and associative links" (Kádár and Haugh 2013: 217).

Awareness From the performer's perspective a relational ritual practice triggers awareness when the performer is reflexively aware that the given practice might become/has become salient to other participants.

Bullying Collective term for destructive behaviour, which amongst other behavioural types includes practices of destructive ritual.

Co-construction Non-demarcated ritual acts come into existence as the interactants co-construct the interaction.

Compulsive rituals Ritual practices, which relate the individual (performer) with others vis-à-vis a ritual practice that is conventional and compulsive for the individual.

Compulsive and delusional rituals Compulsive ritual practices with delusional beliefs relate the individual (performer) with an imaginary entity (or a group of entities), i.e. the realm of the 'imaginary'.

Conformance Conventional behaviour implies a particular emphasis on conformance, i.e. the need to conform to network expectations.

Consciousness From the performer's perspective a relational ritual practice triggers consciousness when it follows normative expectations.

Constructive rituals Relationship-forcing acts, the performance of which stimulates interpersonal relationships to develop.

Contrastive identity formation Distinctive ritual mimetic practices, adopted by members of relational networks intentionally, in order to make their group saliently different from other groups, as well as 'society' per se.

Convention Those forms of recurrent schematic behaviour which follow patterns associated with relating.

Conventionalisation The process during which a form or a behaviour type recurs until what it implies becomes accepted as a 'standard' meaning.

Covert ritual Ritual type, which includes clinical (compulsive, and compulsive and delusional) cases, as well as non-clinical ('imaginary') cases.

Deconstructive ritual Rituals that reshape relationships through the ludic deconstruction and recombination of relational configurations.

Demarcatedness Collective category for ritual acts which are clearly codified and institutionalised, and which are meant to be performed at a definite point of time.

Deritualisation According to this concept, which is challenged in the present book, rituals have largely disappeared from contemporary social-communicative practices.

Destructive rituals Relationship-corrupting acts, the performance of which stimulates interpersonal relationships to break down; destructive rituals stigmatise one in-group member (or several in-group members), i.e. they have a target, and they destroy the victim's relation with, and symbolic role within, the group.

Discursive approach The examination of ritual as a relational action constructed in interaction; it aims to capture the features of ritual phenomena by analysing the interactants' behaviour in culturally and socially diverse contexts, hence avoiding a priori predictions.

Diversity Various groups within a society orient to different cultural values, and so it can be argued that a given culture is constituted by an aggregation of subcultures; due to this conventional and ritual practices are subject to diversity.

Emic (Culture/network) insider expectations of ritual behaviour.

Emotivity The individual rather than relational (affective) emotive effect of ritual practices.

Enduredness Destructive relational ritual practices were and continue to be endured rather than supported by the public, especially by those in power within a society whose voice counts as 'normative'.

Ethos Ritual practices represent socially dominant or network ethos through mimetic performance.

Etic (Culture/network) outsider expectations of ritual behaviour.

Evil ritual Folk-theoretical/theoretical (second-order) term, which includes rituals of violence, as well as other ritual practices that are condemned by the public in a given society or social network.

Expectations Conventional and ritual acts tend to be used according to normative expectations within a relational network; expectations not only differ across networks, but there is also an important distinction that can be drawn between practices (a) which network members regard as *likely* to happen (empirical norms), and others (b) which they consider *ought to* happen (moral norms).

First-order perspective The interactional definition/evaluation of ritual by participants themselves and emic/etic expectancies of rituality.

Fluctuation In co-constructed ritual interactions emotions and affection tend to fluctuate.

Formal fixity Rituals are more often than not formally fixed; they are expressed with institutionalised lexical items, and they can have certain predetermined prosodic and other linguistic properties.

Game and play Game and play can be ritualistic and ritual is a form of game and play in a wider sense; in the sphere of game and play the rules and habits of 'ordinary life' are no longer valid.

Historicity Every ritual act has its historicity, and what matters for a relational theory of in-group ritual is relational history, the existence of which is a precondition for in-group rituals to operate.

Identity practices Identity practices manifest themselves in two ways at the level of language use: "Negative identity practices are those that individuals employ to distance themselves from a rejected identity, while positive identity practices are those in which individuals engage in order actively to construct a chosen identity" (Bucholtz 1999: 211–12).

Imaginary ritual The type of non-clinical covert ritual practices.

Impoliteness Collective technical term for offensive behaviour, which is used in accordance with Culpeper (2011: 79–80).

In-group ritual The type of ritualised relational practices which are formed locally within the social unit of relational network.

Long-term emotions An alternative term for affectivity.

Markedness/unmarkedness These categories correspond to the participant(s)' point of view in terms of recognition of a ritual practice.

Mimesis Performance by means of which ritual re-enacts certain social or interpersonal values.

Mock impoliteness "Mock impoliteness, or banter, is impoliteness that remains on the surface, since it is understood that it is not intended to cause offence" (Culpeper 1996: 352).

Moral refusal Destructive ritual practices tend to be evaluated as immoral in public discourse.

Non-contrastive identity formation Ritual practices which form a network's identity without positioning the network against others.

Onlooker perspective The (second-order) perspective of those in-group members who do not actively participate in the performance of destructive ritual acts.

Participants The persons who participate in a relational ritual interaction.

Performance Unlike conventional behaviour, which implies a particular emphasis on conformance, ritual behaviour represents another important way in which recurrent schemata operate in interaction, vis-à-vis mimetic performance.

Performer The person who performs a given relational ritual act.

Personal ritual The type of ritual practices which are performed by an individual alone; these ritual practices (unlike covert rituals) are not saliently different from what relational networks normatively expect, and they have two types: (1) personal rituals that relate the individual to the realm of invisible, and (2) other rituals that relate the individual with others in personal (arbitrary) ways.

Politeness Here it is a technical term, which encompasses all types of interpersonal behaviour through which we take into account the feelings of others as to how they think they should be treated in working out and maintaining our sense of personhood as well as our interpersonal relationships with others.

Potentiality The interactional application of relational rituals offers a potentiality – more precisely, a regularity of potentiality – in terms of gaining recognition within a relational network.

Recognition Interactional (or post-interactional) awareness of a ritual practice.

Recurrence A key mechanism through which the practices of convention and ritual operate.

Recurrent covert offence A destructive ritual practice, which recurrently discredits the stigmatised person as one of 'the normal' through making repeated soft attacks on her or him.

Recurrent non-doing An important form of destructive ritual, which implies *not* to perform an act which is perceived and, perhaps even more importantly, anticipated as a proper (normative) convention.

Recurrent reference to the stigma The most direct practice of destructive ritual, when the stigma is named by the performer.

(Re-)enactment By performing the symbolic act of ritual we enact and re-enact certain beliefs and ideologies.

Reflexivity The performer's reflexive awareness of the possible evaluation/reaction a given ritual act triggers.

Relational history The prior relationship experiences and prospects of a relational network, which influence the formation and perception of ritual practices.

Relational network The basic social unit of analysis in the present framework; society is constituted through an intersecting nexus of relational networks.

Relational perspective The study of the interactional construction (or destruction) of interpersonal relationships vis-à-vis ritual practices.

Ritual moment Ritual acts create an atmosphere in which states of mind alter; this ritual moment represents "a temporary destruction of awareness of the wider meaningful relations of one's individuality and the reduction of the self to the immediate physical experience of the here and now" (Koster 2003: 219).

Ritualisation Ritual practices come into existence through ritualisation; ritualisation can operate directly, i.e. when a group of people who animate the voice of an institution create a certain ritual practice, as well as indirectly, i.e. once a convention is adopted by a social network, and when it takes on mimetic functions, it becomes ritual.

Ritualised aggression The ritual enactment of conflict, which plays an important part in the avoidance/settlement of actual conflicts.

Routine A great deal of our everyday activities are recurrent, and it is recurrence that provides the routine practice behind linguistic (and other behavioural) schemata; routines by their nature operate with "basic schematic forms that constitute the organizational building blocks of coordinated action" (Fairhurst and Cooren 2004: 143).

Schemata Pre-existing pattern of language and behaviour, which is the manifestation of an action rooted in routine practice.

Schematic Collective term for organising information according to certain routinised actions.

Second-order perspective Theoretical and/or technical understanding of ritual, which in the present work implies rationalising the interactional meaning and function of relational ritual practices.

Sequencing The interactional structure of a relational ritual act; ritualistic interactions tend to be governed by strict formulation and/or sequencing principles.

Short-term emotion(s) Emotive responses to a relational ritual act.

Social action The present framework approaches ritual as social action triggered by interactional practices.

Social emotions Emotions evoked by the production and evaluation of social actions; social emotions are generated by external stimuli, such as an interaction, and they are cognitively higher order than self-conscious emotions.

Social ritual The category of ritual practices which accord with dominant social values; these practices tend to be transparent and accessible to culture insiders.

Sounding The competitive exchange of ritual insults.

Static Collective term for the unmarked/conscious recognition of relational ritual acts.

Stigma When a person is "reduced in our minds from a whole and unusual person to a tainted, discounted one" (Goffman 1963: 12); destructive ritual practice comes into operation when the person who sticks out for any reason, or who is regarded as being different or simply vulnerable, is stigmatised by the performer of a given abusive ritual.

Stigmatisation The victimisation of a network member vis-à-vis destructive relational ritual practices.

'The normal' Goffman's (1963) term; in the present work used as a collective name for those network members who stigmatise a victim or a group of victims.

Transparency The degree of understandability of a ritual act for an observer/network outsider.

Visibility Although mimetic performance is present in every relational ritual practice, its visibility (from the observer's perspective) is subject to variation.

References 参考文献

Alemán, Melissa W. 2001. Complaining among the elderly: Examining multiple dialectical oppositions to independence in a retirement community. *Western Journal of Communication* 65(1): 89–112.

Alexander, Martin S. 1998. *Knowing Your Friends: Intelligence inside the Alliances and Coalitions from 1914 to the Cold War*. London: Frank Cass Publishers.

Andrews, Molly 2000. *Lines of Narrative: Psychological Perspectives*. New York and London: Routledge.

Andrews, Stephen 2001. The language awareness of the L2 teacher: Its impact upon pedagogical practice. *Language Awareness* 20 (2/3): 75–90.

Angouri, Jo, and Meredith Marra (eds) 2011. *Constructing Identities at Work*. Basingstoke: Palgrave Macmillan.

Aouragh, Miriyam 2011. *Palestine Online: Transnationalism, the Internet and the Construction of Identity*. London and New York: I.B. Tauris (Palgrave Macmillan).

Archer, Dawn 2011. Facework and im/politeness across legal contexts: An introduction. *Journal of Politeness Research* 7(1): 1–19.

Arundale, Robert B. 2006. Face as relational and interactional: A communication framework for research on face, facework, and politeness. *Journal of Politeness Research* 2(2): 193–216.

Arundale, Robert B. 2010. Constituting face in conversation: Face, facework, and interactional achievement. *Journal of Pragmatics* 42(8): 2078–105.

Attardo, Salvatore 1994. *Linguistic Theories of Humour*. Berlin and New York: Mouton de Gruyter.

Aune, Michael B., and Valerie DeMarinis (eds) 1996. *Religious and Social Ritual: Interdisciplinary Explorations*. Albany: State University of New York Press.

Austin, John L. 1962. *How to Do Things with Words*. Cambridge, MA: Harvard University Press.

Bandura Albert 1991. Social cognitive theory of moral thought and action. In: Kurtines, William M., and Jacob L. Gerwirtz (eds) *Handbook of Moral Behaviour and Development: Theory, Research, and Applications*. Vol. 1, 45–103. Hillsdale, NJ: Erlbaum.

Barnes, Marian, Janet Newman, and Helen Sullivan 2007. Discursive arenas: Deliberation and the constitution of identity in public participation at a local level. *Social Movement Studies* 5(3): 193–207.

Bax, Marcel 2004. Out of ritual. A semiolinguistic account of the origin and development of indirect language behavior. In: Bax, Marcel, Barend van Heusden, and Wolfgang Wildgen (eds) *Semiotic Evolution and the Dynamics of Culture*, 155–213. Bern and Oxford: Peter Lang.

Bax, Marcel 2010a. Rituals. In: Jucker, Andeas H., and Irma Taavitsainen (eds) *Handbook of Pragmatics*, Vol. 8: *Historical Pragmatics*, 483–519. Berlin and New York: Mouton de Gruyter.

Bax, Marcel 2010b. Epistolary presentation rituals. Face-work, politeness, and ritual display in early modern Dutch letter-writing. In: Culpeper, Jonathan, and Dániel Z. Kádár (eds) *Historical (Im)politeness*, 37–85. Berne and Oxford: Peter Lang.

Bell, Catherine 1992. *Ritual Theory and Ritual Practice*. Oxford: Oxford University Press.

Bell, Catherine 1997. *Ritual: Perspectives and Dimensions*. Oxford: Oxford University Press.

Bendix, Regina 1992. National sentiment in the enactment and discourse of Swiss political ritual. *American Ethnologist* 19(4): 768–90.

Bennett, Lance W. 1980. Myth, ritual, and political control. *Journal of Communication* 30(4): 166–79.

Berthomé, François, and Michael Houseman 2010. Ritual and emotions: Moving relations, patterned effusions. *Religion and Society: Advances in Research* 1(1): 57–75.

Bierbauer, Günter 2007. Reactions to violation of normative standards: A cross-cultural analysis of shame and guilt. *International Journal of Psychology* 27(2): 181–93.

Blackmore, Susan J. 2007. Imitation makes us human. In: Pasternak, Charles (ed.) *What Makes us Human?* 1–17. Oxford: Oneworld.

Bloch, Sidney, Sally Browning, and Graeme McGrath 2011. Humour in group psychotherapy. *British Journal of Medical Psychology* 56(1): 89–97.

Bodor, Péter, and Barcza Virág 2011. Érzelmi fejlődés és a kicsinyítő képzők elsajátítása [Emotional development and the acquisition of diminutives]. *Pszichológia* 31(3): 195–236.

Bosk, Charles L. 1980. Occupational rituals in patient management. *The New England Journal of Medicine* 303(2): 71–6.

Bourdieu, Pierre 1978. *Outline of a Theory of Practice*. Cambridge: Cambridge University Press.

Bourdieu, Pierre 1991. *Language and Symbolic Power*. Cambridge: Polity Press.

Bousfield, Derek 2008. Impoliteness in the struggle for power. In: Bousfield, Derek, and Miriam A. Locher (eds) *Impoliteness in Language. Studies on its Interplay with Power in Theory and Practice*, 127–53. Berlin and New York: Mouton de Gruyter.

Bousfield, Derek 2010. *Impoliteness in Interaction*. Amsterdam and Philadelphia: John Benjamins.

Bovey, Alixe 2002. *Monsters and Grotesques in Medieval Manuscripts*. Toronto: University of Toronto Press.

Brakke, David 2012. *The Gnostics: Myth, Ritual and Diversity in Early Christianity*. Cambridge, MA: Harvard University Press.

Brody, Elaine M. 1970. The etiquette of filial behaviour. *The International Journal of Aging and Human Development* 1(1): 87–94.

Brown, Penelope, and Stephen C. Levinson 1987. *Politeness: Some Universals in Language Usage*. Cambridge: Cambridge University Press.

Bucholtz, Mary 1999. 'Why be normal?' Language and identity practices in a community of nerd girls. *Language in Society* 28(2): 203–23.

Buckley Ebrey, Patricia 1991. *Confucianism and the Family Rituals in Imperial China*. Princeton, NJ: Princeton University Press.

Burke, Peter 1987. *Historical Anthropology in Early Modern Italy*. Cambridge: Cambridge University Press.

Byon, Andrew Sangpil 2012. Korean honorifics and politeness in second language learning. *Language, Culture and Curriculum* 25(2): 205–7.

Caillois, Roger [1958] 1961. *Man, Play and Games*. New York: The Free Press.

Chan, Alan K. L. 2000. Confucian ethics and the critique of ideology. *Asia Philosophy: An International Journal of the Philosophical Traditions of the East* 10(3): 245–61.

Chan, Marjorie K. M. 1998. Gender differences in Chinese: A preliminary report. In: Lin, Hua (ed.) *Proceedings of the Ninth North American Conference on Chinese Linguistics*, 35–52. Los Angeles: The University of South California.

Charvat, František, and Jaroslav Kučera 1970. On the theory of social dependence. *Quality and Quantity* 4(2): 325–53.

Ciarocchi, Joseph W. 1995. *The Doubting Disease: Help for Scrupulosity and Religious Compulsions*. Mahwah: Paulist.

Clark, Herbert H., and Dale H. Schunk 1980. Polite responses to polite requests. *Cognition* 8(2): 111–43.

Clarke, Matthew 2008. *Language Teacher Identities: Co-Constructing Discourse and Community*. Clevedon: Multilingual Matters.

Clift, Rebecca 2012. Identifying action: Laughter in non-humorous reported speech. *Journal of Pragmatics* 44(10): 1303–12.

Clift, Rebecca, Paul Drew, and Ian Hutchby 2006. Conversation analysis. In: Östman, Jan-Ola, and Jef Verschueren (eds) *Handbook of Pragmatics*, 1–17. Amsterdam and Philadelphia: John Benjamins.

Collier, Judith, and Murray Longmore 2006. *Oxford Handbook of Clinical Specialities*. Oxford: Oxford University Press.

Collins, Randall 2004. *Interaction Ritual Chains*. Princeton, NJ: Princeton University Press.

Collinson, David L. 2002. Managing humour. *Journal of Management Studies* 39(3): 269–88.

Copestake, Anne, and Marina Terkourafi 2010. Conventional speech act formulae: From corpus findings to formalization. In: Kühnlein, Peter, Anton Benz, and Candace Sidner (eds) *Constraints in Discourse 2*, 125–40. Amsterdam and Philadelphia: John Benjamins.

Couldry, Nick 2012. *Media Rituals: A Critical Approach*. New York and London: Routledge.

Cova, Bernard, and Robert Salle 2000. Rituals in managing extrabusiness relationships in international project marketing: A conceptual framework. *International Business Review* 9(6): 669–85.

Crane, Susan 2002. *The Performance of Self: Ritual, Clothing, and Identity during the Hundred Years War*. Philadelphia: University of Pennsylvania Press.

Crystal, David 2003. *English as a Global Language*. Cambridge: Cambridge University Press.

Culpeper, Jonathan 1996. Towards an anatomy of impoliteness. *Journal of Pragmatics* 25(2): 349–67.

Culpeper, Jonathan 2005. Impoliteness and entertainment in the television quiz show: 'The Weakest Link'. *Journal of Politeness Research* 1(1): 35–72.

Culpeper, Jonathan 2008. Reflections on impoliteness, relational work and power. In: Bousfield, Derek, and Miriam Locher (eds) *Impoliteness in Language. Studies on its Interplay with Power in Theory and Practice*, 17–44. Berlin and New York: Mouton de Gruyter.

Culpeper, Jonathan 2011a. *Impoliteness: Using Language to Cause Offence*. Cambridge: Cambridge University Press.

Culpeper, Jonathan 2011b. Politeness and impoliteness. In: Aijmer, Karin, and Gisle Andersen (eds) *Sociopragmatics*, Vol. 5 of *Handbooks of Pragmatics*, 391–436. Berlin and New York: Mouton de Gruyter.

Culpeper, Jonathan, and Jane Demmen 2011. Nineteenth-century English politeness: Negative politeness, conventional indirect requests and the rise of the individual self. *Journal of Historical Pragmatics* 12(1/2): 49–81.

Damasio, Antonio 2006. *Descartes's Error*. New York: Vintage Books.

Danblon, Emanuelle, Bernard De Clerk, and Jean Pierre Van Noppen 2005. Politeness in Belgium: Face, distance and sincerity in service-exchange rituals. In: Hickey, Leo, and Miranda Stewart (eds) *Politeness in Europe*, 45–57. Clevedon: Multilingual Matters.

Das, Veen 1982. *Structure and Cognition: Aspects of Hindu Caste and Ritual*. Oxford: Oxford University Press.

Deflem, Mathieu 1991. Ritual, anti-structure, and religion: A discussion of Victor Turner's processual symbolic analysis. *Journal for the Scientific Study of Religion* 30(1): 1–25.

Derrida, Jacques 1967. *Of Grammatology*. Trans. Spivak, Gayatri Chakravorty (1978). Baltimore and London: Johns Hopkins University Press.

Donald, Merlin 1991. *Origins of the Modern Mind*. Cambridge, MA: Harvard University Press.

Douglas, Mary 1970. *Witchcraft, Confessions and Accusations*. London: Tavistock.

Drew, Paul, and Traci Walker 2009. Going too far: Complaining, escalating and disaffiliation. *Journal of Pragmatics* 41(12): 2400–14.

Durkheim, Émile 1912 [1954/2001. Carol Cosman trans.]. *The Elementary Forms of Religious Life*. Oxford: Oxford University Press.

Eberhard, Wolfram 1965. Chinese regional stereotypes. *Asian Survey* 5(12): 596–608.

Eckert, Penelope 2000. *Language Variation as Social Practice: The Linguistic Construction of Identity in Belten High*. Oxford and New York: Blackwell Publishing.

Eckert, Penelope, and Etienne Wenger 2005. Communities of practice in sociolinguistics: What is the role of power in sociolinguistic variation? *Journal of Sociolinguistics* 9(4): 582–9.

Edmundson, Mark 1995. *Literature against Philosophy, Plato to Derrida: A Defence of Poetry*. Cambridge: Cambridge University Press.

Eelen, Gino 2001. *A Critique of Politeness Theories*. Manchester: St Jerome Publishing.

Eglash, Ron 2002. Race, sex, and nerds: From black geeks to Asian American hipsters. *Social Text* 71(2): 49–64.

Elias, Norbert 1994 [2000]. *The Civilizing Process: Sociogenetic and Psychogenetic Investigations*. Oxford and New York: Blackwell Publishing.

Escandell-Vidal, Victoria 1998. Politeness: A relevant issue for Relevance Theory. *Revista Alicantina de Estudios Ingleses* 11: 45–57.

Fairclough, Norman 2009. A dialectical–relational approach to Critical Discourse Analysis in social research. In: Wodak, Ruth, and Michael Meyer (eds) *Methods for Critical Discourse Analysis*, 162–86. London: Sage.

Fairhurst, Gail T., and François Cooren 2004. Oganizational language in use: Interaction analysis, conversation analysis and speech act semantics. In: Grant, David, Cynthia Hardy, Cliff Oswick, and Linda Putnam (eds) *The Sage Handbook of Organizational Discourse*, 131–52. Thousand Oaks, CA: Sage.

Fakhr-Rohani, Muhammad Reza 2005. Persian religious honorifics: A preliminary pragmatic inquiry into the linguistic manifestations of two Islamic articles of faith. In: Azadarmaki, Taqi (ed.) *Actes du colloque organisé par l'INALCO (ERISM), l'Université de Téhéran et l'IFRI*, 37–42. Louvain: Peeters.

Fitzmaurice, Susan 2002. *The Familiar Letter in Early Modern English: A Pragmatic Approach*. Amsterdam and Philadelphia: John Benjamins.

Forand, Nancy 2002. The language ideologies of courtship ritual: Maya Pentecostals and folk Catholics. *Journal of American Folklore* 115(457/458): 332–77.

Forgács, Tamás 2005. *"Állati" szólások és közmondások: A felfuvalkodott békától a szomszéd tehenéig* [Animal Idioms and Proverbs: From Bloated Frog to the Neighbour's Cow]. Budapest: Akadémiai Kiadó.

Foucault, Michel 1973. *The Order of Things: An Archaeology of the Human Sciences*. New York: Vintage Books.

Foucault, Michel 1975. *Surveiller et punir – Naissance de la prison*. Paris: Gallimard. Trans. Alan Sheridan 1976. *Discipline as Punish: The Birth of the Prison*. London: Penguin.

Fox, Suzy, Paul E. Spector, Angeline Goh, and Kari Bruursema 2007. Does your coworker know what you're doing? Convergence of self- and peer-reports on counterproductive work behaviour. *International Journal of Stress Management* 14(1): 41–60.

Frankfurter, David 2001. Ritual as accusation and atrocity: Satanic ritual abuse, gnostic libertinism, and primal murders. *History of Religions* 40(4): 352–80.

Fraser, Bruce [1981] 2012. Insulting problem in a second language. *TESOL Quarterly* 15(4): 435–41.

Friedman, Edward 1995. *National Identity and Democratic Prospects in Socialist China*. New York: M. E. Sharpe.

Garfinkel, Harold 1964. Studies in the routine grounds of everyday activities. *Social Problems* 11(3): 225–50.

Garner, Thurmon 1983. Playing the dozens: Folklore as strategies for living. *Quarterly Journal of Speech* 69(1): 47–57.

Geertz, Clifford 1973. *The Interpretation of Cultures: Selected Essays*. New York: Basic Books.

Gilmore, David D. 1990. *Manhood in the Making: Cultural Concepts of Masculinity*. New Haven, CT: Yale University Press.

Gleason, Jean Berko, and Sandra Weintraub 1976. The acquisition of routines in child language. *Language in Society* 5(2): 129–36.

Goffman, Erving 1963. *Stigma: Notes on the Management of Spoiled Identity*. London: Penguin.

Goffman, Erving 1967. *Interaction Ritual. Essays on Face-to-Face Behavior*. Garden City, NY: Doubleday.

Goffman, Erving 1974. *Frame Analysis: An Essay on the Organization of Experience*. New York: Harper & Row.
Goffman, Erving 1979. Footing. *Semiotica* 25(1/2): 1–30.
Goffman, Erving 1981. *Forms of Talk*. Philadelphia: The University of Pennsylvania Press.
Goleman, Daniel 1998. *Working with Emotional Intelligence*. New York: Bantam Books.
Goleman, Daniel 2011. *Social Intelligence: The New Science of Human Relationships*. London: Random House.
González, M. P., E. Barrull, C. Pons, and P. Marteles 1998. What is Affection. Retrieved from: <http://www.biopsychology.org/biopsychology/papers/what_is_affection.html>
Goodrick-Clarke, Nicholas 1985. *The Occult Roots of Nazism*. London: Tauris.
Goodwin, Marjorie H. 2006. *The Hidden Life of Girls: Games of Stance, Status, and Exclusion*. Oxford: Blackwell Publishing.
Gou, Chengyi 勾承益 2002. *Xianqin lixue* 先秦礼学 [The Study of 'Li' in Pre-Qin Times]. Chengdu: Ba-Shu shuse.
Grabenhorst, Fabian, Edmund T. Rolls, and Benjamin A. Parris 2008. From affective value to decision-making in the prefrontal cortex. *European Journal of Neuroscience* 28: 1930–9.
Grimes, Ronald L. 1990. *Ritual Criticism: Case Studies in its Practice, Essays on its Theory*. Columbia, SC: University of South Carolina Press.
Gross, Steven 2000. Intentionality and the markedness model in literary codeswitching. *Journal of Pragmatics* 32(9): 1283–303.
Gruenwald, Ithamar 2003. *Rituals and Ritual Theory in Ancient Israel*. Leiden: Brill.
Gu, Yueguo 1990. Politeness phenomenon in modern Chinese. *Journal of Pragmatics* 14(3): 237–57.
Guttmann, Allen 2004. *From Ritual to Record. The Nature of Modern Sports*. New York: Columbia University Press.
Hajdú, Mihály. 2003. *Általános és magyar névtan* [General and Hungarian Onomatology]. Budapest: Osiris Kiadó.
Handelman, Don 1979. Is naven ludic? Paradox and the communication of identity. In: Kapferer, Bruce (ed.) *The Power of Ritual: Transition, Transformation and Transcendence in Ritual Practice*, 177–91. Adelaide: University of Adelaide.
Harré, Rom, Fathali M. Moghaddam, Tracey Pilkerton Cairnie, Daniel Rothbart, and Steven R. Sabat 2009. Recent advances in positioning theory. *Theory & Psychology* 19(1): 5–31.
Harris, Sandra 1984. Questions as a mode of control in magistrates' court. *International Journal of the Sociology of Language* 48: 5–27.
Harris, Sandra 1995. Pragmatics and power. *Journal of Pragmatics* 23(2): 117–35.
Haugh, Michael 2003. Anticipated versus inferred politeness. *Multilingua* 22(4): 397–413.
Haugh, Michael 2010. Jocular mockery, (dis)affiliation and face. *Journal of Pragmatics* 42(8): 2106–19.
Haugh, Michael 2013 (forthcoming). Interpersonal evaluations and the participant order. In: Haugh, Michael, Dániel Z. Kádár, and Sara Mills (eds) *Journal of Pragmatics: Special Issue – Interpersonal Pragmatics*.
Haugh, Michael, Dániel Z. Kádár, and Sara Mills (eds) 2013. *Journal of Pragmatics: Special Issue – Interpersonal Pragmatics*.

Heidegger, Martin [1927] 1991. *Being and Time*. New York: John Wiley & Sons.
Henderson, David R., Robert M. McNab, and Tamás Rózsás 2005. The hidden inequality in Communism. *The Independent Review* 9(3): 389–412.
Hepburn, Alexa, and Sally Wiggins (eds) 2007. *Discursive Research in Practice: New Approaches to Psychology and Interaction*. Cambridge: Cambridge University Press.
Herring, Susan C. 1997. Computer-mediated discourse analysis: Introduction. *Electronic Journal of Communication* 6(3): 1–3. <http://www.cios.org/www/ejc/v6n396.htm>
Herring, Susan C. 2002. Computer-mediated communication on the Internet. *Annual Review of Information Science and Technology* 36: 109–68. <http://ella.slis.indiana.edu/~herring/arist.2002.pdf>
Holmes, Janet 2000. Politeness, power and provocation: How humour functions in the workplace. *Discourse Studies* 2: 159–85.
Holmes, Janet 2012. Politeness in intercultural discourse and communication. In: Paulston, Christina Bratt, Scott F. Kiesling, and Elizabeth S. Rangel (eds) *The Handbook of Intercultural Discourse and Communication*, 205–27. Oxford: Blackwell Publishing.
Holmes, Janet, and Meredith Marra 2004. Relational practice in the workplace: Women's talk or gendered discourse? *Language in Society* 33(3): 377–98.
Holmes, Janet, Meredith Marra, and Bernadette Vine 2011. *Discourse, Ethnicity and Leadership*. Oxford: Oxford University Press.
Holmes, Janet, and Stephanie Schnurr 2005. Politeness, humour and gender in the workplace: Negotiating norms and identifying contestation. *Journal of Politeness Research* 1(1): 121–49.
Hubert, Henri, and Mauss, Marcel 1899. *Essai sur la nature et le fonction du sacrifice* [Sacrifice: Its Nature and Function]. Trans. Wilfred D. Halls (1964). Chicago: University of Chicago Press.
Huggins, Kyle A. 2008. *The Emotional Experience Model: An Interaction Ritual Perspective on how Consumer Subcultures can Emotionally Re-Energize the Daily Routine*. Ann Arbor, MI: ProQuest.
Hughes, Geoffrey 1992. *Swearing: A Social History of Foul Language, Oaths and Profanity in English*. New York: J. Wiley & Sons.
Hugh-Jones, David, and Reinstein, David 2012. Anonymous rituals. *Journal of Economic Behaviour and Organization* 81(2): 478–89.
Huizinga, Johan 1938 [1955]. *Homo Ludens*. Boston: Beacon Press.
Ide, Risako 1998. 'Sorry for your kindness': Japanese interactional ritual in public discourse. *Journal of Pragmatics* 29(5): 509–29.
Ide, Sachiko 1989. Formal forms and discernment: Two neglected aspects of linguistic politeness. *Multilingua* 8(2/3): 223–48.
Illich, Ivan 1975. *Medical Nemesis: The Expropriation of Health*. New York: Pantheon Books.
Jacobs, Andreas, and Andreas H. Jucker 1995. The historical perspective in pragmatics. In: Jucker, Andreas H. (ed.) *Historical Pragmatics. Pragmatic Developments in the History of English*, 1–33. Amsterdam and Philadelphia: John Benjamins.
Jefferson, Gail. 2002. Is 'no' an acknowledgement token? Comparing American and British uses of (+)/(−) tokens. *Journal of Pragmatics* 34: 1345–83.
Josephus, Titus Flavius. *The Wars of the Jews*. Trans. Geoffrey A. Williamson 1959. London: Penguin.

Jucker, Andreas H. 2010. 'In curteisie was set ful muchel hir lest', Politeness in Middle English. In: Culpeper, Jonathan, and Dániel Z. Kádár (eds) *Historical (Im)Politeness*, 175–200. Berne and Oxford: Peter Lang.

Kachru, Braj B. 1985. Standards, codification and sociolinguistic realism: the English language in the outer circle. In: Quirk, Randolph, and Henry Widdowson (eds) *English in the World: Teaching and Learning the Language and Literatures*, 11–30. Cambridge: Cambridge University Press.

Kachru, Braj B. 1992. Teaching world Englishes. In: Kachru, Braj B. (ed.) *The Other Tongue: English across Cultures*, 355–66. Urbana, IL: University of Illinois Press.

Kádár, Dániel Z. 2007a. On historical Chinese apology and its strategic application. *Journal of Politeness Research* 3(1): 125–50.

Kádár, Dániel Z. 2007b. *Terms of (Im)Politeness: On the Communicational Properties of Traditional Chinese (Im)Polite Terms of Address*. Budapest: Eötvös Loránd University.

Kádár, Dániel Z. 2009. *Model Letters in Late Imperial China – 60 Selected Epistles from 'Letters of Snow Swan Retreat'*. Munich: Lincom.

Kádár, Dániel Z. 2010a. *Historical Chinese Letter Writing*. London and New York: Continuum.

Kádár, Dániel Z. 2010b. Exploring the historical Chinese polite denigration/elevation phenomenon. In: Culpeper, Jonathan, and Dániel Z. Kádár (eds) *Historical (Im)politeness*, 117–45. Berne and Oxford: Peter Lang.

Kádár, Dániel Z. 2011a. A graphic–semiotic analysis of the Chinese multimodal elevation and denigration phenomenon. *US–China Foreign Language* 9(2): 77–88.

Kádár, Dániel Z. 2011b. *Xue-guanhua* 学官话 : *A Ryūkyūan Source of Language Education*. Newcastle: CSP.

Kádár, Dániel Z. 2012a. On the positive formation of Chinese group identity. In: Pan, Yuling and Dániel Z. Kádár, *Chinese Discourse and Interaction*, 271–91. London: Equinox.

Kádár, Dániel Z. 2012b. Historical Chinese politeness and rhetoric. *Journal of Politeness Research* 8(1): 93–110.

Kádár, Dániel Z., and Marcel Bax 2013 (in press). In-group ritual and relational work. In: Haugh, Michael, Dániel Z. Kádár, and Sara Mills (eds) *Journal of Pragmatics: Special Issue – Interpersonal Pragmatics*. http://dx.doi.org/10.1016/j.pragma.2013.03.011

Kádár, Dániel Z. and Jonathan Culpeper 2010. Historical (im)politeness: An introduction. In: Culpeper, Jonathan, and Kádár, Dániel Z. (eds) *Historical (Im)politeness*, 9–36. Berne and Oxford: Peter Lang.

Kádár, Dániel Z., and Michael Haugh 2013. *Understanding Politeness*. Cambridge: Cambridge University Press.

Kádár, Dániel Z., and Sara Mills 2013 (forthcoming). Rethinking discernment. *Journal of Politeness Research* 9(2).

Kanter, Jodi 2007. *Performing Loss: Rebuilding Community through Theater and Writing*. Carbondale: South Illinois University.

Kertzer, David I. 1988. *Ritual, Politics, and Power*. New Haven, CT: Yale University Press.

Kienpointner, Manfred 1997. Varieties of rudeness: Types and functions of impolite utterances. *Functions of Language* 4(2): 251–87.

Kis, Tamás 1992. *Bakaduma: A mai magyar katonai szleng szótára* [Private Jaw: Dictionary of Contemporary Hungarian Army Slang]. Budapest: Zrínyi Kiadó.

Koster, Jan 2003. Ritual performance and the politics of identity. On the functions and uses of ritual. *Journal of Historical Pragmatics* 4(2): 211–48.

Koutlaki, Sofia A. 2002. Offers and expressions of thanks as face enhancing acts: Tæ'arof in Persian. *Journal of Pragmatics* 34(12): 1733–56.

Kowalski, Robin M., Susan P. Limber, and Patricia W. Agatston 2008. *Cyberbullying: Bullying in the Digital Age*. Oxford: Blackwell Publishing.

Kress, Tricia M. 2011. *Critical Praxis Research: Breathing New Life into Research Methods for Teachers*. London: Springer.

Kryk-Kastovsky, Barbara 2006. Impoliteness in Early Modern English court trial discourse. In: Kryk-Kastovsky, Barbara (ed.) *Historical Courtroom Discourse. Special issue of Journal of Historical Pragmatics* 7(2): 213–45.

Krzyżanowski, Michał 2010. *The Discursive Construction of European Identities: A Multi-Level Approach to Discourse and Identity in the Transforming European Union*. Berne and Oxford: Peter Lang.

Kyriakidis, Evangelos (ed.) 2007. *The Archeology of Ritual*. Berkeley: University of California Press.

Labov, William 1972. Rules for ritual insults. In: Labov, William: *Language in the Inner City*, 297–353. Philadelphia: University of Pennsylvania Press.

Langlotz, Andreas 2010. Social cognition. In: Locher, Miriam, and Sage Lambert Graham (eds) *Interpersonal Pragmatics*, 167–202. Berlin and New York: Mouton de Gruyter.

Langlotz, Andreas and Miriam Locher 2013 (forthcoming). The role of emotions in a discursive approach to relational work. In: Haugh, Michael, Dániel Z. Kádár, and Sara Mills (eds) *Journal of Pragmatics: Special Issue – Interpersonal Pragmatics*.

Lawson, Thomas E., and Robert N. McCauley 2002. *Rethinking Religion: Connecting Cognition and Culture*. Cambridge: Cambridge University Press.

Leech, Geoffrey 1983. *Principles of Pragmatics*. Harlow: Longman.

Locher, Miriam A. 2004. *Power and Politeness in Action: Disagreements in Oral Communication*. Berlin and New York: Mouton de Gruyter.

Locher, Miriam A. 2010. Introduction: Politeness and impoliteness in computer-mediated communication. *Journal of Politeness Research* 6(1): 1–5.

Locher, Miriam A. 2011. Situated impoliteness: The interface between relational work and identity construction. In: Haugh, Michael, Andrew John Merrison, and Bethan Davies (eds) *Situated Politeness*, 187–208. London and New York: Continuum.

Locher, Miriam, and Andreas Langlotz 2008. Relational work at the intersection of cognition, interaction and emotion. *Bulletin vals-asla, bulletin suisse de la linguistique appliquée* 88: 165–91.

Locher, Miriam A., and Richard J. Watts 2005. Politeness theory and relational work. *Journal of Politeness Research* 1(1): 9–33.

Locher, Miriam A., and Richard J. Watts 2008. Relational work and impoliteness: Negotiating norms of linguistic behaviour. In: Bousfield, Derek, and Miriam A. Locher (eds) *Impoliteness in Language. Studies on its Interplay with Power in Theory and Practice*, 77–99. Berlin and New York: Mouton de Gruyter.

Locke, John 2011. *Duels and Duets: Why Men and Women Talk So Differently*. Cambridge: Cambridge University Press.

Lytte, Jim 2007. The judicious use and management of humour in the workplace. *Business Horizons* 50(3): 239–45.

McClenon, James 1997. Shamanic healing, human evolution, and the origin of religion. *Journal for the Scientific Study of Religion* 36(3): 345–54.
McKenzie, Jon 2004. The liminal norm. In: Bial, Henry (ed.) *The Performance Studies Reader*, 26–31. New York and London: Routledge.
Marks, Isaac Meyer 1987. *Fears, Phobias, and Rituals: Panic, Anxiety, and Their Disorders*. Oxford: Oxford University Press.
May, Jacob L. 2011. Speech acts in context. In: Anita Fetzer and Etsuko Oishi (eds) *Context and Contexts: Parts Meet Whole?* 171–80. Amsterdam and Philadelphia: John Benjamins.
Mazzone, Marco 2011. Schemata and associative processes in pragmatics. *Journal of Pragmatics* 43(8): 2148–59.
Menesini, Ersina, Virginia Sanchez, Ada Fonzi, Rosario Ortega, Angela Costabile, and Giorgio Lo Feudo 2003. Moral emotions and bullying: A cross-national comparison of differences between bullies, victims and outsiders. *Aggressive Behavior* 29(6): 515–30.
Miller, Jean B. 1984. The development of women's sense of self. Wellesley, MA: Stone Center Working Paper Series.
Mills, Sara 2003a. *Michel Foucault*. New York and London: Routledge.
Mills, Sara 2003b. *Gender and Politeness*. Cambridge: Cambridge University Press.
Mills, Sara 2011. Discursive approaches to politeness and impoliteness. In: Linguistic Politeness Research Group (ed.) *Discursive Approaches to Politeness*, 19–56. Berlin and New York: Mouton de Gruyter.
Mills, Sara, and Dániel Z. Kádár 2011. Politeness and culture. In: Kádár, Dániel Z., and Sara Mills (eds) *Politeness in East Asia*, 21–44. Cambridge: Cambridge University Press.
Milroy, Lesley, and James Milroy 1992. Social network and social class: Toward an integrated sociolinguistic model. *Language in Society* 21(1): 1–26.
Muir, Edward 2005 [1997]. *Ritual in Early Modern Europe*. Cambridge: Cambridge University Press.
Myers Scotton, Carol 1998. Introduction. In: Myers Scotton, Carol (ed.) *Codes and Consequences: Choosing Linguistic Varieties*. Oxford: Oxford University Press.
Naipaul, Vidiadhar S. 2005. *V. S. Naipaul: Critical Essays*. Delhi: Nice Printing Press.
Oberoi, Harjot 1994. *The Construction of Religious Boundaries: Culture, Identity, and Diversity in the Sikh Tradition*. Chicago: The University of Chicago Press.
Ohashi, Jun 2008. Linguistic rituals for thanking in Japanese: Balancing obligations. *Journal of Pragmatics* 40(12): 2150–74.
Okamoto, Shigeko 1999. Situated politeness: Manipulating honorific and non-honorific expressions in Japanese conversations. *Pragmatics* 9(1): 51–74.
Ollendick, Thomas H., and Carolyn S. Schroeder 2003. *Encyclopedia of Clinical Child and Pediatric Psychology*. New York and London: Routledge.
Ong, Walter J. 1981. *Fighting for Life: Contest, Sexuality, and Consciousness*. Ithaca, NY: Cornell University Press.
Packer, Lesley E. 2012. Obsessive–compulsive behaviour: Overview. Retrieved from: <http://www.schoolbehavior.com/disorders/obsessions-and-compulsions/obsessive-compulsive-disorder-overview/>
Pan, Yuling, and Dániel Z. Kádár 2011. *Politeness in Historical and Contemporary Chinese*. London and New York: Continuum.

Paternoster, Annick 2012. Inappropriate inspectors: Impoliteness and overpoliteness in Ian Rankin's and Andrea Camillieri's crime series. *Language and Literature* 21(3): 311–24.
Penner, Hans H. 2012. Ritual. *Encyclopaedia Britannica*. Retrieved from: <http://www.britannica.com/EBchecked/topic/504688/ritual>
Peregrin, Jaroslav 2012. The normative dimension of discourse. In: Allan, Keith, and Kasia M. Jascczolt (eds) *The Cambridge Handbook of Pragmatics*, 209–26. Cambridge: Cambridge University Press.
Pike, Kenneth 1967. *Language in Relation to a Unified Theory of the Structure of Human Behavior*, 2nd edn. Berlin and New York: Mouton de Gruyter.
Pizziconi, Barbara 2011. Honorifics: The cultural specificity of a universal mechanism in Japanese. In: Kádár, Dániel Z., and Sara Mills (eds) *Politeness in East Asia*, 45–71. Cambridge: Cambridge University Press.
Planchenault, Gaëlle 2010. Virtual community and politeness: The use of female markers of identity and solidarity in a transvestites' website. *Journal of Politeness Research* 6(1): 83–104.
Potolsky, Matthew 2006. *Mimesis*. New York and London: Routledge.
Poyurovsky, Michael, Abraham Weizman, and Ronit Weizman 2004. Obsessive-compulsive disorder in schizophrenia: Clinical characteristics and treatment. *CNS Drugs* 18(14): 989–1010(22).
Presthus, Robert, Richard Simeon, and David Braybrooke 1976. Exchange. *Canadian Journal of Political Science* 9(1): 127–31.
Purdy, Charles 2004. *Urban Etiquette. Marvellous Manners for the Modern Metropolis: A Commonsense Guide to Courteous Living*. Tulsa and San Francisco: Wildcat Canyon Press.
Rákosi, György 2008. Some remarks on Hungarian ethical datives. <http://ieas.unideb.hu/admin/file_364.pdf>
Rampton, Ben 2006. *Language in Late Modernity: Interaction in an Urban School*. Cambridge: Cambridge University Press.
Rapoport, Judith L. (ed.) 1989. *Obsessive–Compulsive Disorder in Children and Adolescents*. Washington: American Psychiatric Press.
Rash, Felicity 2004. Linguistic politeness and greeting rituals in German-speaking Switzerland. *Linguistik Online* 20 (3/04). Retrieved from: <http://www.linguistik-online.de/20_04/rash.html>
Rasmussen, Susan J. 1992. Ritual specialists, ambiguity, and power in Tuareg society. *Man* 27(1): 105–28.
Redding, S. Gordon, and Michael Ng. 1982. The role of 'face' in the organizational perceptions of Chinese managers. *Organization Studies* 3(3): 201–19.
Reijnders, Stijn 2007. Media rituals and festive culture: Imagining the nation in Dutch television entertainment. *International Journal of Cultural Studies* 10(2): 225–42.
Rossano, Matt J. 2009. Ritual behaviour and the origins of modern cognition. *Cambridge Archeological Journal* 19(2): 243–56.
Rossner, Meredith 2008. Why emotions work: Restorative justice, interaction ritual and the micro potential for emotional transformation. Dissertation, Penn State University.
Rothenbuhler, Eric W. 1998. *Ritual Communication. From Everyday Conversation to Mediated Ceremony*. Thousand Oaks, CA: Sage.

Ruhi, Şükriye 2009. A place for emotions in conceptualizing face and relational work. Plenary lecture, International Symposium on Face and Politeness, Griffith University, Brisbane.
Sanguinetti, Angela, and Wendy Reyes 2011. Functional assessment of drug-trafficking terms: A substantive and methodological expansion of a verbal behavior research program. *Behavior and Social Issues* 20: 102–17.
Schechner, Richard 1995. *The Future of Ritual – Writings on Culture and Performance*. New York and London: Routledge.
Schegloff, Emanuel A. 1995. Discourse as an interactional achievement III: The omnirelevance of action. *Research on Language and Social Interaction* 28(3): 185–211.
Schermerhorn, John R., Hunt, James G., and Osborn, Richard N. 2011. *Organizational Behaviour*. New York: J. Wiley & Sons.
Scheve, Christian von 2011 (in press). Collective emotions in rituals: Elicitation, transmission, and a 'Matthew-Effect'. In: Michaels, A., and C. Wulf (eds) *Emotions in European and South-Asian Rituals*. London. <http://www.affective-sociology.org/uploads/2/5/4/4/2544442/scheve_emotionsrituals_preprint.pdf>
Schmidt, Bettina E., and Ingo Schröder 2001. *Anthropology of Violence and Conflict*. New York and London: Routledge.
Searle, John 1969. *Speech Acts: An Essay in the Philosophy of Language*. Cambridge: Cambridge University Press.
Searle, John 1975. Indirect speech acts. In: Cole, Peter, and Jerry L. Morgan (eds) *Syntax and Semantics*, Vol. 3: *Speech Act*, 59–82. New York: Academic Press.
Sears, William, and Martha Sears 2005. *The Good Behaviour Book: How to Have a Better-Behaved Child from Birth to Age Ten*. London: Thorsons (HarperCollins).
Sifianou, Maria 2012. Disagreements, face and politeness. To the memory of Christina Kakavá, a pioneer in research on disagreements. *Journal of Pragmatics* 44(12): 1554–64.
Silverstein, Michael 1981. The limits of awareness. Sociolinguistic Working Paper 84. Washington: National Institute of Education.
Smith, Peter K., Helen Cowie, Ragnar F. Olafsson, and Andy P. D. Liefooghe 2002. Definitions of bullying: A comparison of terms used, and age and gender differences, in a fourteen-country international comparison. *Child Development* 73(4): 1119–33.
Smith, Peter K., Kristen C. Madsen, and Janet C. Moody 1999. What causes the age decline in reports of being bullied in school? Towards a developmental analysis of risks of being bullied. *Educational Research* 41(3): 267–85.
Smith, Peter K., Jess Mahdavi, Manuel Carvalho, Sonja Fisher, Shanette Russell, and Neil Tippett 2008. Cyberbullying: Its nature and impact on secondary school pupils. *The Journal of Child Psychology and Psychiatry* 49(4): 376–85.
Spencer-Oatey, Helen 2005. (Im)politeness, face and perceptions of rapport: Unpackaging their bases and interrelationships. *Journal of Politeness Research* 1(1): 95–119.
Spencer-Oatey, Helen [2000] 2008. Introduction: Language, culture and rapport management. In: Helen Spencer-Oatey (ed.) *Culturally Speaking*, 1–10. London and New York: Continuum.

Spencer-Oatey, Helen 2011. Conceptualising 'the relational' in pragmatics: Insights from metapragmatic emotion and (im)politeness comments. *Journal of Pragmatics* 43(14): 3565–78.

Spencer-Oatey, Helen, and Peter Franklin 2009. *Intercultural interaction: A Multidisciplinary Approach to Intercultural Communication*. Basingstoke: Palgrave Macmillan.

Staal, Fritz 1979. The meaningless of ritual. *Numen* 26(1): 2–22.

Streeck, Jürgen 1980. Speech acts in interaction: A critique of Searle. *Discourse Processes* 3(2): 133–53.

Streeck, Jürgen 1996. A little Ilokano grammar as it appears in interaction. *Journal of Pragmatics* 26(2): 189–213.

Sugimura, Ryoichi 1986. Japanese honorifics and situation semantics. In: *Proceedings of International Conference on Computational Linguistics 1986*, 507–10. Bonn: University of Bonn.

Tao, Lin 2010. Politeness in Chinese and Japanese verbal communication. *Intercultural Communication Studies* XIX: 37–54.

Tavuchis, Nicholas 1993. *Mea Culpa: A Sociology of Apology and Reconciliation*. Palo Alto, CA: Stanford University Press.

Taylor, Paul Beekman 1994. Repetition as cure in Native American story: Silko's *Ceremony* and Momaday's *The Ancient Child*. *SPELL: Swiss Papers in English Language and Literature* 7: 221–42.

Taylor, Stephanie 2007. Narrative as construction and discursive resource. In: Bamberg, Michael (ed.) *Narrative – State of the Art*, 113–22. Amsterdam and Philadelphia: John Benjamins.

ten Have, Paul 1991. Talk and institution: A reconsideration of the 'asymmetry' of doctor–patient interaction. In: Boden, Deidre, and Don H. Zimmerman (eds) *Talk and Social Structure: Studies in Ethnomethodology and Conversation Analysis*, 138–63. Cambridge: Polity Press.

ter Haar, Barend J. 1998. *Ritual and Mythology of the Chinese Triads: Creating an Identity*. Leiden: Brill.

Terkourafi, Marina 2001. Politeness in Cypriot Greek: A frame-based approach. Doctoral dissertation, University of Cambridge.

Terkourafi, Marina 2005. Beyond the micro-level in politeness research. *Journal of Politeness Research* 1(2): 237–62.

Thomas, Angela 2007. *Youth Online: Identity and Literacy in the Digital Age*. Berne and Oxford: Peter Lang.

Thornborrow, Joanna 2002. *Power Talk: Language and Interaction in Institutional Discourse*. London: Longman.

Thornbury, Scott, and Diana Slade 2006. *Conversation: From Description to Pedagogy*. Cambridge: Cambridge University Press.

Tonkin, Humphrey 1987. One hundred years of Esperanto: A survey. *Language Problems & Language Planning* 11(3): 264–82.

Tracy, Karen, and Julie Naughton 2009. The identity work of questioning in intellectual discussion. *Communication Monographs* 61(4): 281–302.

Traube, Elizabeth G. 1986. *Cosmology and Social Life: Ritual Exchange among the Mambai of East Timor*. Chicago: University of Chicago Press.

Tuchman, Gaye 1972. Objectivity as strategic ritual: An examination of newsmen's notions of objectivity. *American Journal of Sociology* 77(4): 660–79.

Tully, Philip J., and Christopher J. Edwards 2009. Schizophrenia, obsessive covert mental rituals and social anxiety: Case report. *Clinical Psychologist* 13(2): 75–7.
Turbott, John 1997. The meaning and function of ritual in psychiatric disorder, religion and everyday behaviour. *Australian and New Zealand Journal of Psychiatry* 31(6): 835–43.
Turner, Victor W. 1967. *The Forest of Symbols: Aspects of Ndembu Rituals*. Ithaca, NY: Cornell University Press.
Turner, Victor W. 1969 [2008]. *The Ritual Process: Structure and Anti-Structure*. Piscataway, NJ: Transaction Publishers.
Turner, Victor W. 1974. *Dramas, Fields, and Metaphors: Symbolic Action in Human Society*. Ithaca, NY and London: Cornell University Press.
Turner, Victor W. 1982. *From Ritual to Theatre: The Human Seriousness of Play*. Michigan: The University of Michigan.
van der Hart, Onno 1983. *Rituals in Psychotherapy: Transition and Continuity*. New York: Irvington Publishers.
van der Hart, Onno 1988. Myths and rituals: Their use in psychotherapy. In: van der Hart, Onno (ed.) *Coping with Loss: the Therapeutic Use of Leave-Taking Rituals*. New York: Irvington.
van Dijk, Teun A. 1985. *Discourse and Communication: New Approaches to the Analysis of Mass Media Discourse and Communication*. Berlin and New York: Mouton de Gruyter.
van Gennep, Arnold 1909 [1960]. *Rite de Passage* [The Rites of Passage]. Trans. Monika B. Vizedom, and Gabrielle L. Caffee. New York and London: Routledge.
Vartia, Maarit 1996. The sources of bullying – Psychological work environment and organizational climate. *European Journal of Work and Organization Psychology* 5(2): 203–14.
Vergaro, Carla 2002. 'Dear Sirs, what would you do if you were in our position?' Discourse strategies in Italian and English money chasing letters. *Journal of Pragmatics* 34(9): 1211–33.
Verschueren, Jef 2000. Notes on the role of metapragmatic awareness in language use. *Pragmatics* 10(4): 439–56.
Voloshinov, V. N. 1986. *Marxism and the Philosophy of Language*. Cambridge, MA: Harvard University Press.
Wallace, Mark 2007. Experience, purpose, pedagogy, and theory: Ritual activities in the classroom. In: Catherine Bell (ed.) *Teaching Ritual*, 73–87. Oxford: Oxford University Press.
Watts, Richard J. 1991. *Power in Family Discourse*. Berlin and New York: Mouton de Gruyter.
Watts, Richard J. 2003. *Politeness*. Cambridge: Cambridge University Press.
Watts, Richard J. 2008. Rudeness, conceptual blending theory and relational work. *Journal of Politeness Research* 4(2): 289–317.
Wenger, Etienne 1998. *Communities of Practice: Learning, Meaning, and Identity*. Cambridge: Cambridge University Press.
West, Richard, and Lynn H. Turner 2010. *Understanding Interpersonal Communication: Making Choices in Changing Times*. Boston, MA: Cengage Learning.
Western, Bruce 2006. *Punishment and Inequality in America*. New York: Russell Stage Foundation.
Wierzbicka, Anna 2006. *English: Meaning and Culture*. Oxford: Oxford University Press.

Williams, Clare 2005. Framing the fetus in medical work: Rituals and practices. *Social Science & Medicine* 60(9): 2085–95.
Wuthnow, Robert 2007. Religion and cognition. *Sociology of Religion: A Quarterly Review* 68(4): 341–60.
Yan, Yunxiang 1993. *The Flow of Gifts: Reciprocity and Social Networks in a Chinese Village*. Cambridge, MA: Harvard University Press.
Yedes, Janet 1996. Playful teasing: Kiddin' on the square. *Discourse and Society* 7(3): 417–38.
Zhang, Yuanzhong 1999. Self-deprecation phenomenon in Chinese face-work: Ritual and pragmatic implications. Retrieved from: <http://www.eric.ed.gov/PDFS/ED475014.pdf>
Zhao Shugong 赵树功 1999. *Zhongguo chidu wenxue shi* 中国尺牍文学史 [The History of Chinese Epistolary Literature]. Shijiazhuang: Hebei renmin chubanshe.
Zhu, Yunxia 2005. *Written Communication across Cultures*. Amsterdam and Philadelphia: John Benjamins.
Zurcher, Louis A. 1985. The war game: Organizational scripting and the expression of emotion. *Symbolic Interaction* 8(2): 191–206.

Index 索引

300 (film), 17, 46, 47

A Beautiful Mind, 102
academic settings, 80, 117, 118, 124, 125
accessibility of rituals, 20, 42, 79, 83–103
action, *see* social action
activation of rituals in interaction, 57–9, 61
affection/affectivity, 11, 13, 17, 20, 47, 64, 71, 92, 104, 105, 111–14, 117, 125–34
African Americans, 54, 55
aggression, 31, 54
Alemán, Melissa W., 68
Alexander, Martin S., 97
ambiguity, 28, 30, 32, 85, 92, 162, 163
Andrews, Stephen, 14
anecdotes, 142, 180
Anglo-Englishes, 36, 39
Angouri, Jo, 64
animating the voice of others/an institution, 45, 46, 56, 59, 63, 122, 147, 153, 158
anthropology, 3, 6, 18, 21, 23, 24, 32, 44–6, 78, 80, 103, 105, 135, 140, 161, 162, 176, 181, 182, 184
anticipating, 114, 130, 131, 149–55, 170, 172
Aouragh, Miriyam, 65
arbitrariness of ritual practices, 85–98
Archer, Dawn, 181
Arundale, Robert, 25
Attardo, Salvatore, 156
audio-recorded interactions, 16, 17
Austin, John L., 85, 107
Australia, 158
awareness of outsider's/public's presence, 61, 162–74

backchannelling, 118
Bandura, Albert, 172
Bax, Marcel, 7, 8, 26, 27, 51, 53, 56, 60, 62, 68, 79, 81, 100, 103
Bell, Catherine, 6, 17, 23, 46, 79, 80, 140
Bendix, Regina, 181
Bennett, Lance W., 181
Berthomé, François, 114
Blackmore, Susan J., 7, 8
Blaikie, Thomas, 42
Bloch, Sidney, 158
blogs, 16, 82, 83, 98, 99, 108, 109, 154, 155
Bosk, Charles L., 80
Bourdieu, Pierre, 64, 73
Bousfield, Derek, 139
Bovey, Alixe, 93
Bridget Jones: The Edge of Reason, 26
Britain/British, 27, 37, 42, 146, 147, 160, 176
British Bulldog, 51
Brody, Elaine M., 38
Brown, Penelope, 63, 177
Bucholtz, Mary, 52, 65, 73, 74
Buckley Ebrey, Patricia, 11
Budapest, 48
Bully Free at Work, 151
'bullying', 135, 136
Burke, Peter, 7, 8, 60
Byon, Andrew Sangpil, 180

Caillois, Roger, 45
Capture the Flag, 51
cartoons, 16
centralisation (of ritual practices), 8
ceremonies, 2, 10
Chan, Alan K. L., 11
Chan, Marjorie K. M., 66
Charlie's Angels, 49

Charvat, František, 8
China/Chinese, 4, 11, 15, 35, 36, 53, 64–77, 100, 164–6, 176, 177, 183
   southern vs northern opposition, 66, 67, 69
Ciarocchi, Joseph W., 88, 90
Clarke, Matthew, 64
Clift, Rebecca, 3, 153
co-construction (of rituals), 2, 14, 19, 47, 51–77, 104, 111, 113, 114, 122, 128, 132, 134, 147, 148, 151, 166, 177, 183
codification (of ritual practices), 8, 40, 45, 51, 52, 56, 88, 98, 113, 125, 128
cognition, 20, 62, 104–34, 173
   cognitive unpredictability, 104
Collier, Judith, 86
Collins, Randall, 4, 5, 56, 113, 114, 128
community of practice, 4, 39, 147, 157, 158
computer-mediated communication, 16, 53, 54, 143
conflict resolution/avoidance, 7, 40, 52, 54, 56, 59, 60, 63, 121, 183
conformance (to expectations), 19, 41–3, 50
Confucianism, 11
consciousness, 111, 114–25
contestedness of ritual practices, 82, 98, 99, 110, 140, 162
context, 14, 19, 110, 116, 119–22, 132
conventions, 9, 14, 18, 19, 28–43, 46, 47, 50, 56, 63, 70, 73–5, 106–10, 114–16, 137, 149, 175
conventionalisation, 4, 5, 11, 12, 20, 36, 82, 91, 103, 106, 138, 178
conversation analysis, 17
Cooren, François, 30
Copestake, Anne, 34
Couldry, Nick, 81
Cova, Bernard, 73
covert ritual, 84–93
   compulsive cases (definition), 86
   compulsive cases with delusional beliefs (definition), 86
Crane, Susan, 24
creativity, 63
cyberbullying, 143

Culpeper, Jonathan, 9, 13, 36, 39, 42, 49, 56, 74, 75, 137, 139, 148, 149, 155, 156, 172
culture, 15, 23, 36, 37, 54, 56, 68, 100, 108, 137, 176–83

data, 9, 15, 16
defaultness, 20, 110–25
Deflem, Mathieu, 142
demarcatedness, 2, 14, 104, 105, 132, 176
Demmen, Jane, 36, 39
deconstructive (ludic) ritual, 142
dependence, 7, 8, 45
'deritualisation', 6–9, 175
destructive ritual acts, 21, 110, 135–74
   reinterpretation of, 167–72
   restrictions of, 164–6
development history of conventional practices, 39
diachronic perspective, 93
dialogic interaction, 16
diminutive, 37, 55
diplomatic rituals, 51
directness, *see* indirectness
discursive perspective, 1–3, 14, 15, 17, 19, 21, 28, 33, 36, 107, 175, 181, 183, 184
discursive resource, 31, 59, 69
discussion boards, 40, 151–4, 167–72
diversity of relational actions, 36–41, 181
dominant social values, 39
Donald, Merlin, 7
Douglas, Mary, 6
Doyle, Sir Arthur Conan, 2
Drew, Paul, 153
Durkheim, Émile, 6, 7, 43, 44, 60, 78, 79, 110, 113, 183
   on positive and negative rituals, 79
   on 'sacred' vs 'profane', 78, 79

East Asia, 10, 11, 54
Eberhard, Wolfram, 66, 70
Eckert, Penelope, 64
economics, 182
educational materials, 16, 164–6
educational studies, 135, 182
Edwards, Christopher J., 86

Eelen, Gino, 26, 42
egalitarianism (ethos), 8
Eglash, Ron, 145
Elias, Norbert, 6
e-mails, 53–64, 122
emergent systems, 123
emoticons, 54, 153, 170
emotions, 17, 20, 47, 89, 92, 96, 105, 111–14, 125–34, 153
'empty' rituals, 3, 44, 176
Encyclopaedia of Taiwan, 100
English, 1, 15, 27, 31, 32, 49, 89–92, 94–6, 99, 102, 105, 108, 109, 130, 162, 167–72, 177
  Early Modern English, 155, 156
Escandell-Vidal, Victoria, 107
Esperanto, 29
ethnicity, 108, 109
ethnography, 5, 17
ethos, 12, 14, 19, 47, 52, 56, 63–5, 74, 76, 114, 132, 136, 138, 145–7, 159, 160, 162, 166
etiquette, 1, 24, 38, 40, 179
evaluations, 10, 18, 26, 35, 38, 42, 88, 93, 96, 98, 110, 112, 117, 120, 130, 132, 139, 149, 150, 161–74
  re-evaluation, 173
'evil ritual', 140, 141
expectancy/expectations, 10, 25, 41, 43, 47, 50, 87, 93, 109–11, 116, 119–22, 131, 153, 162
  moral expectations/sentiment, 42, 44, 110, 111, 117, 128, 138, 139, 155, 171
expression of emotions as ritual, 71

Fairhurst, Gail T., 30
Fakhr-Rohani, Muhammad R., 180
favours and gifts, 67
films, 16, 17
flexibility of ritual practices, 63
flux of emotions and affection, 112, 113, 131, 132
flyting, 54
folk theorisation of ritual, 84, 140, 141, 182
Forand, Nancy, 181
formal fixity, 11, 13, 14, 19, 34, 51, 52, 56, 105, 138

forms of address, 56, 131, 156, 159, 181
forms of salutation, 82
Foucault, Michel, 8, 9, 141
frame/framing, 62, 64, 105, 117, 121
France, 163
Frankfurter, David, 141
Fraser, Bruce, 137
French, 39, 40, 42
Friedman, Edward, 66

game and play, 3, 45, 46, 48, 49, 51, 52, 61, 130, 169
Garfinkel, Harold, 30, 39
Garner, Thurmon, 55
Geertz, Clifford, 93
gender/gendered, 37, 38, 41, 54, 73, 131, 132
generations, 38, 42, 82
gestures, 54
Gilmore, David D., 80
girls' cliques, 55
Goffman, Erving, 5, 21, 59, 104, 105, 136, 143–8, 159
Goleman, Daniel, 112
Gong, Weizhai 龚未斋, 67–77
González, M. P., 13, 104
Goodrick-Clarke, Nicholas, 140
Goodwin, Marjorie H., 55
Gou, Chengyi, 11
Grabenhorst, Fabian, 13
graphic representation, 35
'grid–group societies', 6
Grimes, Ronald L., 60, 80
Gruenwald, Ithamar, 44
Gu, Yueguo, 183
Guttmann, Allen, 6

hallucinations, 88
Harré, Rom F.M.M., 170
Harris, Sandra, 181
Haugh, Michael, 1, 3, 10, 18, 24, 25, 32, 37, 42, 83, 106, 109, 139, 149, 150, 158
Heidegger, Martin, 9
Henderson, David R., 8
Hepburn, Alexa, 14
Herring, Susan, 54, 122
hierarchy, 8–9

historical pragmatics, 6, 177
historical sociology, 8
historicity, 9, 12, 136, 173
history research, 3, 162
Holmes, Janet, 25, 156, 178
Holmes, Sherlock, 1
Homo Ludens, 45
Hong Kong, 73
Hot Water, 32
Houseman, Michael, 114
Hubert, Henri, 80
Huggins, Kyle A., 114
Hughes, Geoffrey, 137
Hugh-Jones, David, 182
Huizinga, Johan, 45, 48
humour, 56–9, 75, 76, 101, 115, 153, 156, 158, 159, 164–6, 170, 171, 179
Hungarian, 12, 15, 37, 39, 41, 48, 50, 51, 53–64, 73, 81–3, 97, 98, 100–2, 115–25, 129–32, 136, 138, 143, 147, 148, 162, 172, 177

iconic, 6
Ide, Sachiko, 177–82
identity formation (of relational networks), 19, 52, 64–77
 positive identity formation practices, 65
ideology, 7, 8, 180, 181
idioms, 75–7
Ilias, 17
Illich, Ivan, 80, 81
impoliteness, 21, 24–8, 36, 42, 111, 137, 139, 143, 148–74, 177
 mock impoliteness, 74–7, 121
 overt/covert impoliteness, 155, 156
indirectness, 27, 34, 37, 39, 148, 149–60, 172
individualism (ideology), 8, 36
in-group (definition), 4
institutionalisation, 113, 114, 125
intentionality, 41, 74, 85, 88, 111–14, 125, 132, 150, 153
Interaction Ritual, 5
interactional frequency, 105, 106
intuition, 106

invitation cards, 35, 36
irony, 121
Italy, 163

Jacobs, Andreas, 9
Japanese, 11, 120, 121, 162, 178–82
Jefferson, Gail, 17
Josephus, Titus Flavius, 84
Jucker, Andreas H., 9, 184

Kádár, Dániel Z., 3, 9, 10, 18, 24, 25, 32, 35, 36, 37, 53, 67, 69, 73, 74, 81, 83, 100, 106, 109, 139, 150, 166, 178–80, 182, 183
Kanter, Jodi, 8
Kennedy, John F., 140
Kertzer, David I., 7, 59
Kienpointner, Manfred, 48
Korea, 11
Koster, Jan, 48, 62, 106, 117
Kowalski, Robin M., 143
Kress, Tricia M., 17
Kryk-Kastovsky, Barbara, 155
Kryżanowski, Michał, 14
Kučera, Jaroslav, 8

Labov, William, 6, 36, 55
Langlotz, Andreas, 111, 112, 125
Lawson, Thomas E., 106
Leech, Geoffrey, 148
Legends of the Fall, 31
letter writing, 16, 53, 64–77
Levinson, Stephen C., 63, 177
li(yi) 礼(仪) (ritual in Chinese), 11, 100
lifespan (of conventions/rituals), 3, 41, 63, 99–102
liminality, 105, 142
literary works, 16, 17
Locher, Miriam, 25, 33, 41, 111, 112, 125
Locke, John, 54
Longmore, Murray, 86
Lytte, Jim, 156

manually recorded interactions, 16
markedness, 20, 110, 111, 114–25
Marks, Isaac Meyer, 6, 87, 88
Marra, Meredith, 64
Mauss, Marcel, 80

Mazzone, Marco, 29
McCauley, Robert N., 106
McClenon, James, 44
McKenzie, Jon, 142
media, 81
medical rituals, 80, 81
memes, 7
Menesini, Ersina V. S., 161
metacommunication, 60
metadiscourse, 20, 37, 94, 102, 104, 105, 109, 110, 115, 121, 122, 128, 143, 154, 155, 161, 173
metapragmatic awareness, 98, 105, 109, 111, 114–25, 170
Mey, Jacob, 115
Midwestern Americans, 98
Miller, Jean B., 2
Mills, Sara, 6, 8, 10, 14, 26, 74, 81, 108, 178, 179
Milroy, James, 4
Milroy, Lesley, 4
mimesis/mimetic, 6, 7, 12, 14, 19, 20, 24, 26, 43–50, 52, 55–64, 68–70, 75, 76, 82, 90, 101, 113–19, 123–5, 128, 129, 136–8, 158, 169, 179
monologic interaction, 16
morality, 140, 143, 161–74
see also moral expectations
Muir, Edward, 7, 8, 9, 10, 162, 163
multidirectional relating, 128
multimodality, 54
mundaneness, 79

Naipul, Vidiadhar S., 8
nationalistic rituals, 69–72, 75
Ng, Michael, 73
norms/normativity, 20, 33, 36, 37, 41, 43, 51, 56, 73, 75, 82, 83, 88, 93, 94, 97, 105–9, 111, 114–18, 122, 125, 131, 139, 150, 151, 162, 163, 166, 175, 178, 181
empirical norms, 41
moral norms, 42
normative/moral order, 123, 125, 166
North America, 108, 109, 125–8, 136, 145, 146, 154, 155, 159
novels, 16

Oberoi, Harjot, 64
observer's paradox, 16
Okamoto, Shigeko, 180
Ollendick, Thomas H., 96
Ong, Walter J., 54
onlookers of ritual practices, 166
organisation studies, 29, 173
overlaps, 118
over-recurrence, 87, 91, 92
Oxford Dictionary, 100

Packer, Lesley E., 91
Pan, Yuling, 180
pauses, 118, 125
Peking, 70, 74
Penner, Hans H., 79
perceptions, 161–74
Peregrin, Jaroslav, 106
performance, *see* mimesis
personal ritual, 84, 93–8
perspectives on ritual, 9–11, 15, 17, 18, 19, 21, 28, 30, 33, 39–41, 43, 45, 51, 56, 83, 84, 91, 104, 106, 110, 114, 116, 118, 128, 136, 139, 140, 157, 162, 171, 172, 175, 176, 180, 183
Pike, Kenneth, 171
Pizziconi, Barbara, 179
Planchenault, Gaëlle, 39, 40, 53, 54
politeness, 14, 18, 24–8, 40, 41, 74, 83, 98, 111, 112, 115, 128, 177
cross-cultural politeness research, 177–82
political rituals, 125–8, 140
positioning
negative positioning, 170
self-positioning, 131
post-event discussions/interviews, 11, 17, 18, 49, 53, 112, 118, 142, 147, 154, 172, 173
post-war Germany, 97
Potolsky, Matthew, 7
power, 147, 158, 163
Poyurovsky, Michael, 6, 87
prayers, 93
Presthus, Robert, 69
privacy, 53, 93
processuality, 63
prosody, 17, 35, 56, 59, 121

psychological needs, 47
psychology, 3, 6, 14, 86–93, 103, 112, 172, 176, 182
　child psychology, 135
'public recognition', 6, 140, 143, 161, 166
Purdy, Charles, 37–9, 42

racist rituals, 136, 145, 146, 160
Rákosi, György, 59
Rampton, Ben, 56
Rapoport, Judith L., 92
rare names (as ritual), 58
Rash, Felicity, 5
Rasmussen, Susan J., 32
rationalisation, 8
reality and 'roasting' shows, 143
realm of imaginary/non-human, 86, 90, 93
recognition, 20, 35, 104–11, 114–25, 136
recurrence, 11, 13, 21, 30, 34, 36, 41, 59, 72, 73, 89, 90, 94, 116, 121, 136, 137, 143, 148–60, 172, 183
recurrent covert offence, 148, 155–9
　see also destructive rituals
recurrent discourse, 67
recurrent non-doing, 148–55
　see also destructive rituals
recurrent reference to stigma, 148, 159, 160
　see also destructive rituals
Redding, S. Gordon, 73
(re-)enactment, 7, 44, 45, 47, 54, 60, 62
reflexivity, 111, 114–25
Reijndners, Stijn, 48
Reinstein, David, 182
relational history, 4, 9, 12, 13–15, 39–42, 47, 53, 56, 64, 95, 100, 101, 109, 117, 123, 132, 136, 143, 155
relational perspective, 2, 3, 24, 27, 46, 50, 60, 78, 82, 85, 86, 100, 140, 141, 175, 176
relational/social network, 4, 30, 37, 39–42, 45, 50, 53, 64, 65, 68, 73, 87, 91, 93, 99, 105, 109, 110, 114, 119, 128, 129, 136–8, 140, 144, 145, 159, 181, 183
　prospects of, 15
　rights of, 94, 97, 103
religious beliefs/practices, 8, 23, 44, 45, 85
restoring membership, 153
retrospective accounts, 17, 91, 105, 171, 172
Reyes, Wendy, 121
rite of breaking wind, 48, 49
rituals of
　challenge, 26, 27, 51, 58, 59
　exclusion, 140–2
　farewell, 47
　forgetting names, 157, 158
　objectivity, 120, 125, 147
　passage, 15, 45, 163
　romance, 49
　sacrifice, 80
　sounding, 54
　violence, 140, 141, 162, 166
'ritual'(as a word/notion), 10, 99–102, 128
ritual bantering, 56, 58, 61, 98, 117, 131, 172
ritual blessing, 180
ritual complaining, 68–72
ritual experience/moment, 17, 45, 48, 52, 60, 62, 89, 106
ritual extravagance, 68
ritual insult, 55, 56
ritual of sexual slave traders, 138
ritual reprimand, 76
ritual style, 55
ritual swear words, 58
ritual teasing, 13
ritualisation, 46–8, 117, 132, 156, 175
ritualised lexical items, 56
Romans, 84, 85
Rossner, Meredith, 114
Rothenbuhler, Eric W., 56
routine practices, 29, 30
Ruhi, Şükriye, 111–13

Salle, Robert, 73
Sanguinetti, Angela, 121
Schegloff, Emanuel A., 2

schematic acts/ language usage, 11, 12, 18, 23–33, 35, 48, 113, 116, 123, 128, 134, 138, 158, 183
schematic, definition of, 29
schematic topics, 19, 68
Schechner, Richard, 141
Schermerhorn, John R., 112
Scheve, Christian von, 114
schizophrenia, 87, 102
Schmidt, Bettina E., 162
schools, 48, 129–31, 145, 146, 161
Schröder, Ingo, 162
Schroeder, Carolyn S., 96
Searle, John, 34, 107
Sears, Martha, 90, 94
Sears, William, 90, 94
self-analysis, 17
self-correction, 125
self-denigration/elevation of the other, 36, 73, 76
self-reflexivity, 10, 184
semi-participants, 162, 171–3
sequentiality, 46, 51, 52, 56, 57, 59, 103
shame, 88, 136, 143, 162–74
Shaoxing 绍兴 area, 66
Sifianou, Maria, 8
silent blessing/curse, 3
Silverstein, Michael, 104, 111
Slade, Diana, 16
Smith, Peter K., 136
social action (of ritual), 3, 4, 15, 18, 26, 34, 46, 52, 92, 132, 151
social class, 56–9, 82, 160
social consciousness, 112
social functionalism, 23
social history, 6
social psychology, 145
social ritual (definition), 4
socialisation, 39
society, 5, 23, 73, 113, 140, 142
sociology, 8, 14, 23, 29, 45, 105, 113, 173
speech acts, 5, 107
Spencer-Oatey, Helen, 3, 11, 18, 25
SpongeBob SquarePants, 144
sports, 48, 52
Staal, Fritz, 2, 104

Standard Arabic, 177, 179–81
Star Wars, 130
stereotypes, 66, 68
stigma, 21, 91–6, 136–74
Stoker, Bram, 89
Sugimura, Ryoichi, 83
symbolic/symbols, 28, 45, 62, 69, 70, 77, 85, 115, 135, 137, 145, 159
symbolic request, 73
symbolic violence, 52
synchronicity/asynchronicity, 53, 62, 122

Tao, Lin, 178
Tavuchis, Nicholas, 153
Taylor, Paul Beekman, 183
Taylor, Stephanie, 31
teenagers, 37, 41
Telegraph, 42, 176
ten Have, Paul, 81
Terkourafi, Marina, 33, 34, 107, 109
The Atlantic Wire, 125–8
The Bully, 143, 144
'the normal' (definition), 147
  see also Goffman
The Shining, 94, 95
Thornborrow, Joanna, 31, 69
Thornbury, Scott, 16
time (concept), 9, 25, 43, 48, 53, 59
Tonkin, Humphrey, 29
transparency of rituals, 20, 39, 41, 43, 83–103
transvestites, 39, 40, 53, 54
Traube, Elizabeth G., 183
Tuchman, Gaye, 120
Tully, Philip J., 86
Turbott, John, 79
Turner, Lynn H., 15
Turner, Victor W., 44, 61, 79, 80, 99, 105, 106, 142
  on life-crisis rituals and rituals of affliction, 79
typology, 4, 19, 78–103, 140–2, 179

United Kingdom, *see* Britain
United States, *see* North America
Urban Etiquette, 37

van der Hart, Onno, 93
van Dijk, Teun A., 29, 30
van Gennep, Arnold, 44, 45, 80
Vartia, Maarit, 144
Vergaro, Carla, 181
Verschueren, Jef, 98
virtual social identity, 145
visibility, 19, 33
   of mimesis, 48–50

Walker, Traci, 153
Wallace, Mark, 24
Watts, Richard J., 14, 16, 25, 26, 28, 34, 111
Wenger, Etienne, 4, 38
West/Western cultures, 1, 8, 10, 11, 73, 98, 100, 163, 176, 177
West, Richard, 15

Western, Bruce, 8
Wierzbicka, Anna, 36
Wiggins, Sally, 14
Williams, Clare, 80
workplaces, 38, 39, 61, 73, 82, 83, 114, 124, 150, 151, 156–8
Woodhouse, P. G., 32

Xuehong-xuan chidu 雪鸿轩尺牍 (*Letters from Snow Swan Retreat*), 67–77

Yedes, Janet, 61
'youth abbeys', 163
Youtube, 136

Zhu, Yunxia, 5
Zurcher, Louis A., 153